My Father's Paradise

My Father's
Paradise

A Son's Search for His Jewish Past

in Kurdish Iraq

ARIEL SABAR

ALGONQUIN BOOKS OF CHAPEL HILL 2008

Published by
ALGONQUIN BOOKS OF CHAPEL HILL
Post Office Box 2225
Chapel Hill, North Carolina 27515-2225

a division of
WORKMAN PUBLISHING
225 Varick Street
New York, New York 10014

Library of Congress Cataloging-in-Publication Data
A CIP record of this book is available from the Library of Congress.

10 9 8 7 6 5 4 3 2 1
First Edition

❖ ❖ ❖

"I searched to discover which was the first of all languages. Many have said that the Aramaic is most ancient, and that it is in the nature of man to speak it without having been taught by anyone. Further, that if a newborn child were placed in the desert with no one but a mute wet nurse, he would speak Aramaic."

—ABRAHAM IBN-EZRA, twelfth-century commentator and linguist

❖ ❖ ❖

CONTENTS

A Note on Method   ix

Introduction   1

ZAKHO

1. What's in a Name   9

2. An Island in a River   12

3. A Book with Shining Pages   16

4. Rotten Corn   19

5. A Surprise   25

6. The Dyer's Son   28

7. Little Thumb Girl   31

8. A Woman's Purpose   42

9. A Prayer to the Prophet   45

10. No Wasted Steps   48

11. Lost in the Land of Assyria   51

12. Speaking with Angels   57

13. Arabs Before Jews   61

14. Plus and Minus   65

15. The Mountains Are
    Our Only Friends   67

16. Freezing in Baghdad   72

17. Hanging   76

18. Let the *Hajji* Speak   80

19. Can't Help This Time   83

20. To Hell with Books   87

21. Let My People Go   93

22. A Suitable Level
    of Civilization   96

23. God Will Provide   102

24. Iraqi Stamps   103

ISRAEL

25. Kissing the Ground   109

26. Where Are the Jewish
    Synagogues?   111

27. Herzl's Beard   117

28. *Ana Kurdi*   120

29. Some of the Best in Zakho   124

30. John Savage   126

31. Sleepwalking out
    Windows   134

32. The Brotherhood
    of Man   145

33. Gold   149

ARAMAIC

34. *Lishana Deni*   155

35. Cleft Sentences   159

36. It's All God's World   164

37. *Hets* and *'Ayins*   172

38. Abandoning the
    Fountainhead   175
39. Exiled and Redeemed   183
40. Systematic Description
    of a Living Dialect   189
41. Getting Lost   192

YALE

42. Aramaic for Dirges   197
43. To a Deep Well   203
44. Missions   213
45. A Memorial Candle   218
46. Are They Kings?   220
47. Some Enchanted Place   223

FATHER AND SON

48. Speechless   229
49. Hollywood on the Habur   241
50. Coming of the Messiah   247
51. Covenants   254

THE RETURN

52. River Keeps Flowing   261
53. Time Travel   267
54. Habur   272
55. Kiss the Eyes of
    Your Sons   274
56. Turkish Delights or
    Jordan Almonds   278
57. Heaven Sent   283
58. Chasing Phantoms   287
59. A Disaster, God Forbid   291
60. Kind of a Problem   296
61. Breakdown   298
62. "The girl, the Jew, is alive." 301
63. Convenient Truths   308

CONCLUSION

64. Paradise Lost   315
65. Ice-Blended Mocha   318
66. Saba's Music   321

Acknowledgments   327
Selected Bibliography   329

A Note on Method

To research this book, I interviewed nearly one hundred relatives, family friends and acquaintances, scholars, and others. I conducted research at libraries, special collections, and government archives in the United States, Israel, and the United Kingdom. I traveled to Iraq, Israel, and cities across the United States to see crucial settings with my own eyes. I collected family letters, diaries, photographs, and official documents. I read transcripts of my grandmother's recorded oral histories. And I spent untold hours harrying my father with questions. I took pains to find every living relative and acquaintance in a position to shed light on my family's story.

But while this book is by and large a work of nonfiction, it is not formal history or biography. Nor is it journalism. In parts of this story where key sources had died or where memories had faded, I built on the framework of known facts and let myself imagine how the particulars of a scene or dialogue would be likely to have unfolded.

A book on one's family is by its nature a subjective exercise. But I have tried in every instance to keep faith with the larger emotional truth of my family's saga.

I changed the names of people who were involved in a family controversy in Israel, because they are dead and did not have a chance to defend themselves. I created a few minor composite characters in an effort to streamline the narrative. Also, in the scenes in modern-day Kurdish Iraq, I changed the names of the people who helped me, out of concern for their security.

KURDISH
AREAS

My Father's Paradise

INTRODUCTION

I AM THE KEEPER of my family's stories. I am the guardian of its honor. I am the defender of its traditions. As the first-born son of a Kurdish father, these, they tell me, are my duties. And yet even before my birth I resisted.

Our first clash — really more of a proxy battle — was over my name. My father wanted to call me Aram, after the swath of ancient Syria where the first Aramaic-speaking tribes dwelt in the second millennium B.C. A son named Aram would be a thread through three thousand years of history, uncoiling through Israel and Kurdistan back to a patch of land between the Habur and Euphrates rivers where my father's native language first graced the lips of man. A son named Aram would pass this awesome birthright to his own son, and that son to his, on and on down the line, like princes in a fairy tale.

This may have been my father's reasoning. But it was not my mother's. She seemed to understand me even before I was born, because she didn't much care for Aram. As an American she knew the cruelty of children to kids with weird names. Aram, she told my father, was a nonstarter.

And so even before I drew a breath, I had landed my first blow.

OURS WAS A CLASH of civilizations, writ small. He was ancient Kurdistan. I was 1980s L.A.

He grew up in a dusty town in northern Iraq, in a crowded mud-brick shack without electricity or plumbing. I grew up in a white stucco ranch house in West Los Angeles, on a leafy street guarded by private police cruisers marked BEL-AIR PATROL.

Our move to Los Angeles in 1972, when I was a year old and he was hired as a professor at UCLA, did not discernibly increase my father's awareness of modernity. He bought suits off the bargain rack at J. C. Penney, in pastel plaids that designers had intended for the golf course, then wore them cluelessly to campus faculty meetings. I bought bermudas and T-shirts at Santa Monica surf shops and wore them like a uniform, even on winter visits to my mother's family in Connecticut.

His hair was a froth of curls that he cut himself with a 50-cent razor comb. I had my mom take me to Beverly Hills salons and sculpted my hair with gobs of KMS gel. My father listened to Kurdish dirges on an off-brand tape recorder whose batteries he lashed in place with rubber bands. I got behind my rock drum set and kept time with bootleg recordings of the Red Hot Chili Peppers.

My father spent the day in his home office in a threadbare bathrobe, inscribing index cards with cryptic notations in Aramaic. I spent the day in the backyard with my skateboarder friends, hammering together a quarter-pipe. His accented English was a five-car pileup of malapropisms and mispronunciations. Mine, a smooth California vernacular, tinkling with grace notes like "rad," "lame," and "mellow." ("Mellow," the verb, as in, "Mellow, dude.")

When we collided, it wasn't pretty. I threw tantrums and unleashed hailstorms of four-letter words. He stewed privately over how any son could behave that way toward his father, then consoled himself with the hypothesis that this was how children were in America.

Mostly, though, I kept my distance. He lived in his world, I in mine.

I can't remember the timing exactly, but at some point, as a teenager, I even stopped calling him *Abba* or Dad. He was just "Yona." He was the odd-looking, funny-talking man with strange grooming habits who lived with us and who may or may not have been my father, depending on who was asking.

Soon enough it didn't matter. I went away to New England for college and got a job with a daily newspaper. I lived for the big story — nerve-jangling, caffeine-fueled pieces about cops shot in the streets, lawmakers caught with their hands in the till, factories spewing illegal waste into rivers.

My father holed up in his home office and, with his sons off to college, burrowed deeper into his studies of the language and folklore of his own obscure tribe: the Jews of Kurdistan. There were days when I wondered whether there had been a mix-up in the hospital's delivery room. Maybe a real Aram, one worthy of the name, anyway, was out there somewhere, being raised by a Porsche-driving Hollywood-agent dad who wished he could get through to his quiet son, if only he could pry the boy from that dog-eared copy of *Linguistic Peculiarities in Aramaic Magic Bowl Texts*.

The sense that I might have gotten my father wrong — and that I might actually be his son — came slowly. A turning point was a chilly night in December 2002, when my wife gave birth to our first child, a boy with fine dark hair and eyes like softly burning lanterns. Would Seth break with me as I had with my own father? Would he, too, think he had nothing to learn and his father, nothing to teach?

"Who are you?" Seth, with those eyes, seemed to be asking, as his mother deposited him into my arms that cold night.

I was thirty-one years old, but I had no answer.

Making things right with my father, and my son, would take work. I lacked the big-heartedness of, say, Barney the Dinosaur or even Dr. Phil. I was defensive. I didn't have it in me to just go home, ask my father's forgiveness, and then embrace through tears as some studio audience burst into applause.

So I did the thing that felt most natural: I reached for a reporter's notepad. If I dug far enough, asked enough questions, I thought I might find the girders that linked his world to mine.

My father had staked his life on the notion that the past mattered more than anything. His people, the Jews of Kurdistan, were the world's oldest Jewish diaspora. Earthy, hardworking, and deeply superstitious, they had lived in isolated mountain villages alongside Muslim Kurds for nearly 2,700 years but never abandoned their ancient tongue: Aramaic. Aramaic had been the lingua franca, or common language, of the Near East for two thousand years. Jesus spoke it. Parts of the Bible were inked in it. Three Mesopotamian empires used it as their official language. But by the time of my father's birth, in 1938, it was all but dead. After Islamic armies conquered the region in the seventh century, Middle Eastern Jews switched to the Arabic of their Muslim neighbors. Aramaic clung to life in just one place: on the lips of Jews, and some Christians, in Kurdistan.

And so the past lived in and through my father's people. Language was their lifeline to a time and place that no longer was.

My father believed that his past anchored him. Without a tether to our ancestors, we were lost, particularly there in L.A.'s suburban desert. That belief helped vault him to the top of his field as a professor of Neo-Aramaic, the fancy name for his language's terminal phase, its death rattle. His efforts to save his mother tongue won him promotions into the highest tier of professors at UCLA, a level reserved for those with international reputations for major advances in their field. His life's work was a Jewish Neo-Aramaic-to-English dictionary, published in 2002, the first of its kind, a gilded graveyard for dying words.

The journal *Mediterranean Language Review* called the dictionary "the culminating point of more than three decades of uninterrupted linguistic activity.... Considering that the Jewish Neo-Aramaic dialects are on the verge of extinction, as a result of massive emigration of the Kurdistani Jews to Israel at the beginning of the 1950s, the author's activity becomes crucial for recording a linguistic and cultural reality which will soon disappear from the face of the earth," the reviewer wrote. "How wonderful it would be if all the endangered languages of the world could boast such a devoted and so highly qualified native to preserve them from oblivion." Over the years, Harvard, Yale, Cambridge, and the Sorbonne, among other elite universities the world over, invited him to lecture.

Academics weren't his only admirers. Because we lived near Hollywood, film and television producers sometimes dropped a line. They were looking, they often said, for a man who spoke the language of Jesus. My father tried to help. When the makers of the movie *The Celestine Prophecy* asked him to translate "nuclear fusion" into Aramaic, my father responded, a little apologetically, that Aramaic's linguistic development preceded nuclear science.

"Make something up," the producer nudged.

So my father approximated. "How about 'seed mix'?" he said. *Seed,* like nucleus, he explained. *Mix,* for fusion.

"That's a take," the producer said.

For the 1977 movie *Oh, God!* he inked the Aramaic quiz with which George Burns, in the title role, proves His bona fides to a panel of skeptical clergy. More recently, for an episode of the HBO comedy series *Curb Your Enthusiasm,* he helped an actor learn the Aramaic for "My foot! My foot!"

"Recite it slowly," the producer coached. "Like you've stepped on, say, a nail and are in pain."

The Hollywood callers never offered my father much money, and in his innocent way, he never bargained for more. He was mostly just happy that here, in Los Angeles, light years from his hometown in Kurdistan, someone — anyone — wanted to speak his language.

Who is my father? How did he wind up so far from home? I wrote this book in part to answer those questions. I wanted to conjure the gulfs of geography and language he crossed on his way from the hills of Kurdistan to the highways of Los Angeles. But I also had other, bigger questions: What is the value of our past? When we carry our languages and stories from one generation to the next, from one country to another, what exactly do we gain?

For many Jewish Kurds of my father's generation, the answer was little. Stigmatized in Israel as back-country rubes, many lost touch with their culture, seeing no use in passing it to their children. Who could blame them? Israel was forging a new national identity on European ideals, and the old country was a millstone best left behind. For complicated reasons, however, my father couldn't let go. For him, the past felt safe, like a hiding place. He found that if handled carefully, if studied in the right angle of light, the past could carry you to new worlds.

Shunning my father and his strange looks and funny accent seemed smart when I was a boy. But what if I had been wrong? What if the past could remake you? What if it could redeem?

In my father's obsession with his mother tongue, I had already glimpsed this: If you knew which levers to pull, you could stop time just long enough to save the things you loved most.

ZAKHO

Road above Zakho, 1957.

1 ❖ What's in a Name

"Which are you, Ariel Sabar or Ariel Sabagha?" the fat man asked, sizing me up with his one good eye. "Which?"

It was a crisp February evening in 2005 in Jerusalem's gritty Katamonim neighborhood. The Katamonim is the heart of Kurdish Jerusalem, rows of tumbledown Soviet-style apartment blocks where Israel had deposited its poorest immigrants in the 1950s and where most stayed until their bodies were carted off by the bearded undertakers of the Kurdish Burial Society. Floral-print house dresses dangled from balcony laundry lines, and courtyard grapevines withered in the unusually cold air. I had come here to learn more about my family. I was particularly keen on stories about my great-grandfather. Ephraim Beh Sabagha had been the only fabric dyer in Zakho, a dusty northern Iraqi town just south of the Turkish border. But he was famous less for the vats of dye in his market stall than for the strange cries that pierced the stone walls of Zakho's synagogue during his nightly prayer vigils. "He spoke," people told me, usually in hushed tones, "to angels."

A few days earlier I had found his only surviving photograph, fastened with rusting staples to a water-stained ID booklet from the Israeli Interior Ministry. The picture was from 1951, the year he came from Iraq. His face has a beatific animation: the mirthful eyes, drooping a little at the corners, as if in rapture at the world's wonders; the faint smile on his lips, as though he possesses some private knowledge he burns to share; the ears pressed out at odd angles by the *poshiya* turban around his head; the unkempt beard, a black tangle made striking by the shock of silver that flares under his chin like a flame. The face is so arresting that it wasn't until much later that I noticed his body, which is pictured only from the chest up. It is a pixie's, with sloping shoulders and a sunken chest. It seemed altogether too small to carry around that extravagant head.

All the Kurds I had spoken to in Israel said that if I wanted to know more about my great-grandfather, I should talk to Zaki Levi. A Zakho native who had helped organize the Jewish exodus from that town, he became a Kurdish *macher* in Israel, a swaggering operator with a roly-poly frame, who liked to drop the names of the Israeli generals and politicians he had dined with over the years. More important, he was said to have an encyclopedic memory of the Jews' last days in Zakho.

So one chilly February evening I walked up the dimly lit steps of Levi's Katamonim apartment.

"Which are you, Sabar or Sabagha?" he repeated, with a dubious glance. He wouldn't let me through the door until I answered. I saw now what he was asking: Are you the great-grandson of Ephraim Beh Sabagha, Ephraim the Dyer of Zakho, or a son of America whose father had seen fit to clean up the family name?

"Sabar," I said.

Levi looked away, and I felt suddenly ashamed.

"Well, okay," he said. "Come in. I'll tell you about *me*."

He led me on a tour of his apartment, pointing out photographs of himself with Moshe Dayan, Chaim Weizmann, and other Israeli dignitaries. When he saw me staring at his clouded-over left eye, he explained that he was getting ready to give a speech at a Socialist rally in one of Israel's immigrant camps in the 1950s when angry Communists began hurling rocks. "Ben-Gurion was speaking first," Levi said gravely. "I stepped between him and the rock."

There was a knock at the door, and in came a parade of prominent Israeli Kurds — a businessman, a poet, a lawyer, the chairman of the National Organization of Kurdish Jews in Israel. Levi bid us sit at a long table his wife had covered with delicacies: golden fried *kubeh*, spiced *urjeh* kabobs, a pile of pita, garlic-eggplant dip, chopped beets, shredded lemon peels dusted with curry. "This feast is like the sultan of Baghdad's!" Levi declared, slapping the table so hard the dishes rattled. "A thousand and one nights!"

I wanted to start in on a long list of questions, but this man with the barrel chest, small nose, and pencil-thin mustache seemed to have other priorities. He sank into a high-backed chair at the head of the table and clicked the TV to the KurdSat satellite channel, broadcast from Sulaymānīyah in the heart of Kurdish Iraq. The screen flashed with Kurdish music videos: a woman in a shimmering dress swaying in the tall grass of a lush mountainside. The words *Kurd Live*, in English, scrolled across the screen.

The photographs, the food, the Kurdish machers, the music. Was this some kind of crash course on my heritage, on the side of me that was Sabagha? All I had come for were a few family stories.

It was two hours later, after we had stuffed ourselves and listened to dozens of Levi's jokes, that he finally leveled his good eye at me.

"Ephraim, your great-grandfather, was a genius," he began suddenly.

I pulled out my notebook.

"He went to Zakho's big synagogue every night. It was big, six *dunams*. It had a courtyard with a *mikveh*. The ark took up an entire room, with the Torah and a place for holy water."

Levi tore a piece of paper from my notebook. He sketched a diagram of the synagogue's layout, drew a square representing a fine Persian rug, and put an *X* on the spot where my great-grandfather sat. Ephraim whiled away the night there, by turns reading books, napping, and conversing aloud with spirits only he could see. "He'd come at two A.M. and stay until morning," Levi told me. "When people started filtering in for prayer at five A.M., they'd hear him all of a sudden start screaming, '*Elohim, baruch, baruch, shmo!*'" Oh, God! How Blessed His Name!

"Did people think he was pious or off his rocker?"

"No!" Levi said. "Pious! He carried himself like a holy man. But he was also a simple man, a working man."

Everyone, it seemed, knew which prayer book was his: The margins were dappled with smudges, from fingers that had spent the day soaking in dyes.

"Please, Mr. Levi," I said, at the edge of my seat now. "What else do you remember?"

But Levi pulled away. He patted the air in front of him in slow motion, as though applying brakes. His point was clear: It was Zaki Levi, and Zaki Levi alone, who would decide when stories about Zakho would begin and when stories about Zakho would end.

"*Leaht, leaht,*" he counseled. Slowly, slowly.

Later that evening he leaned over his ample stomach toward a tray of decanters filled with brightly hued liquids.

"What you like?" he said, turning to me. "Wine? Cocktail? Arak?" I had never tried the anise-flavored liqueur, but I remembered reading that it was a favorite after-dinner drink among the Kurds, some of whom also drank it during and before dinner.

"Arak," I replied.

Levi smiled at me for the first time. Then he poured the liquid into a row of hourglass-shaped snifters, dropping in ice cubes and a splash of water, which turned the drink a cloudy pear color.

The liquor burned my throat and I winced.

Levi was beaming. "Hah!" he said. "Now, you are Sabagha."

If only it were that easy.

2 ❖ An Island in a River

"The appearance of Zakhu in the present day coincides in a remarkable manner with what it was described to be in the time of Xenophon."

—WILLIAM FRANCIS AINSWORTH,
Travels in the Track of the Ten Thousand Greeks, 1844

It is tempting to look out across my father's hometown and see a landscape of fairy tale: an ancient island in a river, in a broad plain, walled by snow-fringed mountains. The Jews lived on the island, a crescent of rock spanning four hundred by eight hundred yards, in a region so isolated that Western visitors (and there weren't many) often fancied they had discovered a tribe of lost Israelites.

"Such Jews!" the Jewish-American professor Walter Fischel wrote after visiting Kurdistan in the 1940s. "Men virile and wild-looking; women wearing embroidered turbans, earrings, bracelets, even nose-rings, and with symbols tattooed into their faces — our brethren and sisters!"

Their language was just as intoxicating, mostly because people had written it off as long dead. Aramaic had been the English of its day, a lingua franca across what was then the world's center of civilization. Its first inscriptions — mostly on stone monuments to gods and kings found near Aleppo, Syria — stretch back to around 1000 B.C., when an obscure tribe of Semitic nomads, the Arameans, began drifting from Syria across the Fertile Crescent. The Arameans' trump wasn't their wealth or power — they never had much. It was their tendency to wander.

As nomads, they had dispersed so widely across ancient Mesopotamia that their language became a de facto common tongue, the world's first esperanto. It was the language on the ground. And no one, it seemed, wanted to mess with it. By the eighth century B.C., a practical decision had been made throughout the Assyrian Empire to adopt the Aramean tongue as the official language of administration. When the Assyrians fell, the Babylonians embraced Aramaic as the official language of their Mesopotamian empire; when the Babylonians fell, the Persians took it up.

That no fewer than three empires came and went without imposing their own language upends a linguistic verity: that language follows power. Aramaic survived precisely because its native speakers lacked political ambition. The Arameans were no-account drifters — "uncouth Bedouins," one historian called them. They were everywhere. But they were so badly organized, so poor, and so powerless that the new emperors saw no threat in their language. Here is what made Aramaic irresistible: It was high-tech. Before it, the closest thing to a Near Eastern lingua franca was Akkadian, which was etched in cuneiform, wedge-shaped characters pressed into clay. Aramaic could be written on papyrus. For an Assyrian or Babylonian bureaucrat with a sprawling empire to administer, it was simply easier to push paper than rock.

The miracle of Aramaic was not lost on Assyrian king Sargon II, who claimed credit for its rapid spread in a stone inscription found near Mosul: "Peoples of the four regions of the world, of foreign tongue and divergent speech, dwellers of mountain and lowland . . . I carried off [and] made them of one mouth."

People were soon speaking and writing Aramaic over wide bands of Asia and northern Africa, from the Caucuses to southern Egypt, from western Turkey to southern India and western China. It crossed borders and bridged faiths as no prior language had. Not only did Jews and Christians speak it as an everyday tongue, but so, at various times, did Zoroastrians, Buddhists, Muslims, Mandeans, Manicheans, and pagans.

For a while, Aramaic appeared destined for immortality. As the common language of the formative years of Christianity and diaspora Judaism, it embedded itself in seminal liturgical texts. An Aramaic translation of the Hebrew Bible was expanded into a landmark work of interpretation known as the Targum, or Translation. The Books of Ezra and Daniel were partly composed in Aramaic. Babylonian Jews wrote the Talmud, the book of commentary and law, in Aramaic. A medieval Spanish poet drafted the Zohar, the chief text of Jewish Kabbalah, in it. The original "writing on the wall" that prophesied the fall of Babylon was in Aramaic. And Jesus Christ himself cried out in the same lilting tongue as he died on the cross: *"Eloi, Eloi, lama sabachthani?"* My God, my God, why have you forsaken me?

The death of Aramaic as one of the world's great languages came suddenly. In the seventh century, Muslim armies from Arabia conquered Mesopotamia and Aramaic was steamrolled by Arabic, which is still the Middle East's dominant tongue. That is why when other Jews, even those from elsewhere in Iraq, first met their Kurdish brethren in the twentieth century, they could scarcely believe their ears. "Though neither Arabic nor Farsi — not Hebrew, either — something in the language struck a chord," the Baghdadi doctor Heskel M. Haddad wrote in his memoir, recalling his first encounter with Kurdish Jews. "Single words were understandable, or almost, and all at once I knew their source. This motley ragged mass was speaking a derivative of Aramaic, the language I'd encountered in the Zohar! Impure, admixed, distorted, but unmistakably the ancient tongue!"

Hearing Aramaic in the twentieth century tended to induce giddiness in otherwise temperate men. "In my view, the history of Aramaic represents the purest triumph of the human spirit as embodied in language," wrote the eminent Yale Arabist Franz Rosenthal, a buttoned-down German Jew normally given to softer pronouncements. "Great empires were conquered by the Aramaic language, and when they disappeared and were submerged in the flow of history, that language persisted and con-

tinued to live a life of its own. . . . The total sweep of Aramaic history . . .
teaches us that the underdog may in fact have the opportunity to play
a decisive role, that it is possible for the word pure and simple to dominate empires and survive their dissolution, that it is possible for the true
achievements of the human spirit to live on. . . ."

Aramaic's longevity owes much to the isolation of places like Zakho:
the island in the river in plains ringed by mountains, a fortress against
the world. More than twelve hundred years after the arrival of Arabic,
Aramaic was still hanging on, thanks in large part to Kurdistan's twenty-
five thousand Jews, a forgotten race of peasants and peddlers who saw
themselves as the direct descendants of the Lost Tribes of Israel.

BY 1930, AT AROUND the time this story begins, Zakho had replaced Arbīl and Amadiya as the center of Jewish activity in Iraqi Kurdistan. But that wasn't saying much. In a town of 27,000 souls, most of them
Muslim Kurds, Jews numbered just 1,471.

The Jews lived on Zakho's island, its oldest district and commercial
heart. Their mud-brick houses lined narrow alleys that zigzagged down
to the Habur River. On the riverbanks, packs of children scampered, loggers tied up rafts, and men at the *chaykhana* sipped glasses of tea while
cooling their toes in the frothing currents. Beyond the Jewish quarter
were a cramped open-air market and an ancient castle housing a small
jail and the offices of the provincial administrator. Stone and suspension
bridges linked the island to Muslim neighborhoods, a small Christian
quarter, and the boys' primary school.

The jumble of low, flat-roofed buildings still gives way to an unremitting flatness. Golden fields of wheat and barley roll across the plains for
miles until they dissolve into an angry terrain of steep gorges and ravines.
Hemming the valley like fortress walls are the Bekher and White mountains, whose peaks tower thousands of feet above the town.

"As a stranger approaches, he is struck with its bold and isolated appearance," the British traveler William Francis Ainsworth, one of the few
Western visitors, wrote of a trip through Zakho in the mid-1800s. "It is
not like Mosul, a town in a partially civilized country; but is an outpost
of warlike Kurdistan."

For a long time Zakho was just a lonely speck of rock on the fringe of the Ottoman Empire, an afterthought some sixty miles northwest of Mosul. When European powers redrew the map of the Middle East after the defeat of the Ottomans in World War I, Zakho found itself within spitting distance of two borders: five miles south of Turkey, twelve miles east of Syria. Its rebirth as a border town only added to its rugged spirit. As it prospered from international trade — much of it illegal — the town had even less of a need for ties with any central government. But isolation had its price: With few exceptions, its people were consigned to lives of mercilessly hard work, ill health, and wild superstition.

Some say *Zakho* is Aramaic for "House of Victory," some, Kurdish for "River of Blood." Both allude to its possible role as the site of some decisive battle in antiquity. The Greek warrior and historian Xenophon is thought to have passed through Zakho with his army of ten thousand mercenaries in 401 B.C., coming under savage attack by the Kurds, or "Carduchians," as he called them.

Others have glimpsed a simpler, more timeless meaning, one better suited to a fairy tale. *Zakho*, they say, is Kurdish for "Bend in the River."

3 ◦ A Book with Shining Pages

The little boy liked roofs. And from the rooftops of his town in Iraqi Kurdistan, the eight-year-old boy with dark hair — his name was Yona — could look down on the whole world. Down there was the store where his father sold the bolts of wool. Over there was the market stall where his grandfather dipped *sherwals* and *shalla u-shappiksas* into drums of dye, brightening the pants and jackets with new colors. And there, doddering in the courtyard of the house by the main road, was one of Yona's favorite men: the storyteller with his pitchfork beard, who lit the boy's imagination with fables of ghouls and beggars and heroes.

Just below, between the stone synagogue and the mulberry tree, stood his own house. A column of steam rose from the courtyard. Though he couldn't see his mother from this angle, he could picture her there, beside a cauldron of boiling burghul, her dress sopping from the heat.

A few yards beyond the house was the edge of the boy's universe: The Habur River. Rivers didn't normally go in circles, but he could see that the one in Zakho did. The Habur peeled in two at one end of town and, precisely at other end, rejoined: Zakho was an island in a river. When the boy peered at the roiling currents, he saw its two branches as arms embracing the town. The river was ruled by the Yimid Maya, the Water Mother. She was a capricious siren who surfaced at night to comb her long, dark hair. The rabbis warned Zakho's boys and girls that violations of Jewish law displeased Yimid Maya. In her fury, she curled icy fingers around the legs of swimmers and dragged them through darkness to their deaths. One day he saw a friend, a blacksmith's apprentice, lose his footing as he reached for a piece of driftwood. Three days later, the boy's bloated body washed up on the banks of a downstream village.

The rooftops were Yona's sanctuary and kingdom. Yimid Maya couldn't touch him here, and some days, high above the town, he felt like a boy aga, a tribal chieftain. The houses were so close together that he could cross the entire Jewish quarter without ever touching ground. He took running starts and, a whisker's breadth before the ledge, sprang up and out. Beneath him, as he flew, the pedestrian goings-on of Zakho's world blurred: the squawking chickens in the courtyards, the peddlers pushing carts of dates, the women scrubbing laundry. Then, in a cloud of dust from his skidding feet, he thumped down on the next rooftop.

You had to be careful. One roof jumper he knew had tripped and snapped his neck. Another boy plunged through uneven thatching and crushed both legs. But in all those years Yona fell only once. It was the day his friend Zacharia showed him the book with the shining pages. The two boys had sat on the riverbank, cooling their feet in the water, and had studied the pictures inside: golden-haired men and women in the strangest costumes. Look at the lips of the women! Look at how tall the men are! Like giants! The boys could make no sense of the words but knew they were English; a teacher had begun showing them the alphabet. Never before had either boy seen photographs of human beings, let alone such splendid ones in such glorious colors, on pages that flashed the sunlight back at your face.

"Give it to me," Yona said, tugging at one of the pages. "Let me see that."

"No, it's mine," Zacharia said. "I found it."

"Where?"

"An Arab gave it to me."

"Please," Yona said, pleading now. "I'll let you play with my bouncing ball later." His father had bought the tennis ball, the only one in Zakho, on a trading trip to Baghdad, inspiring envy in all the other boys.

"I'll trade you," Zacharia said. "You can have the book if I can have the ball."

"Okay, okay," Yona said, reaching out. "Just let me have a turn."

But then Zacharia reconsidered. He loved having something that Yona wanted. It was all too often the other way round. Yona's father was always returning from Mosul and Baghdad with new toys, jackets, and rubber shoes for his son. Now it was Zacharia's turn to inspire envy. "Who cares about a stupid ball," Zacharia yelled, getting up and sprinting down the riverbank, the pages fluttering. "I've got the book with shining pages."

Yona stewed, furious that the other boy had gotten the upper hand. Then, that evening, like a miracle, he heard the news: Zacharia had scaled the roof of his own house and hidden the book under a *makabbeh*, an overturned wicker basket for keeping cats away from fresh food. When Zacharia came back to check on it an hour later, the book was gone. Rumors were circulating that Salim Judo, the bully, had swiped it.

Yona laughed. He climbed the courtyard steps to the roof, cupped his hands at the sides of his mouth, and broadcast the happy tidings. "Zacharia lost his shining book! Did you hear, everyone?"

But Yona had to see for himself that the book was gone: It would feel good to lift up that makabbeh and look at the nothingness underneath. He hurtled across a few more rooftops and landed with light feet on Zacharia's. The basket was in the corner. But before he reached it, something in the courtyard below caught his eye. Just below the crude gutter was Zacharia's mother, Sabria, fat, naked, and astride a pail of steaming water. He tiptoed closer, watching as she ladled hot water onto her ample frame. It cascaded down the ripples of coffee-colored flesh. He had never before seen a woman like this — without clothes, that is. What a curious sight! The folds of soft skin reminded him of an accordion that one of the town's musicians had shown him. He could not tear his eyes away. She ran a sponge over her arms and breasts. She splashed her feet about like one of those jolly sea monsters the town's storyteller had told him about. Or maybe this was Yimid Maya herself?

Then came an awful groaning sound: twisting metal. Yona felt something give way beneath his feet. The rusted-out gutter was collapsing. He felt a prickle of heat as something hard pierced his jaw. Sabria's figure grew larger and larger. He blacked out too soon to hear her scream.

He opened his eyes to the hazy sight of a man in a long coat hooking a needle and thread through his chin. "He was lucky," he overheard the man tell his father, who was slouched in the corner of the candlelit room. "If he had fallen on a skinny one, he might have been dead."

"God saved my son," Yona's father said.

"By sacrificing a cow," the man in the coat said, and the men laughed.

What did they mean exactly? Yona wondered, as he closed his eyes against the pain. Did he mean Sabria? Had he fallen on top of her? Did everyone in Zakho know the story?

The man in the white coat let out a weary sigh as he tied off the last stitch. "His jaw will take time to heal, so give him small things to eat that need little chewing, like yogurt, bread crumbs, and *kaimach*," sour buffalo cheese.

"And," he added, as he turned to go. "Tell the boy to keep his mouth shut for at least a month."

4 ◈ Rotten Corn

If Yona was spoiled or felt a little superior, it was not his fault. He had succeeded at something that had eluded nearly everyone else his mother had ever cared about: He lived. For this simple reason, Miryam and her husband, Rahamim, pampered him. They led him to believe he could fly where others faltered.

The Jewish cemetery in Zakho was checkered with freshly turned earth where babies had been buried in unmarked graves. So many infants died in Zakho that the Kurdish Jews fashioned elaborate rituals to boost fertility. Some women ornamented their necks with silver and copper amulets inscribed with magic incantations. Some took part in exotic rites, melting bullets or tying snake skins around their stomachs. In a few cases, a mother would sell her newborn to a female relative for a nominal sum. The relative would then hire the mother to nurse and raise the baby, a ruse to confound the *jinne* — the demons — and protect the child.

But the trials of motherhood in Kurdistan seemed to cut Miryam more deeply than it did other women. Birth and death had always gone hand in hand, ever since the day she watched her mother die.

July 1928 was so hot that the people of Zakho hoisted bed frames onto the roofs. Miryam Beh Nazé was three years old, a dark-eyed beauty even then, with hair the color of mahogany. When she walked toward her mother's wails in the next room, she saw a circle of women on their knees, mumbling prayers and dabbing at somebody with wet rags. The women were her aunts, Miryam saw now. And between them, writhing on a sheet on the hard-packed dirt floor, was her mother, Rifqa. It was the Fast of Tisha B'Av, a day of mourning for the destroyed temples of Jerusalem, and the men were at synagogue.

"Bless this boy," a midwife said, lifting the newborn baby, Yusef, from between her mother's legs and tying an amulet made of cow's fetus to his ankles. The aunts nodded their amens. "Keep him from evil."

But the blood kept trickling, and Rifqa's chest jerked. A stain spread like spilled wine across the white sheet. The midwife looked at the ceiling and asked God for mercy.

"Mommy?" Miryam said, sobbing now.

The aunts turned together, noticing their niece in the shadows. "Come here, *kurbanokh*, hold your mother's hand," one said.

"It is not clean, she mustn't," the midwife said. "Go from here, girl, go outside! Pray!"

But Miryam could not move. Her older brother, Shmuel, dashed in, soaked in sweat — someone had summoned him from his game of knucklebones. He clasped Miryam's arm. "Mommy? Mommy?" he said. "We're here, Mommy, me and Miryam. Can you see us?"

As the long afternoon shadows spread across the room, Rifqa's eyes went blank. Her sisters' screams carried all the way to the courtyard of the synagogue, where men in worship were chanting the Book of Lamentations.

The baby Yusef, born moments before his mother died, was fair-skinned and fine-featured, like his father. Miryam took to pretending that she was his mother, spoon-feeding him boiled wheat and calling him "my little baby."

When he turned three, a rash bloomed on Yusef's forehead. His breathing grew shallow and he started to cough. Miryam's father, Menashe, had to leave town for week-long spells to load logs onto rafts upriver, so a neighbor was paid to look after Yusef. Shmuel walked Miryam over to the house in the afternoons, so she could stroke Yusef's hair and make him laugh with a funny noise she made squeezing air through her teeth.

She dreamed sometimes that her father had come back with a beautiful new wife and that they were again a family.

"He'll be back soon," Shmuel told his younger sister. "A few more days."

But their father stayed away and Yusef got sicker. The rash crept from his forehead to his legs. A few weeks later, he was all ribs and knees. One morning, when the neighbor woman left his cradle to boil tea, the boy died.

FOR MIRYAM, STILL a young girl, the world was not the cascade of wonders it was for some children. She awoke in a sweat some mornings, looking around the house to check that everything was still in its place. Forces beyond her understanding had already spirited away her mother and her little brother. She worried that her father might be next, and his long absences suspended her in a state of fear. She gazed up at the Bekher mountains that edged the plains, searching for the tallest peak and imagining that the evil eye reigned there in a glistening castle of ice. Up so high, it had a clear view of Zakho's townspeople as they bustled through their daily rounds. Up so high, it could choose victims at will. There was nothing anyone could do but wait her turn.

A few years after her mother's death, Miryam's father married a razor-tongued woman with high cheekbones and a cleft chin. Her name was Arabe, and she walked with an almost military bearing, chest forward, shoulders back. Some townspeople saw in it a posture of pride, but most saw hostility, which was fine with Arabe. When Arabe gave birth to a line of four healthy boys, it only adding to her hauteur.

"How is your daughter?" a neighbor once had the temerity to ask.

"I don't have one."

"The girl you send to wash the clothes in the river, the one who cooks for you?"

"She came with my husband."

Arabe had taught Miryam to cook for one reason: So she wouldn't have to. The more housework she could unload onto her compliant stepdaughter, the better. Miryam needed to learn that she was a guest in Arabe's house. She would have to pull her weight.

On many afternoons Miryam waited by the doorway for her half brothers to return from the Jewish school in Zakho's synagogue.

"*Yaprach, Yaprach,*" they would chant, demanding stuffed grape leaves as they filed through the door and tossed their book bags onto the dirt floor. Arabe was occasionally out of the house at this hour. And when she was, Miryam set out the plates and then bargained with the boys. She'd cook if they told her something they'd learned in school that day.

Even when she was a girl, the kitchen was a source of pride and power. A separate vestibule off the main room, it cocooned her in glorious aromas. She had proven herself a skillful and painstaking chef, famous in the family for yaprach that tickled the tongue with notes of tomato, lemon, and dried sumac. Shmuel and her half brothers teased that Miryam's date-size yaprach were tiny, like her. Miryam didn't mind the ribbing; she rolled grape leaves at half their usual size precisely so that her family would recognize them as hers, rather than her stepmother's or her aunts'.

Fridays brought the week's most elaborate meal, a Byzantine interlacing of ingredients that turned the kitchen into an alchemist's lair. As long as there were Fridays in Jewish Kurdistan, there was *hamusta*. The tart brew of dense meat dumplings in a light citrus soup of turnips, leeks, and beetroot was the traditional pre-Sabbath meal. Miryam slipped into a reverie amid the glazed spice jars and wood-burning clay stove. She took pride in the precision with which she cut the leeks into halves, snipped off the roots, and softened the brittle leaves in cold water. She shaped the beef into cubes, rolled in specks of finely diced celery and garlic, fried them in oil. Then she folded the chewy bulgur dough around the seasoned meat to form saucerlike dumplings called *kubeh*. When the soup simmered, sending a bouquet of lemon through the house, Miryam dropped in the kubeh and smiled to herself as she watched the dough turn to gold.

"First, you have to tell me what your teacher said today," Miryam would tell her half brothers.

"We don't have to do anything until we eat," one boy said.

"Do you want a bloody nose?" Shmuel said, leaning over the younger boy and watching the bravado seep away. "Then tell her."

And so by dribs and drabs, the boys unwound tales of good and evil, of kings and slaves, of wars and famine, and of God.

ONE THURSDAY MORNING in the spring, not long after she turned twelve, Miryam walked to the river to scrub the family's laundry. Her back ached as she shouldered the sopping load up the riverbank and past the market to the house. Why was her stepmother treating her like this? If Miryam's father weren't away so often on his logging trips, he could protect her. His temper, she knew, was the only thing Arabe feared.

Blessedly, her stepmother was out, probably at the market. Miryam drew a breath of warm air and let the laundry sack slide off her back onto the floor of the courtyard. And then a thought overtook her. She stepped on a stool to reach the shelf where Arabe kept a jar of henna. She grabbed it, hid it under a fold in her dress, and retreated to the secluded bend in the river where women bathed. Miryam untied the white scarf from her head. She combed her index finger through her tightly braided hair and tugged downward until the coils peeled free. The thick mahogany strands reached her waist.

Something about her reflection startled her. She was still tiny, yes. But her chest and hips were beginning to take on a rounder form; her mouth seemed fuller, her chin stronger. *Maybe I will look like my mother,* she thought. She had remembered the leathery texture of her mother's hands at bath time, but was never able to conjure more than a gauzy picture of her face. Maybe by becoming a woman, she would also in some way find her.

Miryam removed the jar of henna and sprinkled the paste with a handful of river water. She stuck her finger in the moist dye, turning her nose away from the smell. Then she streaked it through her hair, pinching the strands between greasy fingers until they turned a coppery orange.

A rustling at the top of the bank made her jump, and when she turned, she saw a boy turn and run. He must have been watching her. She hurriedly covered the jar, knotted her hair back into a crude braid, and refastened the scarf. But when she stepped into her courtyard, she noticed that the jar of henna she thought she'd tucked into her dress was missing. Arabe was in the main room, glowering over the wet pile of clothes Miryam had left by the door.

"You stupid girl," Arabe said, turning around. "Where have you been? Your father will need those clothes tomorrow for work, and your brother has no clean diapers. Everything is still here, as wet as a mop. How dare you leave without my permission?"

"I just went to the river for a rest," Miryam said. "I'm sorry. I'll hang the clothes now."

"A rest?"

When she looked up at her stepmother's face, the woman's features twisted into a mockery of a pleading child. Miryam felt suddenly paralyzed. There was a world outside the house — books and boys and flowers and mountains — and the only plan this woman had for her was housework.

"Don't look at me like that," Arabe said. "How dare you look at me like that." Then she slapped Miryam across the cheek so hard that the girl, a waif who weighed no more than the brother half her age, spun around and crumpled to the ground. Her henna-stained braid slipped out from under her scarf.

"And what did you do to your hair, you silly girl? Where did you get that henna!" Arabe stalked over to the shelf and found the jar missing.

"Thief!" Arabe shouted, her voice a wolf's growl. "Henna won't make you pretty, idiot girl. It didn't make your mother pretty either. Get up! Get up!"

But Miryam couldn't move. "So full of tears, this one is," Arabe said. "Maybe we'll just hang you up to dry instead of the laundry."

Arabe bent down and coiled Miryam's hair around a forearm built like a cedar log. She dragged the girl by the hair to the courtyard and pinned the tip of her braid to the laundry line. "See, I told you hanging laundry wasn't hard."

Just then Miryam's father materialized in the doorway and saw his sobbing daughter in the humiliating pose. "Arabe, you crazy witch," Menashe growled. He dug his nails into his wife's shoulders and slammed her against the wall. "You won't disrespect me this way."

The fracas had brought a knot of neighbors to the courtyard. Miryam, sprawled in the dirt and humiliated, buried her face in her arms.

"If you touch my children again," her father said, "I'll throw you into the streets."

"You thought you planted wheat," Arabe said. "But what you got was rotten corn."

Menashe wore the stunned expression of a man in disbelief at an underling's temerity. He slammed the back of his hand into the sharp ledge of his wife's cheekbones.

"Just rotten corn," she said, spitting out blood. Miryam noticed she was staring right at her, her eyes boring into the girl like a pair of awls.

5 ⬦ A Surprise

A few weeks later Miryam's stepmother asked her to plug holes in the roof. When she returned home with two pails of tar, her father called to her.

"Set those by the house," he said. "We're going to take a walk."

"Tomorrow," he told his daughter after a few steps, "I am taking you to your uncle Ephraim and aunt Hazale."

"Yes, father," she said. She swallowed back the bile in her throat. "But what have I done?"

"Nothing, my daughter."

"Then why . . ."

"It is a surprise," he said, squeezing her shoulder.

"You have heard of Ephraim Beh Sabagha, yes?" It was a fair question. Her father wasn't close to his sister, Hazale, and had spoken of her even less after she married Ephraim, the fabric dyer who had moved to Zakho from the village of Atrush after his first wife, a Mosul woman, had died.

"He is a good man, one of Zakho's most pious," he said, his voice cracking as though something were stuck in his throat. "And his sons, they're hard workers. His eldest is turning into a successful merchant. His father sends him to Turkey for all those fancy textiles he dyes in his shop. You must have seen his eldest boy, Rahamim, on your errands in the market?"

A hazy image of a runtish man with a moonlike face and thin mustache flashed before her. Perhaps, yes, she thought, she had seen him unloading goods once or twice. But he hadn't made much of an impression.

"I don't know," she said.

"You will enjoy it there," her father said. "It may be easier for you."

"But . . ."

"Enough," he said, his gruffness back. "You have chores today. Didn't your stepmother tell you yesterday that the crack in the roof needs tar?"

Miryam scarcely knew this Ephraim. Sure, everyone had heard stories about the crazy old man with the wooly beard who claimed to speak to angels. But she had never so much as set foot in his house. And what was so great about his sons? She had dozens of first cousins, and these, no one ever talked about or even visited.

And then came a bout of breathlessness, like a donkey's buck to the stomach. *My stepmother is behind this,* she thought. *She convinced my father to throw his own daughter out of his house. I wasn't a good enough servant for her. So she is putting me to work as a maid.*

A sob erupted inside her chest. Her father was several paces ahead of her now, but well within earshot.

"Daddy," she gasped. She looked searchingly after him, waiting for him to turn around, to see her tears. His head twitched as though at nothing more vexing than a fly's buzz. Then he vanished through the crooked timber door frame.

The next morning a mottled white mare was waiting for the journey to the Beh Sabagha house. Miryam, clad in her best *sudra*, a dress with red embroidery that had belonged to her mother, pressed a couple of lesser shifts into the saddlebags and hoisted herself astride the huffing animal. She did not look at her father.

Maybe this would be a fresh start, she had told herself when she got up that morning. She wanted this aunt and uncle to like her. The horse, she thought, was a promising sign. It would have been easy enough to walk to the Beh Sabagha house, just a few paces down their own street. But these relatives had seen fit to dispatch a horse — perhaps not the prettiest in Kurdistan, but a horse nonetheless.

A few doors past Zakho's big synagogue, her father helped her off. She straightened her dress with her palms as she took in the house, which was bigger than her own family's. When her father led her over the threshold, she started. Spread before her on a low table in the courtyard was the biggest feast she had ever laid eyes on: heaping plates of roasted chicken and seasoned lamb, bowls of steaming hamusta and sliced watermelon, knee-high stacks of freshly baked flat bread. Around the table, smiling, stood more aunts, uncles, and cousins than she had ever seen gathered in one place.

At the sight of the thirteen-year-old, the women raised a ululation that could be heard half way down the street. "Klilililili, klilililili!" they cried. "Klilililili!" The crowd parted suddenly, and shuffling to the front with an uneasy smile was a short man in a shalla u-shappiksa of such brightly colored stripes that Miryam had to resist twin impulses — the first to giggle, the second to flee. The traditional billowy trousers and short sheep's-wool jacket radiated every color of the rainbow. Someone, it seemed, had gotten a little carried away in Mr. Beh Sabagha's dye shop.

The man met her gaze for a moment as he advanced, then dropped his eyes to the dirt floor. Miryam recognized him now as the moon-faced man with the thin mustache she had seen at the market. Then, from a seat at the head of the table, a wiry older man with kind eyes and a square beard rose to his feet.

"Miryam, I am Ephraim Beh Sabagha, the head of this house," he said. "Your father and I have reached an agreement. Yes, we have! We are very happy that you will be joining our household — and our family. I am told you are a good cook and a hard worker. Before you," he continued, sweeping his hand toward the squat man in the rainbow suit, "is someone whom you will be happy to serve for the rest of your life. May I present my eldest son, Rahamim."

The short man — perhaps a decade older than she but not much taller, Miryam saw — tilted forward in a mincing bow.

And then the women raised their cries and the room rang with a song Miryam had heard at her cousin's betrothal ceremony.

> *Why does the girl go hide*
> *Alone beneath the rock?*
> *Why is she shy?*
> *Why are you running to the mountains?*
> *Don't hide — it won't help.*
> *Why are you standing against the wall in tears?*
> *Go with the parents of the groom,*
> *That will be best for you.*

Miryam felt sick at the dawning reality of what was happening. She had been summoned here not as a servant but as a bride.

"Hallelujah, yes!" Ephraim said when the women finished their song, "In six months, Miryam, you will move in with us and become Rahamim's wife."

6 ❖ The Dyer's Son

When Rahamim was a newborn, his parents had waited too long to stitch an amulet into his blanket. The evil eye had crept into his crib and cast a spell. Why else, Rahamim mused during the dull stretches of his mule trips into Turkey, would he, the eldest of Ephraim and Hazale's three sons, be the shortest? His younger brothers towered over him. In a needless stroke of cruelty, the evil eye had given Eliyahu a baritone voice that turned heads a kilometer away, and to Israel brooding good looks that . . . well, did the same. These facts, one could not argue. But industry and wiles, these Rahamim believed were his province. He had plans for the Beh Sabagha family. He believed he could lead his family out of Zakho's middle class and into the ranks of the town's wealthiest and most honored Jews. Men like Moshe Gabbay, who owned the land and the storefronts where lesser men peddled their goods. Men like Beh Avo and Beh Hoja, who were so well respected that the alleys they lived on were known as *Makhalit Beh Avo* and *Makhalit Beh Hoja.*

The Beh Sabaghas were not nobodies. Their reputation, if you could call it that, was for spirituality. Not piety, mind you. But spirituality, a self-styled mysticism that derived from Ephraim's overnight prayer vigils at the synagogue. Some townspeople claimed to overhear him conversing with angels. Others — Rahamim laughed when he thought about it — just shook their heads at the blue smudges on the pages of the prayer books and wondered why the man didn't scrub his hands harder after his long days in the dye shop. His father was perhaps the only merchant in Kurdistan who stuffed books into his donkey's saddlebags on peddling trips through the mountain villages. His business partner complained bitterly about the waste of precious cargo space.

"The only wasted cargo space on this journey, my friend," Ephraim would snap back, tapping a forefinger against his partner's temple, "is in a head too empty to read."

Rahamim liked his father's independent streak and belief in self-improvement, but spirituality, virtuous as it was, had to be balanced against pragmatism. This business of accepting one's father's trade — and identity — as one's own did not sit right. Rahamim *Beh Sabagha* — Rahamim, of the Dyer's House. As if no other destiny were possible. Rahamim had learned math so well in school that by the time he was a teenager, he was helping manage his father's accounts. He could read and write well enough that illiterate people from across the Jewish quarter sought his help composing letters. And to be called no more than an occupant of the Dyer's House?

Yet in Zakho, if you weren't careful, names stuck. And once townspeople had latched on, you could find yourself going nowhere, like a rooster in mud. Just look at the sorry lives of Mordechai *Bkah'ena*, Mordechai the One-Eyed, Nachum *Jojo*, Nachum the Pants Wetter, and Faho *M'arto*, Faho the Farter.

The worst, though, was Shlomo. He had been a respected woolens merchant and called The Weaver. Then, one day, while drying a patch of wool on his roof, a powerful gust swept it up into the mountains. Afterward, if you had told Zakho's townspeople that you were looking for Shlomo the Weaver, you would get a blank expression. That was no longer a name anyone recognized. "Ah-hah," the townspeople would eventually reply, "Ah, yes. You must mean Shlomo *Poha*," Shlomo the Wind.

Shlomo's business was never the same.

Recalling the story one blustery afternoon while returning by mule from a trading trip to Turkey, Rahamim shook his head and laughed. *Fool,* he huffed to himself.

Suddenly the bark of a man's voice jolted Rahamim out of his daydream.

"Hey, you, Kurd! Where do you think you're going?"

A Turkish soldier on horseback, a bandolier across his shoulder, was racing toward him from the other side of the dusty ravine.

Customs.

Rahamim ground his teeth. How could he have been so careless this close to the border? He tugged on the mule's reins, slumped forward in the saddle, and let his jaw hang slack in his best imitation of the dumb village Kurd.

"What do you have in those bags?" said the soldier, a young man with fair skin and hair slicked back and parted.

"Nothing, sir," Rahamim said. "Just walnuts and garbanzo beans."

"And where are you going?"

"Zakho," Rahamim said, waving a limp hand south.

"Open the bags."

The soldier dismounted and plunged his hands into the bulging saddle bags; the nuts and beans were so densely packed that the officer withdrew his hands almost instantly.

"You penny-pinching Kurds don't waste any space, do you?" the soldier said.

"No, sir."

No, sir, indeed, Rahamim thought as the soldier waved him across the border. Had the soldier reached any deeper, he would have discovered a wardrobe's worth of fine Turkish silk scarves, a bundle of delicately woven funeral shrouds, and a set of heavy wool blankets embroidered with the likeness of the handsome Ataturk. Had the officer asked Rahamim to disrobe, he would have found his chest wrapped like a giant kubeh in layers of mink and fox pelt.

Smuggling could land you in jail. But only if you were caught. That is why Ephraim put his eldest and shrewdest son — and not his brothers, however tall and handsome — in charge of such risky international transactions. Yes, every day, he was, by hard work and ingenuity, muscling his family closer to the loftier perch he felt was their due. As Zakho's patchwork of low-slung houses appeared on the horizon, ringed by the glistening river, his thoughts turned to his new wife. And he was reminded of another reason for financial prudence: A baby was on the way.

7 ◈ Little Thumb Girl

If her father and stepmother's house felt at times like a slave quarters ruled by a madwoman, Miryam's new house was like a rowdy, cluttered bazaar ruled by no one. Her in-laws were merchants, black-market peddlers, and textile dyers. Miryam glimpsed no separation between market and home. Sheep's and goat's wool was waiting to be combed; hens and chicks crisscrossed the floors. A procession of customers tramped through the house, dickering over the price of nuts, wool, animal skins.

The many visitors made her feel part of an important enterprise. She had found an ally in her new husband's only sister, Rachel. The two girls were the same age and the recipients, both felt, of more than their share of housework. When Rahamim was away on trading trips or in Mosul for army training, they would slide their sleeping rugs together and swap stories about the trials of a girl's life in a house full of boys.

"Maybe I will find a husband with many young sisters," Rachel said, one night.

"Yes," Miryam said, giggling, the candlelight glinting in her eyes. "Make them your slaves while you sleep until noon."

"It must be nice to have a husband," Rachel said, after a while. (With the unrelenting housework and without her sister-in-law's more refined features, it would be another dozen years before Rachel would marry, and then to a widower fifteen years her senior.)

"Yes," Miryam said, as if considering the idea for the first time. "It is nice sometimes." Miryam had slowly warmed to her husband. He was not the most handsome or the tallest. But he was earnest and wanted to better himself. And no man in her life besides her brother Shmuel had been as kind.

Their marriage was not an hour old when the women of Zakho, seeing the couple in their wedding clothes, started in with a familiar blessing. "May you have seven boys!" they said, because more boys meant more workers for the family business. Miryam waited for the day when she could give her husband the thing he wanted most. And when her belly finally curved, at fifteen years old, some two years after their wedding day, she wept.

In the fading light of the room the family had built for the newlyweds, Rahamim threaded his arms under his wife's and pressed her forehead to his lips. "Please, God, grant us a boy," he said, looking up. "Big, healthy, strong. A real Sabagha."

For a moment, safe in her husband's arms, Miryam thought she could hear a baby's cry. The keening sounded like wind swirling down from the snowy mountains beyond the river. Was it her unborn child trying to reach out to her? When Rahamim let go, her face was wet with tears.

On a late spring morning, Miryam awoke to two equally unpleasant sensations: pain like a fist kneading the insides of her abdomen, and the idiotic rantings of her portly neighbor.

"Oh goodness, it's *gurgur* day! It's *gurgur* day!" came Sabria's singular squeal. Sabria was a woman who saw the making of gurgur, a couscous-like cracked wheat, as a community project. But why, Miryam wondered, did Sabria always feel the need to shout her every thought?

"Look at that," Sabria continued, her voice slicing through the hot, thick air. "Haha! Looks like we'll be able to parboil enough wheat to feed the entire Jewish quarter."

"If there's any left after you serve yourself," Miryam grumbled to herself, as she steered her throbbing belly out from under the covers. Then she flushed, embarrassed at her intemperance.

From the rooftop, where the family had set up their beds to escape the house's heat, Miryam now saw the reason for Sabria's stridency.

Waddling toward them in the street below were two sturdy matrons bearing an empty iron cauldron the size of a calf. The *qaqibe* was suspended by rings from a wooden pole that rested on the women's shoulders like a yoke on oxen.

"We got it from Abd al-Karim Agha," one of the matrons huffed, beads of moisture on her forehead.

Miryam recognized the name: Abd al-Karim was a big man in the family of Muslim agas who for more than a century had ruled the rugged patch of Kurdistan anchored by Zakho. The advent of an Iraqi state after World War I had sent a couple of unlucky Baghdadi bureaucrats to a small government outpost, or *qichla*, at Zakho's periphery, but it did little to upset the supreme power of the region's Sindi, Gulli, and Slivani tribes.

"'A gift for my Jews,' al-Karim Agha told us," the other cauldron bearer announced. "May God grant our Muslim friend life in Heaven. But he says we must have the qaqibe back tomorrow by sundown."

"Oh, my!"

"Let's go."

"Ladies, work is the salt of life."

The women of the street were whipping themselves into a lather. Their fevered mutterings and puff-chested bustle seemed to mock the pain spreading into Miryam's legs.

She reached behind with one hand to settle back into bed, but felt someone smack her on the side of the neck.

"Move, girl!" It was her mother-in-law, Hazale. "We've got a day to boil a month's worth of wheat. No time for sleep. Move! Today we boil!"

In the sunburned streets below, Miryam joined the procession of women advancing with brass jugs toward the river. From behind, Miryam thought, they all looked the same: the thick ankles, the duck walk, the sacklike dresses draping stout frames. In her enlarged state, she imagined herself indistinguishable from the other women of the town. Burning bands of pain streaked across her belly and back, as if from the lash of a whip. To make the feeling go away, she imagined herself a link in a chain, towing the links behind it and being towed by those in front. A link does work but has no feeling and no will. Miryam held on to this thought for the next hour, as her dress grew sticky with sweat. One jug hung by curled fingers at her side, the other was slung over her shoulder. When she came back from the river for the sixth time, the women told her she was done. The cauldron was full.

Rachel measured wheat with the other women and emptied it into the water. Someone set fire to the logs. The giant iron vessel soon reached a noisy boil. The women stood in a circle around it, cheered, and exchanged satisfied looks.

"Rachel! Rachel!" Miryam finally said, breaking into a sob. "My belly!"

Their neighbor Rima stepped away from the cauldron and elbowed Rachel aside, asserting her authority as the eldest female present. "Someone run for the midwife," Rima shouted, turning her attention just as quickly back to the cauldron, which by now was giving off an awful heat. "Sit, Miryam, don't worry. We will take care of the gurgur."

At noon a baby girl was born. She was so beautiful, with such long legs and such milky skin that Miryam could not stop looking at her. She strung an amulet of silver bells around the baby's ankle that rang with each little kick. She was so pretty, and so helpless. But when Rahamim returned from his donkey trip at sundown, he turned his eyes away.

"Please, just look at her," Miryam said. "She's ours."

"She's a beauty, like you," Rahamim replied, without really looking. He kissed his wife on the cheek.

The three of them slept on the roof that night, beside the pasty sheets of gurgur drying out after the day's boiling. The sky was a velvety dome of jewels. Miryam looked into her daughter's dark eyes, pressed the baby's lips to her breast, and suddenly remembered one of her own mother's lullabies.

"Nursing baby, nursing baby, so fresh and young and pretty," Miryam sang. "To the market of Mosul we'll take her, to buy her clothes and jewelry. Nose just like a hazelnut, lips as fine as paper. To keep her far away from harm, would I be sacrificed to her Creator."

She clasped her husband's arm with her free hand and gave him a look of such vulnerability that he thought she might cry.

"My love," she whispered.

"Yes."

"Can we name her after my mother?"

"Arabe? I thought you hated her."

"Not her, for shame. My real mother."

"I've never heard you speak of her."

"Rifqa," she said, her eyes moistening. "Her name was Rifqa."

RAHAMIM KEPT HIS HEAD low that week, avoiding the market and taking less traveled routes across town. Shame greeted the birth of girls. Not long ago he had watched children bait one of his poorer customers after a daughter's birth. "*Tuha, tuha, khiryeh bilihyet abuha!*" the boys had chanted. "A daughter, a daughter, dirt in her father's beard!"

Zakho's prejudices were far from Miryam's mind that first week. Every day, she saw proof of her daughter's all-consuming need for her. Rifqa sucked so fiercely that Miryam wondered how so small a creature could have so great a thirst. But eight days after her birth, the girl looked smaller. Miryam's nipples had been sore for a couple of days, and when she examined them, she saw dark splotches and cracks in the skin. She squeezed, but the milk couldn't get through. She wondered how long her baby had been sucking in vain.

"'Split,' they call it," her mother-in-law said, seeing Rifqa struggle at Miryam's breast. "You're not the first."

Neighbors recommended hen's fat, sesame paste, and curses against the evil eye, but nothing restored Miryam's milk. Ephraim had looked in the Jewish neighborhood for a wet nurse. But mothers who had hired themselves out in years past had not recently had children and were no longer with milk.

The family then resorted to what they saw as the last recourse: reaching beyond the Jewish quarter for a Muslim wet nurse. Gentiles in the out-lying villages had nursed a number of Jewish babies from Zakho, returning them to their parents once they were old enough for solid food. It was hard to know whom to trust sometimes, and travel beyond Zakho was risky, so the idea made many Jews uneasy.

But Miryam saw a stark choice: give up her baby for a few months or watch her die. Ephraim asked a Jewish peddler with contacts in the Muslim villages to put out word. The next day a woman with a deeply lined face and blank eyes appeared at their door, with a toddler in her arms.

"I am Gamra," the woman said. She seemed to be wearing every stitch in her wardrobe: canvas blouses and dresses were layered atop one an-other. As the woman's hems dragged across the floor, like a mop, Miryam and her mother-in-law traded a look of disgust. The heap of clothes was giving off the smell of sour milk.

"You are from Tusani?" Hazale inquired, after sitting in the courtyard and serving her tea.

"We are nomads," Gamra replied. "But we have been with our buffalos, working the pastures in Tusani for many months."

"Miryam, give her Rifqa," Hazale said, switching from her broken Ara-bic to Aramaic, so the wet nurse wouldn't understand. "Let's see if she can take this woman's milk."

Miryam, holding back tears, passed her squirming daughter to Gamra. She fixed the older woman with a beseeching look, but Gamra's expres-sion was blank.

Gamra tugged a breast from beneath the sour-smelling clothes and stuck it in Rifqa's mouth. The girl sucked greedily. But after a minute

Gamra's own boy, who wore an odd hat with a chin strap and a goat-hair suit studded with white sea shells, squinted at the intruding child. Soon he was pounding with little fists, trying to dislodge Rifqa from his mother's breast. Gamra elbowed her son aside.

When Hazale went inside to fetch more tea, Miryam followed.

"Auntie," Miryam said. "I'm scared."

"I know," Hazale laughed. "They sent us a real stinker. The woman smells like she hasn't bathed since Creation."

"She says she's a new mother, but her face . . . She looks like a *taplapa*," a walking corpse, Miryam said. "We shouldn't even let her spend the night here."

The next morning Ephraim handed Gamra two months' pay, a small barrel of dates, and a sack of the hand-sewn clothes and gifts the towns-people had given Rahamim and Miryam to welcome their firstborn.

The family — it seemed like a dozen uncles and aunts had joined the procession — all marched with Gamra to the Habur River. Ephraim told her to bring Rifqa back in two months or the family would come looking for her.

An *abra* made of inflated sheepskin lashed to a set of logs docked at the river's edge. Gamra stepped aboard the raft, with Rifqa asleep in a shoulder sling.

As her baby disappeared with the stranger down the long river, Miryam heard herself laugh. For so many sleepless nights, she had been up, feeling the ache in her breasts, listening helplessly to her daughter cry in hunger. *Now I can rest*, she thought. *Now I have help. Now my breasts will heal and soon I can have my baby back.*

Like her namesake in the Book of Exodus, Miryam had sent her baby down the river and into Gentile hands so that it might live. She giggled at the thought of Rifqa as a girl Moses. She was already picturing the day of her triumphant return.

A MONTH PASSED with no news from Gamra. Then another. Zakho's peddlers returned from their summer trading trips, and the leaves of the poplars were turning crimson.

In the courtyard, on the last day of the cheerful harvest festival of Suk-kot, Ephraim rose from his carpet and stamped his feet. He was shaking.

"All this celebration, all this food, it is not right," the old man thun-dered to his sons. "We made a deal with that stinking Bedouin, and her time is up."

The urgency in Ephraim's voice worried his eldest son. Rahamim had planned to meet a black-market textiles dealer in Turkey later that week, a man who could help him enter the lucrative trade in carpets and rugs. To stand up this man, who was making the trip to the mountains just for this meeting, could kill the deal and sully Rahamim's reputation among his Turkish business contacts. He would be happy to set aside a few days to retrieve Rifqa afterward. But he could not ignore business. His father and brothers didn't seem to realize that he worked hard not for himself, but for them, for the family's good name. But he sensed that now was not the ripest time for that argument.

"But, Babba," Rahamim said. "Miryam is only now starting to heal. Wouldn't it be better to wait a little longer, until Miryam's all better, be-fore bringing back that sick girl?"

"That nomad has broken her contract with us," Ephraim said. "You say you want to be a great businessman with a big store and a house with three rooms. Maybe one day you will be. But if you don't hold people to their word, you'll be riding that ass of yours the rest of your life."

"Babba, I . . ."

"Enough! You will go tomorrow."

The next morning, the peaks of the mountains on the Turkish border were frosted with a light snow. Rahamim pulled on a new wool shalla u-shappiksa, folded a wad of dinars into his vest pocket, and walked to the house of his cousin Murdakh. Murdakh's combed-back blond hair, neatly trimmed mustache, and twinkling blue eyes drew the approval of many of Zakho's women, who said he looked like a British soldier. But Rahamim was there for other reasons: the man was built like an oak, owned a bandoleer, and had one of the town's most powerful mules. All would come in handy, Rahamim thought, on the twenty-mile journey to Tusani, which lay in the dangerous tribal lands near the intersection of the Iraqi, Turkish, and Syrian borders.

The men traveled for four hours along iced-over streambeds and ravines before stumbling onto a cluster of tumbledown mud shacks at the edge of a river.

"Do you know where we can find Gamra, the nomad, the wife of Hsen?" Murdakh asked at one doorway.

An old man pointed across to the rolling pastures beyond the settlement. "You'll find the Bedouin up there," he said. "But few are left. It's winter in the mountains here. They've taken their stinking buffalo south, thank God."

As they trekked up a steep hill to the pastures, the men made out a single black tent through the veil of snow. Murdakh reached over his shoulder and touched his rifle. Yes, it was there.

They parted the heavy tent flaps, and when their eyes adjusted to the darkness, they noticed a woman in the corner with gray streaks in her hair. She started at the sound of their footsteps, and looked up with unseeing eyes the color of milky tea. "Who's there?" she asked, her head swiveling from side to side. She patted the ground until her hand settled on a pair of rusted wool shears. "Who's there?"

"We are from Zakho," Rahamim said, his voice coming out thinner than he had hoped. He turned a pleading glance toward Murdakh, one that begged him to take over speaking duties, but Murdakh only nodded for Rahamim to continue. "We are looking for Gamra, the wife of Hsen."

The woman made a *tih-tih-tih* sound as though spitting out watermelon seeds. "Gamra is gone. Acchh, she was barely here."

"Where did she go?" Rahamim said.

"I don't know her business. She had a sick girl with her, a baby Jewess. Her tent was just across from ours. But she left this pasture before the last moon."

"That girl was my daughter," Rahamim said. "Please, if you can help us . . ."

There was a long silence. "The baby dried up as soon as Gamra brought her here," the old woman said. "Or maybe a month after. I don't remember. But the baby girl dried up and died. That's what people said. Then Gamra ran away. In shame, they said. In shame, she ran away."

Rahamim thought of his wife and felt something grind in the pit of his stomach. "We have to go back," he said to Murdakh, shivering suddenly. "It's cold and getting dark."

"Yes, yes, go. Go back to Zakho," the old woman said. "My sons will be back soon, and they are not nice like me."

Something exploded inside Murdakh. He lunged toward the woman and grabbed her hair. "Don't tell us lies, woman," he said, twisting the oily strands, which gave off a sour smell. "Where is Gamra? You tell me where she is or I'll shear you like a sheep."

The woman clenched up. "I don't know," she said. "She said she was going south, to another pasture, where her husband was. I don't know any more."

"We're going to find her," Murdakh said. He clasped his cousin by the arm and headed for the opening in the tent. But they were stopped by the woman's voice.

"I will warn you not to look any further," she said. "The way I hear people talk, it's not safe here for Jews. Nowadays, they tell me, you have not so many friends as before."

Was she just angry at Murdakh? Or had this simple shepherdess here in no-man's-land actually heard of the Arab riots in Palestine, the protests against the influx of European Jews? Rahamim, though he considered himself a worldly man, wouldn't have heard if not for his recent trip to Mosul, where it was the talk of the Jewish teahouses.

"Murdakh, the world is not well," Rahamim said. "What would they say in Zakho if two big men like us, men with families, got killed looking for this little thumb girl? Which would be the bigger shame? Didn't you hear the woman? The girl died. Now let's go."

"But how could we look at your father without turning over every stone? If it were my daughter . . ."

"But it isn't," Rahamim interrupted.

They were standing in the pasture, and the winds were picking up, driving whorls of snow across the sloping fields. Rahamim reached into the mule's saddlebags and pulled out a sack of stuffed grape leaves Miryam had packed for their trip. They were nearly frozen now.

Rahamim extended a handful to his cousin, but Murdakh turned away.

BACK HOME IN ZAKHO the women had stayed up late by the fire, eating apples and drinking raisin juice, giddy at the prospect of the baby's homecoming. Was she much bigger? they wondered. Whom did she look like?

Hazale made jokes about scrubbing Rifqa with a *xarota*, a loofa sponge, soaked in tallow to rid her of Gamra's stench. Rachel was picking stray bits of yarn out of a wool suit she had woven to keep Rifqa warm through the winter.

Miryam tittered at her in-laws' jokes. She couldn't sit still. Every few minutes, she peeked outside at the dark, snowy road, impatient for the first sight of her husband and their baby girl atop that handsome Murdakh's mule.

God or sesame paste or time — she did not know which — had rid her breasts of the swelling. And the three months of good sleep had strengthened her body. Her childhood with Arabe had taught her that a daughter must make sacrifices for her mother's comfort. But giving away Rifqa for Miryam's comfort had come to feel wrong. She realized that Arabe had it exactly backward: A mother had to sacrifice for her child. This was what sixteen-year-old Miryam vowed to do, from the minute her husband laid Rifqa in her arms to the day Rifqa left home to marry some kind man. Maybe even a man the girl would choose for herself, Miryam thought, smiling and cradling the *kallota*, the doll she had made a month earlier by braiding scraps of cloth into the crude likeness of a baby girl. It was to be her gift to Rifqa, something the girl could hold when her mother was busy, so she would never feel alone.

At around midnight Miryam heard a thump and the faint clopping of hooves. She dropped the doll and dashed into the courtyard. The clouds over Zakho were cleaving apart in a few places, and rays of moonlight danced a silent fugue across the snow-blanched rooftops. Then, there he was. Her husband's chest looked shrunken, collapsed on itself like a kicked dog. There was nothing in his hands, she saw now, except for the empty sack she'd used to pack his lunch.

"Where?" Miryam said, her chest heaving. "Where is she? Please. Where?"

"Go inside," Rahamim barked, his breath turning to steam. "You'll freeze to death."

The other women crowded into the doorway. "He's right, Miryam," Hazale said, timidly. "Come in now."

"No," Miryam shrieked, glowering at her husband. "I will stand here until Rahamim tells me everything. Everything."

Rahamim reached out sheepishly to touch his wife's cheek. But she swatted his hand away, then crumpled into the knee-deep snow, shaking.

8 ❧ A Woman's Purpose

For the next few days Miryam and her husband scarcely spoke. At night she lay on her mat, unable to sleep, with the kallota held tight to her chest. She silently asked its forgiveness and pleaded with God for some sign that Rifqa was still alive, that Gamra was on her way to Zakho at that very moment, that there had been a mistake. As her husband snored on a mat across the room, the image of the wet nurse's face swam before her in the darkness. Miryam searched it for meaning. Would this woman hurt her baby? She already had a boy, so what would she want with a "little thumb girl"? Or was it just some unspeakable accident? But what kind? Perhaps the woman rolled over on the little girl in her sleep and smothered her, the layers of foul rags so thick that she could not hear the baby's screams. The scene grew vivid in Miryam's imagination — the baby invisible beneath the nomad's heap of clothes, her kicks soft, useless under Gamra's weight, the nomad's look of surprise the next morning at the sight of the blue-lipped, lifeless form wedged between two cushions.

In these dark days she thought of how her brother Shmuel had protected her as a girl, and one day went to see him at her old house. When she told him about Rifqa, he pulled her into his arms.

"This place is cursed," he said. "We don't belong here."

"Why?" she said, startled, clutching his arm. "What do you mean?"

He said that a *shaliach*, an emissary from Palestine, had come with word that Iraq was no longer safe. Muslims had killed Jews in Baghdad. A bomb had been tossed into a crowded synagogue there on Yom Kippur but had not, thank God, exploded. The emissary would help anyone leave, and Shmuel had already signed on to go. Plans were being made to one day evacuate the whole region. Shmuel said he would cross the River Tigris and make his way to Al Qāmishlī, a city some seventy-five miles away in Syria, where an aunt lived. Then he would travel southeast across the Syrian desert to the Land of Israel.

Miryam let out a disbelieving laugh. "Are you crazy?" she said. "Muslims, killing Jews? I don't believe it." The Muslims and Jews in Zakho got along fine, she reminded him. Muslims shopped at Jewish stores, went to Jewish tailors. They sent the Jews gift baskets of bread, milk, and eggs at the end of Passover. On the Sabbath the Muslims in the teahouse even stubbed out their cigarettes in respect as Jews filed past on their way home from the synagogue. Yes, the Jews sometimes had to "volunteer" their labor when the aga needed a new irrigation ditch dug or a new addition on his house. But this was a small price for Shemdin Agha's protection, which was backed by such force that neighboring tribes knew that robbing or murdering a Zakho Jew would invite retributory bloodshed.

Miryam reminded her brother that Shemdin Agha employed a Jew, their cousin Saleh, as his trusted personal secretary. "Now stop this foolish talk, Shmuel," she said. "And, the Land of Israel? You've been reading too much Torah."

She was grateful for the chance to laugh.

But Shmuel didn't smile. A few snowflakes were now falling, and he led her from the center of the courtyard to the *birbanke*, the brushwood veranda, which was propped up by a row of wooden posts.

"It's also Arabe," he said.

"What? More?"

"Worse than before," Shmuel said. A few days earlier, he said, Arabe had punished him for some infraction by ordering him to stand outside in the sleet until he was soaked through and shivering.

"But I thought she was afraid of you, Shmuel."

"She was," he said. "But something has happened to Babba. It's like he's forgotten we came from a different mother. 'Arabe's your mother now,' he told me. 'And you will obey her as though she was your own.'"

The old memories swarmed around Miryam. Why hadn't he just told her the truth first, instead of making up stories about missionaries and bombs and murdered Jews? Shmuel looked like a young man now, with a deep voice and a handsome mustache. Was she the only one who could still see the little boy beneath?

"Don't go," she said abruptly.

"You have a new family now," Shmuel said. "A better one. Let them take care of you. I am no good to you anymore. I am no good to anyone."

Miryam put her fingers to her eyes, trying not to cry. She understood him perfectly. She rested her head against his chest, and they held each other for a long time.

She would not see him again for fifteen years.

THE BEH SABAGHA FAMILY worked like a finely calibrated assembly line. Eliyahu, the giant, trundled in wheelbarrow after wheelbarrow of freshly slaughtered ewe and cow. The strapping Israel unloaded the carcasses onto the snowy ground and flushed the blood away with jugs of river water. Rahamim dragged the cleansed slabs to another corner of the courtyard, leaving a pink trail in the snow. He slipped a hooked knife beneath the animals' skin, and sloughed off the rippling layers of fat.

Then the women took over. Miryam carried the chops to pots of boiling salted oil. Rachel sliced the cured meat into cubes. Hazale stuffed the cubes into jars, sealed them with wax, and stacked them in a storage chamber off the kitchen: enough salted meat to feed the family until the melting of the snows.

There was something indeed miraculous about the Beh Sabaghas, Miryam thought as she shuttled between her husband and the pots of hot oil. Rahamim and his two brothers moved like one man. They were each so sure of the others' movements that they could work this way for hours without exchanging a word. She longed for a bigger part in the Beh Sabagha family's purposefulness. But how? She had already failed at every bride's first duty. If she couldn't make healthy babies, she wondered, what could she offer beyond one extra pair of hands?

A few nights later, Miryam awoke in terror and bolted upright on her sleeping mat.

"I can't breathe," she shrieked, waking her husband. "The air won't stay down."

"Shhh, shhhh," Rahamim said, rubbing her back and staring curiously into her brown eyes. "Steady yourself, woman. You have been dreaming."

"It was she," Miryam said. "The taplapa."

"What about her?" Rahamin said.

She pressed her face against his neck and he could feel her wet cheeks.

"We knew nothing about her, Rahamim. Nothing! How could you have given her our baby? How? How?"

"I don't know," he said. "It was a mistake. We learned something. All of Zakho did." She listened for heartbreak but heard only regret — like a businessman's when a deal sours.

She cried until all the fight drained from her. Finally she lay down again, her head against the crook of her husband's elbow, so that he cradled her.

"You are still a young lamb," Rahamim said. "We can have more."

"Yes," she said, looking up at him through the semidarkness. "Maybe this time a boy."

9 ⋄ A Prayer to the Prophet

The road south from Zakho skirted the edges of the mountains, then sliced through gorges and past streambeds rushing with melted snow. Miryam inhaled the warm air through the windows of the bouncing bus, her heart quickening at the sight of the narcissus, anemone, and cyclamen dappling the roadside in spectacular effusions of yellow, red, and white. She had never set foot outside of Zakho. But with no sign of a new pregnancy after a year of trying, Miryam needed help. She wanted to go where other Zakho women had gone in times of distress: to the Shrine of the Prophet Yona. Rahamim told her to come along on his next trading trip to Mosul; Nineveh was just beyond the city limits.

The half day's journey to Mosul had made Miryam's stomach churn. But then the walls of the ancient city of Nineveh, with their gray-stone battlements and their forbidding gates named after Assyrian gods, rose on the horizon. She and Rahamim got off the bus and climbed the dusty path to the ruins of the onetime capital of the Assyrian empire, where kings had lived in eighty-room palaces.

A babel of languages swirled around them as they passed a row of vendors in stalls beside the arching gate. They walked toward the crenelated minaret that loomed like a giant stovepipe over the city, and entered through the gate below.

"Is this a mosque?" Miryam whispered, wavering as she remembered Shmuel's warnings the year before about Muslims in the big cities.

"Yes, of course," Rahamim said.

"But Yona was a Jew."

"He was a prophet for Muslims, too. Yunis, they called him."

When Yona (Jonah to English speakers) had defied God's command to preach against the wicked ways of the people of Nineveh, God roiled the seas and Yona was thrown from his ship. But God gave Yona a second chance. A whale trailing the ship swallowed Yona whole. When the prophet repented, the whale spit him ashore to continue on God's path. Miryam had asked her husband to tell her the whole story on the bus ride there.

Now she knelt in the shadows and pressed her forehead against the old tomb, draped in luminous silk carpets, with tapers burning in copper candlesticks at the four corners. "All I ask, dear prophet," Miryam whispered, "is for a healthy baby in my belly. A baby no better or worse than the other strong children of Zakho."

She stood to go, then spotted her husband sitting against a far wall of the mosque, his lips moving silently as he read from the small Hebrew prayer book he always carried in his shirt pocket. She spun around and knelt again before the sepulcher.

"If you grant me a boy, dear Yona," she said, "I will name him after you."

TEN MONTHS LATER, on one of the coldest nights of the year, the cries of a newborn boy rang through the Jewish quarter.

"Listen to that voice," Ephraim bellowed, laughing at the sound of a boy he felt sure had inherited his windpipe. "His voice will fly to the gates of Istanbul!"

Miryam looked at the baby's slick body, at the whorl of black hair matted against his forehead, and pressed him to her chest. She worried for a moment that her love would crush him. The baby's heart — she could feel it against her chest — was pulsing twice as fast as her own. But they were in sync. Perfect sync. Just like the rhythms of the *dola*, the Kurdish drum played with two wooden sticks, one big, the other small. She closed her eyes. Her muscles unclenched and her breathing steadied. Everything bad was flushing from her.

When she opened them again, she saw her husband's fingers gently stroking the baby's cheeks. She noticed something in his eyes she had never before seen in their three years of marriage: tears.

After sunset, as Rachel and Hazale began preparing a celebration feast, Rahamim retreated to his sleeping mat and slipped the small prayer book from his pocket. He thought about the Torah portion the rabbi had recited at synagogue that morning. This week's was titled "Vayetze": "And he came out." The verses of Genesis dealt with Jacob's dramatic departure from his father-in-law's home after two decades of indentured servitude. But Rahamim had to laugh. "And he came out" summed up the day about right. It was somewhere between December 1938 and February 1939. But the closest thing to an official record of Yona Beh Sabagha's birth was the one Rahamim inscribed in pencil in the margins of his prayer book.

"This little Yona," Rahamim wrote, grinning, "was born today, on Shabat Vayetze," the Sabbath of He Came Out.

10 ❖ No Wasted Steps

Yona's birth seemed to usher in a period of new prosperity for the Beh Sabaghas. Rahamim had streamlined his peddling business to make more money in less time — and with less work. For a few years, when he visited the farms just outside Zakho to buy eggs and wheat wholesale, he tried to interest the farmers in a rotating selection of fabrics draped over his donkey's back. Once in a while he made a sale. But more often he headed back to town in a funk, with merchandise that some farmer's wife said wasn't the right size or color or texture.

Children in a Jewish village in Kurdish Iraq, 1934.

"Why can't you just bring what I want?" a farm matron carped one day. The remark drew a scolding from her husband, who, like many Kurdish men, believed their women should be "an egg without a mouth," a smooth and delicate object that emitted no sound.

The woman's forwardness irritated Rahamim, but she was on to something. Instead of guessing at his customers' needs, he tried something novel among the peddlers of Zakho: He took advance orders. When he went to buy eggs and wheat from the farmers now, his donkey carried exactly the fabrics they had ordered a week earlier. When he took produce to the vendors in town, he was fulfilling the vendors' precise requests. The shift in business strategy raised his standing among his brothers and put a bounce in his father's stride. With that single stroke, he had doubled his efficiency, reduced risk, and ensured a more predictable flow of income.

By the mid-1940s he and his brothers had salted away enough dinars to take an even bolder step. They opened two stores in Zakho's bustling riverfront market. Rahamim had built up enough business contacts, from the mountain villages around Zakho to the broad boulevards of Baghdad, to offer more goods at better prices than all but a few local merchants. "Heh! Let the customers come to us!" he announced to his brothers. And come they did.

Rahamim stocked the shelves in the cramped stall with bolts of soft cotton, skeins of local yarn, Turkish funeral shrouds, and ladies' fine scarves. He stayed in step with local tastes, and adapted on the fly as a growing number of wealthier customers abandoned their traditional goats-hair shalla u-shappiksas for Western-style wool blazers and slacks.

His handsome brother Israel ran the general store next door. Cloth sacks along the walls overflowed with dates, garbanzo beans, nuts, shirt buttons, sewing needles, pots of glue.

And Eliyahu stationed himself each morning atop Zakho's arching stone bridge, the famous upside-down *V*, where he intercepted the daily stream of villagers carting fox and mink pelts into town. Why haul all this merchandise into the big city, he would tell them, in a most sympathetic tone, when you can sell it all to me right here and return home to your families?

The family's growing success gave little Yona a feeling of power. It's hard to see when I look at my father now, a slouching man full of anxious self-doubt despite his many achievements. But when he was a child, before he had left a single mark on the universe, or in Zakho, for that matter, he looked at his reflection in the Habur River and believed himself possessed of gifts.

A distant uncle, a local Kabbalist, flattered the boy's self-assurance by enlisting him in his business: summoning spirits to help families find lost valuables. The uncle poured oil into a bottle of water and asked Yona to act as an "innocent child" divining meaning from the patterns. When the man from the Iraqi lottery passed through town, nine-year-old Yona believed he knew the winning numbers.

Most Zakho boys left school after fourth grade or just skipped it altogether. The moment they were strong enough to lift a bucket or stock a shelf, they were yanked from the classroom into the family business. But Rahamim and his brothers were making enough money to keep Yona in school: first the Jewish school at the synagogue, then the state school across town. Yona knew from early on that his father dreamed of his becoming a doctor. It was an aspiration so out of proportion to the family's station that his father confided it only to his son.

Miryam would bury three boys and two girls in Zakho. Several were stillborn, the others died of disease. Only one — a girl named Fawziya — lived long enough to be given a name. Miryam wept after each burial, cursing a body that mocked her yearning for more children. Then, each time, she redoubled her devotion to her eldest son, whose survival came to seem ever more of a miracle.

She spoiled him with his favorite dishes. She helped him into the new coats and boots that Rahamim brought home from his trips to the big cities. She called him kurbanokh, asking God to sacrifice her before any ill came to him.

"*Pishlé Isho mshiha,*" her stepmother, Arabe, sputtered one day, watching Miryam lace her son's new rubber-soled shoes. "You're turning him into a little Jesus."

11 ❖ Lost in the Land of Assyria

And it shall come to pass, that in that day a noise shall be made with a great trumpet, and they that were lost, shall come from the land of the Assyrians, and they that were outcasts in the land of Egypt, and they shall adore the Lord in the holy mount in Jerusalem.   —ISAIAH 27:13

My father and his schoolmates could not then know that they were the end of the line for Iraqi Jewry. But you could hardly blame them. When a people live in one place for twenty-seven hundred years, shielded from the world beyond the mountains, there is no reason to believe anything will ever change.

The man who sent their ancestors to Kurdistan in the eighth century B.C. had no particular grudge against the Jews. For the Assyrian King Tiglath-Pileser III, the Kingdom of Israel with its Ten Tribes was no more than an irritant to his vision of a Middle Eastern empire stretching from the Nile Valley to the Caspian Sea. Brilliant, methodical, and ruthless, Tiglath-Pileser advanced the science of warfare with a singular invention: population exchange. By marching thousands of conquered subjects from one corner of the empire to another, he accomplished twin goals: He cut off ethnic groups from the familiar settings from which they drew identity and power; and he fortified the empire's frontiers with infusions of new inhabitants.

His policy of mass deportation had already transplanted tens of thousands of conquered Syrians, Persians, and southern Mesopotamians by the time King Pekah of Israel ran afoul of him in 734 B.C. In retaliation, Assyrian armies raided Israel's Galilee and marched its inhabitants hundreds of miles to Assyria, a region centered on what today is Kurdish Iraq. Assyrian troops swept back into ancient Palestine again about a decade later, after another rebellious king of Israel, Hoshea, jilted his imperial

masters by allying with Egypt and ending his annual *madattu*, or trib-
ute, to the Assyrian crown. Tiglath-Pileser's successors, Shalmanaser and
Sargon II, mounted a three-year siege of Samaria, the capital of Israel's
Northern Kingdom, finally conquering it in 721 B.C.

And so the remaining tribes of Israel were herded out of the Holy Land
and northeast across a vast expanse of desert. If you believe the Hebrew
Bible, there is no mystery about where they ended up. "In the ninth year
of Hoshea," according to 2 Kings 17:6, "the king of Assyria captured
Samaria, and deported the Israelites away to Assyria. He settled them
in Halah, in Gozan on the Habor River and in the towns of the Medes."
Translation: They were deported to Kurdistan.

Scholars generally agree that the Habor River of the Bible is none other
than the Habur that rings Zakho before crossing into Syria. Gozan is
modern-day Tell-Halaf, Syria, a prehistoric pottery-making city some 150
miles to Zakho's west. The Medes lived in northwestern Iran. And Halah,
some scholars believe, is Nineveh, where Miryam had prayed at Yona's
tomb for the birth of a son.

The exiled Jews gave up Hebrew for Aramaic, the common language of
the Assyrian empire, but saw themselves as inhabitants of a biblical landscape. They looked up at Mount Ararat, just over the Turkish border, and
saw the craggy peaks where Noah's Ark is said to have run aground. They
could claim Abraham as a native son, since the eastern Turkish city of
Urfa — ancient Edessa — was very likely the "Ur of the Chaldees" where
he was born. They made pilgrimages to a constellation of holy sites that
seemed to sanctify the very earth they trod: the shrines of the prophets
Yona (Jonah) in Nineveh; Nahum in Alqosh; Daniel in Kirkuk; Queen
Esther and Mordechai in Hamadan. In the mornings they nibbled on
sweet grits that gelled in the tree branches with the morning dew; Jews
believed it was no less than the heaven-sent sustenance — manna — that
rained down on the desert-wandering Israelites in the Book of Exodus.

The spiritual capital of this Israel in mountain exile, in my father's day,
was Zakho. Jews converged there in large numbers in the mid- to late
1800s, fleeing Muslim tribal unrest in nearby Amadiya and Arbīl, and
turned Zakho into a regional center of Jewish activity. Jews in remote
villages began to travel to Zakho for certification as kosher slaughterers

or for rabbinical training. From 1888 to 1906, its Jewish population grew from fifteen hundred to twenty-four hundred. In 1930, Jews made up just 5 percent of Zakho's population. But they believed they lived in the "Jerusalem of Kurdistan."

Scholars like to speak of the Jews of Iraq as a single people. But history had dealt a very different hand to the Israelites, from Samaria (northern Palestine), than it did to the Judeans, from southern Palestine. About a century after the Israelites were marched to what today is northern Iraq, the Judeans were deported to what today is central Iraq: the prosperous urban centers of Babylon (near modern-day Al Hillah, fifty miles south of Baghdad) and Nippur (one hundred miles southeast of Baghdad). The Bible waxes lyrical about the Judean exile: "By the rivers of Babylon, there we sat down, yea, we wept, when we remembered Zion," Psalm 137 says. "We hung our harps on the willows . . . How shall we sing the Lord's song in a strange land?"

It didn't take long for them to figure it out. The Jews deposited in Babylon, at the crossroads of Mesopotamian civilization, would leave a well-known legacy: They would write the Talmud, establish a worldwide hub of rabbinical activity, and build major synagogues and yeshivas. They would eventually abandon Aramaic for the Arabic of their Muslim neighbors and rise into the highest circles of Iraqi business and government.

The Israelites, by contrast, never left the wilderness. They lived in villages scattered across remote mountains, largely cut off from one another and from the crosswinds of civilization. The Bible reserves no poetry for their exile. The Israelites, says Isaiah 27:13, were simply "lost" in Assyria. In some translations, the word *lost* is rendered, more glumly, as *perished*. The Babylonian Talmud, drafted just a few hundred miles to the south, makes scant mention of the Kurdish Jews. It's as if they had just been written off. So little was heard from them in Palestine, where a few Jews had returned from exile, and Babylon — then the centers of Jewish civilization — that they were dubbed the "Lost Tribes" and consigned to the realm of fable. Some rabbis ascribed their disappearance to conquest or assimilation, others to the mythical river Sambatyon, a seething torrent that permanently severed them from the rest of Jewry. Either way, the Lost Tribes were symbols of an irrecoverable past.

Over the years, Jewish enclaves as far flung as China, India, Venezuela, and Ethiopia have asserted ancestry in the Lost Tribes. But the Jews of Kurdistan might be said to have the strongest claim. For better and worse, they stayed right where the Assyrians had put them. They had not perished. They were not even lost. They were just too far outside the beltway for anyone to notice.

A COMPLETE HISTORY of the Jews of Kurdistan is impossible. They never recorded their own story and were too few to rate more than a passing mention by Muslim writers. Kurdish Jews appear in the historical record only in the fleeting moments when their lives intersected with some larger current of history. The few known fragments are as confounding as they are tantalizing. Whether they are representative or idiosyncratic is hard to tell. Still, they hint at a buccaneering strain of messianic Judaism that hewed to nobody's rules but its own.

The first historical blip after the Bible declared the Israelites "lost" comes centuries later. The Babylonian Talmud makes a brief, enigmatic reference to a rabbinical ruling that "proselytes may be accepted from the Cordyenians." If rabbis indeed mounted a campaign to convert "Cordyenians" (Kurds) to Judaism, they hit pay dirt in the first century A.D. in Adiabene, a Kurdish kingdom centered on Arbīl, about one hundred miles southeast of Zakho. The queen and crown prince, Helen and Izates, Parthian pagans, embrace Judaism and are promptly converted by a couple of Jewish merchants. According to the first-century historian Flavius Josephus, when Izates tells his advisers that he's gotten a secret circumcision, there is fear in the royal court that "his subjects might not submit to be governed by a man who was so zealous for a strange religion." But the matter blows over and, like many converts before and since, the queen and her son set out to out-Jew the Jews. They build a palace and tombs in Jerusalem. During a famine in the Holy City, they send corn, dried figs, and other humanitarian aid. And when the Jews in Palestine mount their famous rebellion against their Roman rulers in A.D. 66, Adiabene's royal family is the only outside power to come to their aid, dispatching troops and supplies. It was a bizarre and quixotic alliance. Neither Jewish Babylonia nor any other diaspora had offered help to the Palestinian Jews, whom the Romans would soon crush in a horrifying bloodbath.

The record of Kurdish Judaism then goes dark for more than one thousand years. When it resurfaces again, briefly, in the twelfth century, the stories are just as extraordinary. Around 1160, one David Alroy, born in the Kurdish city of Amidiya, north of Mosul, goes to yeshiva in Baghdad and returns an intellectual. He learns seventy languages. He is as well read in Jewish Law and the Talmud as he is in "the wisdom of the Mohammedans" and "the writings of magicians and soothsayers."

With those credentials and considerable charisma, he comes home and proclaims himself the Messiah. He announces that he will lead his fellow Kurdish Jews in a "fight against all the nations," writes Benjamin of Tudela, a Jewish traveler who visited the area around that time. "He showed signs by pretended miracles to the Jews, and said, 'The Holy One, blessed be He, sent me to capture Jerusalem and to free you from the yoke of the Gentiles.'"

Alroy wins fanatical followers across the region. But his plans for world war and apocalyptic deliverance don't sit particularly well with the king of Persia, who threatens to slay every Jew in his empire unless the head of the Baghdad yeshiva persuades his former student to stop his foolishness. When that doesn't work, the king resorts to simpler means: He pays Alroy's father-in-law ten thousand gold pieces to kill Alroy in his sleep and the deed is done.

The story inspired the nineteenth-century British statesman Benjamim Disraeli, his country's first and only Jewish prime minister, to write a novel, *Alroy or The Prince of the Captivity*. "Being at Jerusalem in the year 1831 and visiting the traditionary tombs of the Kings of Israel," Disraeli, a Sephardic Jew, writes in the preface, "my thoughts recurred to a personage whose marvellous career had, even in boyhood, attracted my attention, as one fraught with the richest materials of poetic fiction."

Then, once again, this time for five hundred years, the annals of Kurdish-Jewish history are blank.

In the seventeenth century, Kurdistan's most illustrious rabbi, Samuel Barzani, a charismatic reformer and yeshiva builder, produces no sons and finds himself unable to continue his line in the usual way. So he drills his beautiful daughter, Asenath Barzani, in Hebrew, Torah, and the Kabbalah. He marries her to his nephew and favorite disciple, Rabbi Jacob, and makes the man swear he'll never make her do housework. When her father and then Rabbi Jacob die, Asenath is the only one in the family with the training to take over the yeshiva the two men had run in Mosul. She becomes what is thought to be the world's first female rabbi. She proves herself a formidable leader, fundraiser, and intellectual, acquiring a reputation as a Kabbalist miracle worker and sage poet and winning over the local Jews. Her ascent forces the bewildered brotherhood of local rabbis to coin a new Hebrew word: *tanna'it*, or "woman Talmudic scholar."

And then, yet again, the record goes blank.

The achievements of the Kurdish Jews cannot be measured by any conventional yardstick. They were largely illiterate. They left behind few written records and had no printing press. Kurdish storytellers carried a spellbinding oral literature across the generations, but the line between fact, folklore, and fantasy is nearly impossible to discern. They were too poor to school their children. They toiled at back-breaking jobs with no real chance for social or political advancement. They were beholden to warring tribal chieftains whose autocratic rule they never had the numbers to challenge. They lived as tiny minorities in some two hundred Muslim towns and villages scattered across the Kurdish regions of Iraq, Syria, Iran, and Turkey, the majority in northern Iraq. Never in the historical record did they band together to press for better living conditions or to assert national rights.

The pinnacle of Kurdish Jewish achievement is not a Hanging Gardens or a revolt against Roman rule. It is something far more simple and poetic: It is the very fact of their survival. It is that after twenty-seven hundred years of being "lost in the Land of Assyria," one can still speak of something called a Kurdish Jew. It is that twelve hundred years after the rest of Iraq's Jews switched to Arabic, the Kurdish Jews still spoke Aramaic, the ancient mother tongue of the Jewish diaspora.

But perhaps that is not as surprising as it sounds. As the legends of

Adiabene, Alroy, and Asenath illustrate, small miracles had a way of raining down on the mountains.

12 ◈ Speaking with Angels

"From Ruwandiz northwards and in most parts of the Mosul *liwa* the trousers are ample, hang straight and are sometimes slightly bell-bottomed. *Choghe* and *rhanik* are almost invariably made of local *buzuw*, the best qualities of which used to be woven by the Jews and Armenians of Zakho in a wide choice of the most attractive designs, colours and waterings."

—C. J. EDMONDS, *Kurds, Turks and Arabs: Politics, Travel and Research in North-Eastern Iraq, 1919–1925*

On some mornings, as Yona's grandfather, Ephraim Beh Sabagha, looked at the vats, kettles, scales, and dye bottles scattered about his shop, he wondered whether God was testing him. He was the only *sabagha*, or dyer, in Zakho, and God would not let him rest. Women hurried in with skeins of yarn. Men in shalla u-shappiksas came in grousing that the sun or rain or perspiration had faded what he had promised were fast colors. Dressmakers lugged in loose cotton and wool and haggled over prices.

That was headache enough. Then came the work: Weighing the crude fabric. Scouring away grease and oil in pails of soapy water. Rinsing out the suds in clean river water and wringing out the moisture. Steeping the cloth overnight in a hot bath of tannic acid wrung from sumac leaves or gall nuts, so the fibers formed a faster bond with the dyestuffs.

Most of his patrons were simple tradesmen and peasants, in search of fresh coats of either indigo or black, the former for holiday and wedding suits, the latter for everyday wear. These days, though, his wealthier customers demanded brilliancy, variety, and fastness. Not so long ago, mulberry fruits, onion peels, pecan shells, pomegranate rinds, peach leaves, and turmeric roots were all a color man needed. A studiously proportioned brew of pure vegetable colors could infuse cloth with a fine range of hues and tints, from Turkey red to Tyrian purple. But the brighter colors Zakho's businessmen had seen on sales trips to Baghdad were, alas, beyond the reach of God's harvest. So Ephraim consulted his dealers in Mosul, who told him that the great German dye works were making the richest and fastest pigments. The names on the sample bottles — aniline, alizarine, benzidine — mystified him. He shrugged his shoulders and ordered a crateful. "If this is what they want, so be it," he told his friend the Muslim barber in the shop next door, throwing up his hands.

Either way, it was alchemy. A customer dropped off a heap of greasy wool or grubby cotton, and Ephraim turned it into finery.

Even as an eight-year-old, Yona was aware of the way other people spoke of his grandfather: The women customers who called Ephraim righteous because he insisted they leave payment on a stand by his seat; to take coins from their hands and risk physical contact would be improper. The schoolteachers who looked at Yona with a new respect after discovering he was the grandson of Beh Sabagha.

There was also the time Babba Ephraim got lost on a snowy night and returned home shivering and faint. Zakho's wealthiest Jew, Moshe Gabbay, summoned an army doctor from a nearby military garrison. The doctor, the grandson of a Baghdad rabbi who had penned a few tomes of Jewish scholarship, restored Ephraim with an injection at no charge.

Uncle Eliyahu was insulted that anyone would see his family as a charity case, but the doctor insisted. "Moshe Gabbay told me that Ephraim is the only person in this whole town who reads my grandfather's books. That is payment enough."

It was a puzzle to Yona. All this fuss because his grandfather read a few books? The Aramaic phrase for deep study was *lyapa blibba*, "learning by heart." Knowledge was stored in memory and transmitted by mouth, not written down and studied for its own sake. All most Jews needed was Aramaic for conversations among themselves and a few basic words of the Kurdish language Kurmanji for business dealings with Zakho's Muslim majority. Arabic was unnecessary if you never left Kurdistan, and most people didn't. Hebrew, you hardly needed, so long as you could sound out a few words at synagogue. Even the local rabbis had read only enough to get through a rudimentary prayer service. Many of Zakho's great storytellers and wise men were illiterate; they had memorized epics, sometimes hundreds of them, that they had heard from fathers and grandfathers, but could not read a word. As a boy, Yona saw things much the same way: Book reading was a chore he performed grudgingly and only under the threat of a teacher's lash. The Kurds even had a proverb: "Study constantly and you'll end up a beggar." His grandfather, however, read every night by choice, for its own sake. Even more of a mystery was that Ephraim gave up a half night's sleep — the salve of old men everywhere, as far as Yona could tell — for books. Books!

And yet, over time, Ephraim cast a spell over his grandson. "*Si hzi pasid shakhina*" — Go and see the face of God — his mother said, as she shook him awake so he could pray with his grandfather before school. She meant the divine likeness that she believed radiated, like a vision, from the Torah scolls. But, for Yona, the phrase evoked only the smiling eyes of his grandfather.

When Yona arrived at temple for 6 A.M. prayers, his grandfather was always at the same spot beside the ark, sitting cross-legged and draped in a heavy robe. He was hemmed in on three sides by books: the prayer manual, the Bible, treatises on Kabbalah and Jewish law, a guide to virtuous Jewish living. He swayed back and forth, the tip of his beard brushing the pages. He muttered the words on the page — and some that weren't on it — and sometimes looked up to the ceiling to shout some exaltation. Arriving worshippers looked at the lantern and coal basket at Ephraim's feet and knew that the town's simple dyer had again spent the entire night at the temple.

Every morning, Yona quietly approached and kneeled on the corner of Ephraim's carpet, prayer book in hand, hoping the old man would turn to say something to him or even to smile. But Ephraim, deep in some rapture, seldom looked up from his books for so much as a nod. It was only after Yona's nearly perfect attendance for a year that Ephraim, who had always been friendly at home, finally spoke to him in the synagogue.

"*Akha sabri kese,*" he said, throwing a glance at the synagogue walls. "This is the only place where my soul is at rest."

"What is in those books, Babba Ephraim?"

"The words of wise men — men far wiser than I," Ephraim said. "But you must not worry about that now. The main thing is to trust in God and pray every day. Do this and you will live longer than your friends."

Yona thought about the smile that played on his grandfather's face when he read.

"Yes, Babba Ephraim, but tell me what the books say."

"No. You must learn to read, yourself. And you must judge for yourself what you believe and what is important."

He thought for a moment about his Hebrew school and the way the teacher made them repeat words in the Bible over and over until they had lost all meaning and were just sounds.

"I don't think I'm good at reading," Yona said.

"Here." Ephraim removed a volume from the center of the stack. Its cover read Book of Psalms. "You want to know what the wise men say, Yona? They say that if you read this book from start to finish every day, God will save a seat for you in the Garden of Eden."

This was one of the times when Yona wondered whether his grandfather might be a little crazy. Ephraim was the only man in town who claimed to have attended a midnight prayer service led by angels who were spitting images of actual people in Zakho. He was the only man who claimed that a phantom likeness of the *shamash*, the synagogue's manager, had once entered the temple before dawn and slapped him on the back of the head, prompting a return punch that sent the wraith flying. His image as a self-styled mystic may have impressed the men and women of Zakho, but Yona knew some of the children felt differently. He had seen a few of his classmates peering into the synagogue windows at dawn and tittering every time the old man launched into dialogue with the angel Rafael, the prophet Elijah, or some other heavenly apparition.

Even so, there was something about Ephraim's eccentricity that appealed to the boy. In a society straitjacketed by tradition, this self-taught man had beaten out a new path. He was a workman-scholar. A dyer-mystic. A nobody-somebody. Ephraim Beh Sabagha had invented a new kind of respectability, one based not on the size of your land or your income, but on the depth of your knowledge and the strength of your faith.

That evening Yona cracked open his grandfather's dog-eared copy of the Book of Psalms and took it to his sleeping mat, along with a small lantern. The neat lines of strange Hebrew words were riddles, but he muddled through, sounding out words and guessing at meanings. By the time he reached the fourth psalm — "O ye sons of men, how long will ye turn my glory into shame? How long will ye love vanity?" — his eyes were heavy. In his dreams that night, Yona was standing in the mountains above Zakho and watching a miniature of himself dashing through a field of golden sunflowers. The Garden of Eden.

Then the scene transformed. The flowers vanished, and he and his grandfather were alone in the synagogue. Sun poured in through the high window, and Ephraim, still cross-legged, floated toward the light.

"Wait for me," Yona shouted. But his grandfather was gone.

13 ❖ Arabs Before Jews

"To a Kurd the mountain is no less than the embodiment of the deity: mountain is his mother, his refuge, his protector, his home, his farm, his market, his mate, and his only friend."

—MEHRDAD R. IZADY, *The Kurds: A Concise Handbook*, 1992

In their idyll in the mountains, the Jews of Zakho heard little about the massive changes sweeping Baghdad, some three hundred miles to the south. After World War I, the Allies carved up the defeated Ottoman Empire and placed the territory of Iraq under a British Mandate. Twelve years later, in 1932, Iraq presented the League of Nations, which it had just joined, a "Declaration on the Subject of Minorities." The document pledged the "full and complete protection of life and liberty [for] all inhabitants of Iraq, without distinction of birth, nationality, language, race or religion."

The very next year, Iraqi troops massacred three thousand Assyrians, Aramaic-speaking Christians with ancient roots in northern Iraq.

The Assyrians had been seeking broader political rights, and a group of eight hundred had taken up arms. The scale and ferocity of the Iraqi response — dozens of Assyrian villages were razed, and civilians and children were among the dead — raised serious questions about its earlier pledge to ensure minority rights.

News of the attack swept through Baghdad's Jewish neighborhoods like a bitter wind. For nearly three millenia, the Jews of central Iraq lived and worked with Muslims. They formed a prosperous class of merchants, bankers, and financiers, exploiting Babylon's role as a commercial crossroads on major international trade routes. They built two large yeshivas, in Sura and Nehardea, that minted new rabbis and kept Judaism alive across this sprawling diaspora. By A.D. 499 Jewish scholars in Iraq had completed the landmark Babylonian Talmud, an Aramaic text recognized then, and now, as the world's most authoritative guide to Jewish laws.

Even after Persia's Cyrus the Great defeated the Babylonian armies in 538 B.C. and let Jewish exiles return to Jerusalem to rebuild their temple, most Jews decided to stay in Babylon. Most stayed even after the Islamic armies conquered the Middle East some eleven hundred years later. So long as Jews paid taxes and gave lip service to the supremacy of Islam, they continued to enjoy broad freedoms of trade and religion. The climate of tolerance survived the rise and fall of empires, and in 1908 the Ottoman rulers put it in writing with a constitution granting equal rights to non-Muslims.

When British troops entered Baghdad in 1917, Jews made up the largest ethnic group: eighty thousand of the city's population of two hundred thousand. According to the historian Nissim Rejwan, wealthy Jews began dressing their children in London fashions and giving them British names such as Edward, George, Daisy, and Claire.

Jews had long held low- and mid-level posts in government. After World War I, with Iraq under British mandate, they rose to greater heights. Sassoon Heskel became the new country's first finance minister, and other Jews took seats in parliament and on the High Court of Appeal. But independence ushered in an era of instability that coincided with growing calls from around the Middle East for pan-Arab unity and an end to Western colonial influence in the Islamic world. Iraq, which saw no fewer than five coups in the 1930s, grew into a haven for Arab zealots and ideologues.

One of the new arrivals was Haj Amin al-Husseini, the fiery Grand Mufti of Jerusalem, who was wanted by British authorities for inciting Arab revolts in Palestine. Another was the Nazi envoy to Baghdad, Dr. Fritz Grobba, an urbane figure who fancied himself a German Lawrence of Arabia. Grobba had purchased the daily newspaper *Al-Alam Al-Arabi* and published Hitler's *Mein Kampf*, in Arabic translation, as a serial. He was soon throwing parties that drew an entranced cast of elite Iraqi politicians, journalists, and military officers. Wide-eyed over Nazi victories in Europe, some Iraqis saw the Third Reich as a possible model for the pan-Arabist cause.

Iraq's chief rabbi, *Hakham* Sassoon Kadoori, and other Jewish leaders took pains to distance themselves from Zionist movements in Europe and Palestine. Even if some Iraqi Jews felt intellectual sympathy with the messianic notion of a Jewish homeland, they were not particularly eager to leave comfortable lives for an uncertain future. Nor did they have any inclination to stir resentment among Muslim friends, neighbors, and business associates.

As early as 1922, Menahem Salih Daniel, a Jewish leader in Baghdad, pleaded with the secretary of the Zionist Organization in London to slow down. "I cannot help considering the establishment of a recognized Zionist Bureau in Baghdad as deleteriously affecting the good relations of the Mesopotamian Jew with his fellow citizens," Daniel wrote, in a letter quoted in Nissim Rejwan's history of Iraqi Jewry.

The Jewish scholar Ezra Haddad reflected popular sentiment in an article he wrote in *Al-Akhbar*, Baghdad's major daily: "When [the Arab Jew] speaks of the Arab lands, he speaks of homelands which from time immemorial surrounded him with generosity and affluence — homelands which he considered and continues to consider as oases in the midst of a veritable desert of injustices and oppressions. . . ." An earlier article by Haddad had carried the pithy title "We Were Arabs Before We Became Jews."

Yosef El Kabir, a Jewish leader and prominent lecturer at the Baghdad

University Faculty of Law, took direct aim at the Balfour Declaration, the landmark 1917 statement of British support for a Jewish national home in Palestine. "The problem which the Balfour Declaration purported to solve is and remains a European problem," El Kabir wrote in 1938 in the *Iraqi Times*.

But the optimism would not last.

In April 1941 a group of four anti-British army colonels calling themselves "The Golden Square" staged yet another coup. The pro-British regent, Crown Prince Abdul Ilah, fled to Transjordan with the help of American diplomats. The Golden Square named the former prime minister, Rashid Ali al-Gilani, a raving nationalist with newfound Nazi sympathies, the country's supreme leader. Shiite clerics and the Mufti of Jerusalem, a Sunni, called for jihad against Britain. Rashid Ali formed what he termed a "Government of National Defense" and shut off Iraq's oil pipeline to the Mediterranean. Nazi ideology took hold in the schools, and Jews were tarred as British collaborators. The Nazis, with their theories of racial purity, bore no love for the Arabs and paid only lip service to Arab ambitions for independence. But the Germans were riding high after a series of military advances across Europe and saw an Arab revolt against the British as another chance to humiliate the Allies. As Rashid Ali and the British raced toward a crisis over England's continued use of Iraqi military bases, Hitler obliged Iraqi requests and sent Baghdad guns, a Luftwaffe squadron, and a team of military advisers. The shipments jolted Winston Churchill into a recognition of the conflict's broader dimensions. He ordered his armies to retake Iraq and cabled his commander there to "beat down Rashid Ali's forces with utmost vigour."

On April 17, 1941, British troops landed unopposed in Basra, and by late May, after a series of devastating bombing raids by the Royal Air Force, the outmatched Iraqi forces surrendered. Rashid Ali, along with the German and Italian envoys and other supporters, slipped across the border into Iran. The Grand Mufti of Jerusalem escaped to Germany, where he was officially received by Adolf Hitler.

On June 1, Crown Prince Ilah returned to Iraq to reclaim the throne. It was the second day of the Jewish festival of Shevuot. Jews were milling through the streets of Baghdad in their finest clothes. A group even traveled to the airport to welcome the regent home. But the sight of Jews celebrating so soon after Rashid Ali's defeat was like a lit match in a fuel depot. As the Jewish well-wishers returned from the airport that afternoon, a group of decommissioned soldiers set upon them. They murdered one Jew and injured sixteen while military police looked on in silence. Mayhem soon spread across Baghdad. Mobs gathered in the slums. High-school students armed themselves with clubs, axes, and knives. Soldiers chafing from their defeat by the British poured into the city. By evening, Baghdad was in the throes of a *farhud*, the Arabic word for "pogrom." Jewish homes and businesses were savagely attacked. Gangs slaughtered infants and raped women in front of their families. In the Abbas Effendi neighborhood, the mangled corpses of six men and one woman were found nailed to a wall. The city's police officers stood on the sidelines, and in some cases they pointed newly arrived rioters toward Jewish homes and businesses. Jewish stores were looted and torched, synagogues desecrated, and Torah scrolls hurled into the streets.

By the time the crown prince finally ordered his army to fire on rioters late the next day, the city was awash in blood. An estimated 150 to 180 Jews had been murdered, along with many Muslims who came to their defense; 896 houses and 583 shops, looted; and nearly 2,400 families, left homeless.

The many Baghdadi Jews who had tried to stay upbeat about their future could no longer keep up the charade. The Farhud was a shot through the heart.

But if you had asked the Jews of Zakho about the massacre, most would have had no idea what you were talking about.

14 ❖ Plus and Minus

For the Beh Sabaghas, the late 1940s were boom years. Their stores were turning such steady profits that the brothers pressed Ephraim, unsuccessfully, to retire. On an August day in 1944, Miryam gave birth to a cross-eyed girl they called Sara. Miryam cursed the evil eye for the cruelty of this particular taunt, until, to her amazement, Sara grew into a vivacious girl. Three years later Avram was born, long and skinny, like a skewer of kabob.

In the afternoons Yona, now nine, kept books for an illiterate Muslim grocer who paid him in *filu* coins and chewy Turkish delights. In the mornings he was being molded into an upright Iraqi citizen at Boys School No. 1. He dressed in the cadet-style uniform, complete with red scouting scarf and tricorne cap. He studied Arabic. And he took part in weekly salutes to the Iraqi flag and King Faisal II, the boy monarch. Yona chanted with the other boys: "We are the heroes of the *fetuwa*" — the youth brigades. "We are the spear tip of the Arab nation / Never bending or softening in the face of the enemy."

When drill instructors rapped his knuckles for confusing his right and left feet on the march home from school, he didn't protest. But when a teacher went to the chalkboard one day and drew a symbol Yona had seen outside the Christian church across the river, the boy felt he had to say something. It wasn't in Koran class, from which all non-Muslim students were excused. It was in math, one of his favorite subjects. The young teacher, a dynamic graduate of a teacher's college in Mosul, drew a + between two numbers on the blackboard. Yona cast a nervous glance at the other Jewish boys. They all grabbed their book bags and stood up as if to leave. A myth had recently circulated in the Jewish quarter about Christians trying to trick Jewish children into conversion. Yona and his Jewish classmates had understood one another without uttering a single word: This teacher was trying to slip a cross into a lesson about numbers.

"What's the matter?" cried the teacher. "Where are you going?"

"We are Jews," Yona said. "We are forbidden to look at the cross."

The teacher's confused expression collapsed into a smile.

"I'm a Jew, too," the teacher said. "My first name is Ya'acov, okay? And believe me, this is not a cross. It's a sign for 'plus.' It has nothing to do with Jesus. Without the up-and-down line, it's a 'minus,' so we don't really have another choice."

The Jewish boys dropped their book bags, but they were not yet ready to trust the teacher's explanation. "Look, just put a half-line above the minus, so that the lines don't actually cross. And I'll know you mean plus. Okay?"

Yona sank slowly, warily, into his seat, and the other boys followed his lead.

15 ❧ The Mountains Are Our Only Friends

"Over the course of several thousand years of Kurdish history—a time long enough for many other ethnic groups to have assimilated entirely into a dominant culture—the Kurds have remained a distinct people. Conversely, almost all who settled among them in the mountains—Scythians, Alans, Arameans, Armenians, Persians, Arabs, Mongols, Turkmens, and Turks—have been kurdified beyond recognition."

—MEHRDAD R. IZADY, *The Kurds: A Concise Handbook*, 1992

Yehoshua Kellman had high hopes for Zakho. Young and idealistic, he had gone there under the auspices of the Jewish Agency, the quasi-governmental Zionist body responsible for Jewish affairs in the Holy Land during the British Mandate. After years of work in Europe, the agency had dispatched him and a few others to Iraq, hoping to turn Jewish discontent over the Farhud into a mass migration to Palestine. Kellman saw the Farhud as a turning point. The Arab world's largest and wealthiest Jewish population might finally wake up to the urgency of aliya, the return to a Jewish homeland.

Zakho, he knew, was important not merely as a center of Jewish life in Kurdistan. Its strategic location on the Turkish border might make the town a critical stop in some future underground railroad to the Holy Land. Some of its Jews had already left for Palestine in the 1930s—though it was also true that a few, unable to find work, had turned around and come back.

When Kellman arrived in Zakho in 1943, he felt encouraged. The Jewish men here were husky and hard working, nothing like the cosseted patrician types he had seen in Baghdad. Strong men were what Palestine needed. A few approached and escorted him to the house of Moshe Gabbay, the wealthy landowner and unofficial leader of the local Jewish community. With a list of business contacts across Iraq, Gabbay had a broader view of the world than did most Zakho Jews. He had heard a little about the Farhud. He had read about the movement for a Jewish state. He had named his son Shmuel, after Herbert Samuel, the British governor of Palestine. And his grandson he called Weizmann, after Chaim Weizmann, the president of the World Zionist Organization.

But when Kellman asked if he could count on Gabbay's help to one day evacuate Zakho's Jews to Palestine, Gabbay shook his head. Naming children after Zionist leaders was a symbolic gesture of support for a new state, he explained, not a sign that he — or anyone else in Zakho — wanted to move there.

Kellman left Zakho after three days, empty-handed and crestfallen.

"I don't understand," his boss said on his return to Palestine.

"They just . . . how do I say this?" Kellman said. "They don't see Zionism the way we do."

KURDISTAN IS A REGION, not a state, and for its religious minorities, that may have been its saving grace. A parabola of mountainous territory at the northern fringe of the Middle East, it spans about two hundred thousand square miles, an area slightly larger than Spain. Roughly following the Taurus and Zagros mountain ranges, it curves from southeastern Turkey and northeastern Syria up to the edge of the former Soviet Union before plunging south across northern Iraq and western Iran.

Cave dwellings dating as far back as one hundred thousand years have been found in the region. But the key to Kurdish identity is not so much a common past, language, racial history, or religion; Kurdistan has seen too much upheaval over the millennia for the textbook bonds of nationhood to apply. Instead, it is the independent character and consciousness forged by hardscrabble lives in the mountains, a frontier mindset where honor and brotherhood count for more than what God you believe in or what language you happen to speak. The identity survived thousands of years of wars and invasions and the division of Kurdish lands into parts of five countries by European powers divvying up the defeated Ottoman Empire after World War I.

In the mountains, hundreds of miles from the religious fanaticism and nationalist movements of big cities, the Kurdish Jews faced almost none of the virulent anti-Semitism that hounded Jews in Europe or even, to a far lesser extent, Baghdad. They went to work, prayed to a Jewish God, and spoke their own language without major disruption for some twenty-seven hundred years.

Seclusion bred fraternity. Muslim, Jew, and Christian suffered alike through the region's cruel cycles of flood, famine, and Kurdish tribal bloodshed. They prospered alike when the soil yielded bumper crops of wheat, gall nuts, and fragrant tobacco. In important ways, they were Kurds first and Muslims, Christians, or Jews second. Muslims sent Jews bread and milk as gifts after Passover. They ate matzoh, which they called "holiday bread," as a delicacy. They sent their Jewish neighbors hot tea during the Sabbath, when Jews were forbidden to light fires. Some Muslims even asked the synagogue keeper to wake them early in the days before Yom Kippur: They viewed early rising on Jewish days of penitence as bringing good luck. And the Jews paid back the respect, forgoing cigarettes, for instance, during the holy month of Ramadan, when Muslims may not smoke.

In Kurdistan, religions from Islam, Christianity, and Judaism to Sufi mysticism, Bahaism, and Yezidism flourished alongside one another, and extremism was rare. Muslim Kurdish women went out without veils, could buy and sell goods in the markets, and were relatively free to talk with men who were not their husbands. Jewish men wore the same baggy trousers and embroidered tunics as their Muslim brethren.

It may be fitting that Kurdistan's greatest historical figure was the warrior-gentleman Saladin. Born in Tikrit in 1138 to a Kurdish governor, Saladin was a strict Muslim and a champion of jihad who united the

Islamic world from Syria to Yemen with diplomacy and the sword. His armies swept the Franks from Jerusalem in 1187 and repelled the ensuing invasion by King Richard the Lionheart and his Crusaders, a reversal of expectations that shocked Christian Europe. Yet Saladin is remembered today less for his military cunning than his chivalry. When Richard's horse was killed, Saladin sent two replacements. When Richard fell ill after his victory at Jaffa, Saladin sent a sorbet of fruit and snow to cool his rival's fever. Christian crusaders had slaughtered thousands of Muslim prisoners, but after his victory, Saladin let Christians exit Jerusalem unmolested.

In spite of the embarrassing setbacks to Christendom's bloody campaign for Jerusalem, Saladin had won the West's respect as an embodiment, however ironically, of Christian values. Dante portrayed him as a virtuous pagan soul in Limbo, the First Circle of Hell: "I saw great Saladin, aloof, alone." Sir Walter Scott cast him as a sympathetic figure in *The Talisman*. When Saladin's plain wooden tomb at the Omayyad Mosque in Damascus fell into disrepair in the late nineteenth century, Kaiser Wilhelm II of Germany offered to replace it with an ornate marble sarcophagus. Even in the thick of America's post-9/11 war on terror, the director Ridley Scott deployed Saladin's story in the movie *Kingdom of Heaven* as an antidote to facile portrayals of "good" Christians and "bad" Muslims in an incurable clash of civilizations.

In fall 2007, with Islamist extremism still raging in the south, Iraq's Kurdish Regional Government added a course on comparative religion to the public-school curriculum, complete with lessons on Judaism and Christianity. "We're trying to reach the point where all the religions can find common ground," Fadel Mahmoud, an instructor at the College of Kurdistan in Sulaymānīyah, told a reporter for McClatchy Newspapers in late 2007. "We are not interested in talking about the points of disagreement."

And so Saladin's legacy lives on.

TODAY, THE TOWNSPEOPLE in Zakho still call the rutted alleys where my father grew up the *mahala Juheeya*, the Jewish neighborhood, despite the exodus of its last Jew more than a half century earlier. Arab political leaders in Baghdad had at some point renamed the district "The Liberated Neighborhood." But the Kurds of Zakho paid no mind. Jews had raised families on those streets for centuries, and the Kurds are in no hurry to erase those memories.

It would have been easy for Kurdistan's Muslims to stamp out its Jews or at the very least their culture and Aramaic language. The roughly twenty-five thousand Jews in Kurdistan in the late 1940s made up less than one half of a percent of the overall Kurdish population of about six million. But well before such late-twentieth-century notions as multiculturalism, Kurdistan was proof that cultures could braid without blurring. It is true that location played a big role: the fortress of mountains walled out bureaucrats, religious fanatics, and other forces of homogenization. But another factor is Kurdistan's statelessness. Government, such as, it was, consisted of independent tribal chiefs who put the needs of their local fiefdoms first and, as a result, were often at war with one another. They had little patience for, or access to, intellectual abstractions concocted in the halls of universities, parliaments, or far-off international organizations like the United Nations.

The Kurds lacked so much as a common set of physical traits. Centuries of invasions and migrations by everyone from the Indo-European–speaking Aryans and Scythians to Mongols, Persians, and Turks had turned the Kurdish population into an ethnic kaleidoscope. Blond, blue-eyed Kurds with semi-Nordic features walked among the brown eyed and the dark skinned. With the exception of a couple centuries of dynastic rule and intellectual ferment in the Middle Ages, the Kurds couldn't even stamp themselves with a uniform national identity; there were simply no central authorities or institutions. This may have complicated later bids for statehood, but for a very long time it had bred a remarkable kind of tolerance.

16 ❖ Freezing in Baghdad

"The Jews of Central Kurdistan . . . have little of the prosperous appearance of
their brethren in Baghdad."

—British Air Ministry, "Military Report on Iraq (Area 9) Central Kurdistan," 1929

Curled up against his father on the overnight train to Baghdad in
the late 1940s, Yona tried to stay awake. He studied the sliver of
moon overhead and thought to ask how it had followed them all the way
from Zakho and why it seemed smaller here. But soon the lights of Mosul, where they had boarded the train, gave way to the dark plains of the
Tigris River Valley, and he could no longer keep his eyes open. In his
dreams, he saw himself as a tiny creature, no bigger than a grain of sand,
being blown across an empty plain.

The voices at the edge of his consciousness were dull at first. Then he
felt an elbow in his ribs and opened his eyes to the sight of three men in
khaki uniforms shouting at his father in Arabic. They were pointing at his
sacks and motioning for him to open them. Yona noticed their sidearms
and pulled his knees against his chest, his pulse racing.

The men punched their hands among the walnuts with which his father always camouflaged his smuggled Turkish textiles. This time his
trick failed. The biggest customs police officer, the one who sounded like a
snarling dog, pulled out one scarf after another, scattering the nuts across
the center aisle and waking several nearby passengers.

"What is it, shorty, do you think we are idiots?" he said, his badge
glowing dully under the row of tiny lights above the aisle. "Do you want
to go to jail? Where are your tariff receipts for all this?"

Yona had never seen his father so frightened, and he began to tremble.
Were they going to take his father away?

"Babba?"

Rahamim reached back to pat his son's knee. He tried to say something in Arabic to the guards, but the words snagged on lips tight with fear. The men looked at one another and laughed. In a moment, they had dumped all his father's merchandise in the aisle and were dividing the fine silks and woolens — perhaps a month's income — among themselves.

"Dumb Kurd," the ringleader said, stalking off with a bundle of fabric under his arm. "We have your name in our books now. Next time, you go to jail. You hear? Jail!"

The train car grew suddenly silent. Yona clutched his father's arm, but he hardly recognized the man it belonged to. His father's shoulders were slumped forward, his eyes vacant. A little bit of life had left him. It was a look of defeat, of hurt pride, that the boy would come to see again — and with greater clarity — as the years wore on. Now, though, he just felt afraid, alone. Why did those men shout at his father as if he were some kind of animal? Yona had come along on this trading trip because he had longed to see the great city of Baghdad for himself. Now he wanted to turn the train around, with a tug of the reins like a trader on a donkey, to be back in Zakho's familiar streets, eating his mother's kubeh, reading his book of psalms so he could get into the Garden of Eden.

He held back tears as he reached for his father's shoulder.

"Babba . . ."

But Rahamim had withdrawn somewhere deep inside himself, and the train clattered on through the darkness.

THE BAGHDAD TRAIN station reeked of the vinegary smell of too many bodies pressed too close together. Yona held his father's hand as Rahamim elbowed his way through the mob to the doors.

Outside, cars and buses — not just one or two, as in Zakho, but hundreds, honking, belching exhaust — jammed the wide, palm-lined boulevard. Rahamim waved down a horse-drawn carriage.

"What are we doing, Babba?" Yona asked, looking down at horses draped in magnificent purple banners. "Are these horses taking me to my wedding?"

Rahamim laughed. "This is not Zakho, Yona. Some places here are too far to walk."

Yona felt a lightness in his stomach at the smack of hooves on cobblestone and the scent of orange blossoms on the summer wind. They crossed a long bridge over the Tigris River, plunged into the circus of bleating car horns on Al-Rashid Street and past the bedlam of the Al-Shorja Bazaar. Soon they emerged in Baghdad's Jewish quarter, at the city's northeastern edge, a district of snaking streets lined with well-kept two-story houses, grand synagogues, and a mosaic-tiled yeshiva.

"Look at these things our brothers in Baghdad have built," Rahamim said. "Like kings of Israel they live."

"Babba, what will you tell Ezra about all your stuff?" Yona said, his stomach sinking as they stepped down from the carriage with their empty sacks. "Will he be mad at you?"

Ezra's official business was his liquor store. But he often left his sons in charge while he pursued his real passion: fencing the scarfs, rugs, and shrouds Rahamim and other Jewish Kurds smuggled from Turkey. Rahamim got a cut, plus food and a place to stay while in Baghdad. But Ezra, a clean-cut man with patrician manners and a fondness for bespoke British suits, was always pressing him to bring more merchandise, take greater risks.

"There is no bottom to the market for these goods," he had told Rahamim over a late-night glass of arak on his last visit. And here he laughed. "Especially the funeral shrouds. There's such a craze, Rahamim, that Baghdadis are buying them for themselves *before* they die. It's not enough to look good during life now, Rahamim. Now one must be well dressed in death." He poured another glass of the clear liquor, which turned milky after he dropped in a few ice cubes. "I'll be honest, friend," he had said. "We can do better."

Rahamim got the feeling that Ezra didn't always appreciate the gambles he took for their sake. He was the one who risked arrest should Turkish or Iraqi customs officials discover the unregistered imports. He was the one who put his life on the line to meet dealers in the lawless borderlands. So many of Zakho's peddlers had been shot or knifed to death by brigands that the Jews even had a saying: Zakho men never die in their own beds.

But all Rahamim told Ezra was, "Next time, I will come with my son. He is a strong boy. He can help me carry an extra sack."

"Now you are talking like a Baghdadi businessman," Ezra replied. "Never underestimate the value of children."

A MAIDSERVANT LED Yona and his father into a *balkon* overlooking a leafy courtyard with a fountain. *What walls!* Yona thought. There was no flaking mud, no scent of moldering clay. The surfaces were perfectly clean and white and smooth. The woman returned a moment later with a tray of gold-rimmed tea glasses. Behind her came a man with slick-backed hair, a chalk-stripe suit, and an air of self-possessed authority.

"Rahamim, friend, how are you?" Ezra said, slapping him on the back.

"Well, Ezra, not so good," Rahamim said, looking at the floor as he unwound the story of the night on the train.

"Here here, stop, please," Ezra interrupted after a moment, reaching into his shirt pocket for a few bills. "Take this as a loan until next time. More careful, okay? We all have to be. Since the Farhud we are living in a new Baghdad. Okay?"

Yona felt ashamed, as if everything had somehow been his fault. Later, when Ezra summoned them to the dining room for lunch, the boy was struck by paralysis.

"Come, Yona, eat, eat," Ezra cried, gesturing toward a mahogany table arrayed with silver, around which sat his exquisitely dressed wife and children.

"It is not polite to refuse," Rahamim said, looking pained as he pulled out a chair. "Come, Yona, please."

But Yona could not will his legs into motion.

"I could smell the fish, so delicious, coming to my nose, and the parsley and that delicious bread," my father told me recently, the memory still vivid more than a half century later. "I was starving. I was hungry. But for some reason, I kept standing in that spot. I don't know what entered me. Maybe I felt inferior or that I didn't belong. They kept saying, 'Yona, come on, we are waiting for you.'"

17 ✤ Hanging

The Baghdad Farhud in 1941 seemed at first to be an aberration in centuries of largely amicable relations among Iraqi Muslims and Jews. In its aftermath, rabid nationalist leaders were replaced by a pro-British monarchy. The Soviet Union's entry into World War II drew legions of Allied troops to Iraqi soil, handing a huge economic windfall to Baghdad's business leaders, many of whom were Jews. Germany's surrender in 1945 was the deathblow to Arab ideologues who had pinned nationalist ambitions to a Nazi victory.

Hope returned to Baghdad's Jewish neighborhood. Jews built new schools; they enlarged their houses and put up new ones in a burgeoning new suburb. Business leaders went to their offices as they always had. Butchers, fruit vendors, and metalsmiths took up their usual spots in the crowded Souk Hinnouni, in the heart of the Jewish quarter. The faithful continued to sleep by their windows so they could hear the shamash's call to morning prayer. They wanted desperately to believe that life for Jews in this beloved land had returned to normal.

But on November 29, 1947, everything changed. By a vote of thirty-three to thirteen, the United Nations General Assembly approved Resolution 181, partitioning Palestine into two states: one Jewish, one Arab. The British had promised to end their mandate by the next year, when the new states would take over. Jews embraced the plan as a fulfillment of biblical prophecy and Zionist yearnings and as a practical necessity after the horrors of Europe. But Arabs rejected it outright. The U.N. delegations of Iraq, Syria, Lebanon, Egypt, Saudi Arabia, and Yemen stormed out after the vote. And across the Arab world, Resolution 181 was denounced as a usurpation by foreign powers and a blow to dreams of Arab hegemony over the Middle East after centuries of imperial rule. Violence flared across Palestine as the British withdrew, leaving hundreds of civilians dead. Zionist commandos massacred 250 Arabs in an attack on the village of Dayr Yasin. Palestinian Arabs responded days later with an ambush on a medical convoy bound for Hadassah hospital in Jerusalem, killing about seventy-seven unarmed Jewish doctors, nurses, and medical students.

The Iraqi government made no secret of its sympathy for the Arab cause. It shut off the oil pipeline from Kirkuk to Haifa. It reduced the number of Jewish teachers at Jewish schools. It barred most Jews from leaving the country. Well-to-do Jews were arrested on an array of trumped-up charges, the cases dropped only after payments of hefty bribes. In Baghdad, cries of "Death to Jews" echoed in the streets. A group of angry demonstrators desecrated a synagogue. And with the government's blessing, Iraqi volunteers joined the pan-Arab auxiliary militia Jaysh al-Inqadh al-Arabi, the Army of Salvation, that was heading to Palestine to make war against the Jews.

The growing tension exposed a generational rift in the Jewish community. Young Baghdadi Jews who came of age after the Farhud reached out to Zionist organizations in Palestine and began planting the seeds of an underground. They met in basements, with lookouts at the doors, and laid the groundwork for arms training, Zionist education, and illegal immigration to Palestine. The signal event in their young lives had been the Farhud. Memories of slaughtered friends and family were fresh. The next time an Iraqi mob came after Jewish lives, property, and dignity, members of groups like Shabab al-Inqad (Youth for Salvation) and Shura (The Line) would be ready, with weapons if necessary.

But Iraq's Jewish leaders, an older generation, viewed the militants as a dangerous fringe and a threat to the future of Iraqi Jewry. The putative head of Iraq's Jews, Rabbi Sassoon Kadoorie, continued to proclaim Jewish loyalty to Iraq and support for the Arab cause in Palestine. Some Jews even sent money to the Arab fighters. But such actions were quickly becoming irrelevant. As far as ordinary Iraqis were concerned, there was no longer a difference between Zionist and Jew.

On May 14, 1948, as the last British high commissioner left Palestine, David Ben-Gurion stood beneath a portrait of Theodor Herzl at the Tel Aviv Museum and proclaimed Israel's statehood to an electrified nation.

"The Land of Israel was the birthplace of the Jewish people," declared the white-haired Ben-Gurion, a Polish-born Zionist who came to Palestine as a twenty-year-old in 1906. "After being forcibly exiled from their land, the people kept faith with it throughout their Dispersion and never ceased to pray and hope for their return to it and for the restoration in it of their political freedom."

Azzam Pasha, secretary-general of the Arab League, went on radio with a call for a pan-Arab jihad. "This will be a war of extermination and a momentous massacre which will be spoken of like the Mongolian massacres and the Crusades," he declared.

Within hours, the armies of Egypt, Lebanon, Syria, Transjordan, and Iraq were massing along the new country's borders. The War of 1948 was supposed to be a glorious moment for Iraq's forces: it was their first conflict on foreign soil. But the war against the new State of Israel quickly turned into a debacle. Some sixty thousand Jewish troops repelled the ill-coordinated armies of five Arab nations, and Iraqi soldiers were soon returning home in boxes.

The defeats were a humiliating blow to a country already riven by domestic upheaval. Martial law gave Iraq's leaders cover for a crackdown, not only on Jews but on Communists and other dissidents. Justice was handed over to military courts, and sprawling detention camps were opened in the south. As nationalist newspapers published editorials critical of Israel's treatment of Palestinian Arabs, Muslim Iraqis started eyeing their Jewish neighbors and friends with suspicion. In July the Iraqi parliament made Zionism a crime. The amendment to Law No. 51 of the Criminal Code set Zionism on par with Communism and Anarchaism as a crime against the state. Offenders faced penalties ranging from seven years in prison to death. Police rounded up wealthy Jews, often in hopes of extorting money for their release. By one estimate, Iraqi officials had extorted the equivalent of some 20 million British pounds from Jews by October 1948. The secret police sifted through mail sacks for letters between Iraqi Jews and relatives or friends in Palestine. Sending or receiving such letters — or even being mentioned in one — became grounds for hundreds of arrests on charges of "contact with the enemy during wartime." In August the minister of finance stripped Jew-

ish banks of permits to deal in foreign currency. The newly appointed
defense minister, Sadiq El-Bassam, an outspoken anti-Semite, ordered
the government to dismiss all Jewish employees for reasons of national
security. The government stopped granting physician's licenses to Jewish medical school graduates and imposed caps on Jewish admissions to
high schools and universities.

The anti-Jewish measures were a form of scapegoating for the government's mounting military losses in Palestine. But they were also a sop to
the pan-Arab nationalists, who saw Jews as undeserving beneficiaries of
Britain's colonial legacy and as a fifth column in the war against Israel.
With its weak hold on power, Iraq's government could afford neither to
anger its critics nor risk a repeat of the Farhud. It was aware of the growing Zionist underground. But police could not keep up with the Zionists'
fast-shifting operatives, who were now receiving cash and guidance from
Israel's Mossad. So it adopted a policy regarding Jews that the Israeli
scholar Moshe Gat has called "controlled oppression."

Anxious Jews in Iraqi's big cities stayed glued to their radios — and
out of sight. Fearing arrest, many destroyed garments bearing the Star of
David, prayer books, and copies of the Bible. If anyone still harbored hopes
of reconciliation, they didn't after September 23, 1948. On that day, Iraq's
wealthiest Jew, Shafiq Adès — a secular man with close ties to the monarch
and the Iraqi business elite — was hanged before cheering crowds outside
his mansion in Basra on trumped-up charges of aiding Israel.

"YOU KNOW WHO this was, Yona?" Sabi said. "He was the biggest Jew in Iraq."

Yona was leaving his job at the grocer's one afternoon when the Jewish
textile merchant in the next stall showed him the grisly photograph in
an Arabic newspaper — a rare sight in Zakho — that one of the educated
merchants had brought from Mosul.

"They hanged this man, Yona," Sabi said. He pointed at the black-and-
white photograph of Adès's limp body dangling from the gallows and
then searched the boy's face for a reaction. "They hanged him not once,
but twice. Twice! Once was not good enough. They killed him, Yona.
Then they humiliated him. Shame! Some even wanted to tie him to a Jeep

and drag him, may his memory be blessed, through the streets. That's what they wanted, the butchers."

"What did he do wrong?" Yona asked, after a pause.

"He was a Jew. That's all," Sabi said. "A big Jew. A wealthy Jew. And in Iraq now — I will translate for you from the newspaper: 'To be a Jew,' it says, 'is to be an enemy of the state.'"

The boy leaned over the open newspaper and looked at the photo again.

"But aren't we Jews, too?" he asked.

18 ⬧ Let the *Hajji* Speak

The tall stranger in the elegant robe and headdress strode purposefully through Zakho's market. He clasped hands with a few wary merchants, bowing deeply, and then stopped at a central spot at the intersection of two dirt alleys.

"All good Muslims gather," he called. "Please, come hear what news I have brought from Palestine."

The storekeepers and customers traded suspicious looks, but, still, a crowd began to gather. "My friends, I have come from Palestine to bring you word of the Jewish atrocities," the Arab visitor began. "The Zionist murderers have thrown thousands of Muslim families from their homes. In a single day, in the village of Dayr Yasin, they massacred two hundred and fifty of our men, women, and children. Every day more of our people die at the hands of the *kilab yahud*," the Jew dogs.

A voice in the crowd cut the man off. "We have no problem with our Jews. Why do you come here?"

"I came because I heard about your Jews. A trustworthy man in Baghdad told me that half now are in prison on charges of aiding the Zionist enemy. This is no problem? Your country's brave Muslim soldiers joined hands with Arab armies to clear Palestine of the kilab yahud. But now our brothers are coming home dead and without honor. This is no problem?"

"That is Baghdad," one of the shopkeepers shouted.

"Let the *hajji* speak," said another, using the Arabic word for "pilgrim." "He has come a long away."

"He tells lies," shouted a third man.

There was a bout of shoving in the crowd.

"Peace, my brothers. Peace," the hajji urged. "News comes slowly to the mountains. But it is time you knew: The Jews here act like your friends. But in the end, they are no different than the occupiers in Palestine. It won't be long before the rest of your so-called friends here rise up and slaughter you as they have our women and children in Palestine. The Zionists know no mercy. . ."

There was a commotion at the back of the crowd. Turning, the men stiffened. It was Abd al-Karim Agha. Though some of Zakho's Muslim tribal leaders saw the aga as a loose canon, the Jews saw him as their chief protector. Tall and possessed of a military bearing, he arbitrated disputes between Jews and Muslims and helped "my Jews" collect debts in Muslim neighborhoods. He had no patience for religious provocation and was known to mete out justice with lashings from his walking stick.

Someone in the market had apparently tipped him to the agitator's arrival, and now he was parting the crowd with swipes of his wooden stick. "I also know no mercy," Abd al-Karim Agha growled once he had reached the front, raising his stick to within an inch of the Palestinian's nose.

The visitor nearly fell as he stumbled backward off the orange crate. He grasped the aga's importance by the crowd's sudden silence and the way several men had already begun to slink back to their shops.

"Who invited you here?" Abd al-Karim Agha went on.

"Aga, I have come this distance to spread the truth about — "

"Palestine is that way, do you understand me?" Abd al-Karim Agha cut him off, furious at the man's effrontery. "This is Zakho. If you don't leave now, it won't be our Jews who will kill you. It will be me."

Abd Al-Karim Agha swiveled around, his walking stick pointed in accusation. He glared at the assembled men, who shrank back at the sight of his twisted red face.

"Shame on you all," he said.

At a nephew's wedding later that week, Abd al-Karim Agha wore an agonized look as he told a few of his sons the story of the Palestinian interloper he had run out of town that morning. It was a nearly moonless night. They were sitting at a table by a bend in the river. The water rumpled as it shifted direction, giving off an orange glow as it passed a row of oil lamps. His sons were a thickset and boisterous lot who had every expectation of riding the family coattails to some position of importance. They had expected this story to end as all their father's did: with his merciless trouncing of the latest fool to question his authority.

Tonight, however, the aga looked less sure of himself.

"Once, once! A man like that would never dare set foot in Kurdistan," he said, looking meditatively at his untouched plate of fried tomatoes and dumplings. "And if he did, he wouldn't have spoken one word before our people cut him down with a beating. But this morning, the men in the market just stood. For how long, Allah knows. But they stood. They listened."

"Babba," interjected an older son, "what is your love for the Jews? Yes, yes, they cut logs, weave clothes, dye fabric. Nothing our Muslims don't do, or couldn't learn to do."

"He doesn't love the Jews, he needs them," said a cousin, a handsome, mustachioed aga who had straggled over after draining several glasses of arak. "Without them, who would bow down to him? Who would pay fees for all his so-called services? Who would work for free on another drainage ditch for our orchards?

"The other agas have no use for our family," the cousin went on. "If we can't get honor from real men, well, we'll always have the groveling Jew dogs."

Speechless with rage, Abd Al-Karim Agha rose from his seat and whipped his walking stick across the table, scattering his uneaten dumplings into the river.

19 ❧ Can't Help This Time

A few months after Shafiq Adès's hanging, as the days grew shorter and snow blanched the mountain tops, a group of fifteen rafts-men, or *tarrahe*, from Zakho's Jewish quarter set out on muleback for Doavmiske, some forty miles to the northeast. Among the group of husky men were Miryam's father, Menashe Beh Nazé, and two of his sons by Arabe, Zaki and Yosef, who had followed him into the trade. A Jewish timber dealer had hired the men to ferry loads of white poplar downriver to Zakho and Mosul. But their trip that winter would be their last.

Zakho's raftsmen were Kurdistan's most celebrated. Zakho, as an is-land in a river, was the perfect training ground for one of Mesopotamia's oldest professions. ("The boats which come down the river to Babylon are circular, and made of skins," Herodotus writes in 430 B.C. in his *History of the Persian Wars*.) Every piece of timber making its way from central Kurdistan to Mosul bobbed over Zakho's snaking riverbeds. The raftsman is so central to Zakho's identity that it figures in one of its cre-ation myths. As the story goes, Jews and Muslims had lived together on the island for centuries. Then, about five centuries ago, a flood destroyed Zakho, flushing every last resident into the river. Eighty years later, Sh-emdin Agha, a tribal leader in nearby Slivani territory, tried to resettle the desolate island with his Muslim family. Every time he built a wall, it collapsed. The aga sought help from a shaman, who said the spirits would not let Zakho rebuild until Jews returned. The aga found a Jewish family in nearby Turkey and moved them to the island. The Beh Dahlikas were timber raftsmen (their name means forester). Dahlika, the strapping pa-terfamilias, went to work right away and built walls, and soon houses, that stood. The Muslim aga's family moved in. Jews followed. As the bal-ance of Jews and Muslims returned to preflood levels, Zakho roared back to prosperity. If the myth is to be believed, Zakho's survival had always depended on two things: Muslim-Jewish harmony and timber raftsmen. Throw one off balance and all of Zakho falls.

On that expedition, in late 1948 or early 1949, the myth would come to seem prophetic. Stranded by a snowstorm a few miles from their destination, the group decided to warm themselves with a song and dance. They crossed and uncrossed their legs to the rhythms of one of Zakho's traditional wedding songs, and Muslim Kurds from a nearby village came out to watch.

"Ti! Ti! Yisrael," the raftsmen sang. "Ti! Ti! Ti! Yisrael." The Muslims joined in, mimicking the sounds of the words, and the singing grew louder. Habib, a loader, picked up his blue-and-white kaffiyeh headdress and tied one end to a stick. He raised it aloft like a flag and waved it as the circle of dancers, Muslim and Jew, widened.

Later, while the raftsmen were feeding their mules, a half dozen Iraqi police on horses rode up. A hard-looking officer clasped his sidearm and ordered the terrified raftsmen to surrender their belongings.

"What is it?" asked one of the men.

"Shut up," the officer said, knocking him to the ground with the butt of his rifle.

"They didn't do anything," one matronly villager pleaded. "They have been our guests here."

"Quiet, woman," the officer said. "Do you want to go to jail with them?"

The officers bound the men together in hand chains, led them into town, and locked them for the night in a horse stable outside the local governor's house. The next day the officers marched them in chains back to Zakho, a ten-hour walk through rain and snow.

Later that week, Zakho's Jews — for the first time in memory — made the Mosul newspapers:

Fifteen Zionist operatives from Zakho disguised as raftsmen were arrested on Saturday, after trying to corrupt local Muslim villagers in Batufe with Jewish propaganda. The police have at least three witnesses, and incontrovertible evidence: a crude Israeli flag and several sticks of dynamite. Authorities in Mosul say that the Zionist conspirators appeared to be planning to bomb bridges between Iraq and Iran. The men are being held at the

Zakho jail, pending transport to Mosul, where they will be tried before a military court.

In Zakho's tiny jail that night, police officers whom many of the Jews had drunk tea with or greeted in the streets over the years were different men.

"You have no idea what you have just brought on yourselves," the ranking officer said, strutting before the main cell. "Military police from Mosul — Mosul, God damn it! — will be here tomorrow morning."

Miryam's half brother Yosef raised his weary body from the bench in one of the cells. "You know we didn't do anything," he said, pressing his face against the metal bars.

"You went to a Muslim village and sang about Israel's triumph over the Arabs," the ranking officer said. "A hundred witnesses saw you. Iraqi soldiers coming home dead every day, and you sing about Israel?"

"That old song was the same one we've sung at weddings here since Adam and Eve. There's not a drop of Zionism in it, my friend, and you know it."

The "flag" the provincial police thought was Israel's was Habib's headdress, Yosef explained. And explosives? That was a joke. "Everyone in Zakho knows we fish with dynamite. Throw a stick in the river, and *wallah*, fish for dinner."

"Stupid, stupid Jews," the ranking officer said, shaking his head. "If you think the men from Mosul are going to believe that, you are damned."

The next morning a barber was summoned to shave the men's heads. Then a trio of officers from Mosul dragged each of the men by his feet into a windowless clay-walled interrogation room. "Who put you up to this? Who are your Zionist contacts?" The men repeated their claims of innocence. The officers clubbed their knees with wooden batons.

The raftsmen were trucked the next day to a prison in Mosul, where a bald man supervised another series of beatings. The men were separated and threatened. Ribs were broken, noses smashed, foreheads gashed open. Their prison rags grew filthy with blood and human waste.

Back in Zakho, the arrests struck with the force of an earthquake. Every Jew knew at least one of the loggers: They were neighbors, business partners, husbands, sons.

Anxious families pleaded with the *qaimaqam*, the provincial governor, for word about their loved ones. Zakho's Jewish leaders begged for help from the Muslim agas who had always protected them. For decades, the Shemdin Agha family had ensured the Jews' safety and freedom. And where the agas couldn't help, a well-placed bribe to the qaimaqam's office usually could.

This time bribes got them nowhere. And all the agas could do was apologize.

We wish we could help, they told a delegation of Jewish leaders who paid a visit not long after the arrests. But this case is in the hands of the secret police in Mosul and Baghdad. Our influence is here in Kurdistan.

Several of Zakho's most powerful Muslim tribesmen were there: Hazim Beg Agha, the dapper fifty-three-year-old leader of the clan and a onetime member of parliament who wore white suits and tooled past his vast land holdings in Zakho's first automobile, a Ford convertible; Hajji Agha, Zakho's mayor in the 1920s; and Hazim Beg's cousin, Abd al-Karim Agha, the longtime protector of the Jews.

As the agas and Jewish leaders filed out of the meeting, Abd al-Karim Agha had never looked so deflated. He put a hand on the shoulder of a man named Murdkah, one of Zakho's well-to-do Jewish merchants and a business associate of al-Karim's family. "Tell them I'm sorry," the aga said.

After three months of brutal interrogations in the damp basement of a Mosul jail, four raftsmen deemed too infirm or too young to be culpable were released. Among them were Miryam's father and her younger half brother, Zaki. Yosef wasn't as lucky. A military judge found him and ten other Zakho raftsmen guilty of Zionist conspiracy and sentenced them to a squalid Baghdad prison. All received three-year sentences, except Yosef. According to his brother Naim, Yosef refused to confess and so was sentenced to an additional year.

In February 2005 I visited Naim, a medium-size man with pale cheeks and an unflagging deadpan, in his small basement apartment across from a kabob shop in Katamonim, the heart of Kurdish Jerusalem. He told me that their sister Shoshana moved to Baghdad to be closer to the prison, and he recalled going with her to visit Yosef.

"I was eight," he said. "I remember looking at him through a huge metal gate. The cell was filthy, not fit for humans. Nobody was taking care of it.

"In prison," Naim continued, "they hit him on the head, poured boiling water and then cold water over him. Right before he was released, they tortured him again. They undressed him, put him in a small room, one meter by one meter, and poured hot water on him."

The torture robbed Yosef of speech. When he came to Israel, more than a year after the rest of Zakho's Jews, Naim told me, "they took him to a convalescent hospital in Gadera until he could talk again."

THE FARHUD AND the Shafiq Adès hanging were hiccups in Zakho. Even the Holocaust was too far away, and the scope of its atrocities too little known, to breed in Zakho's Jews a broader sense of society's interconnectedness. Only something as pointedly local as the loggers' arrest and torture could deliver the world to Zakho's doorstep.

20 ❖ To Hell with Books

On March 2, 1950, Salih Jabr, the Iraqi interior minister, introduced a draft bill to parliament whose dryly technical name, Supplement to Decree 62 of 1933, belied its colossal significance for Iraq's Jews. The preamble read:

> It has been noticed that some Iraqi Jews are attempting by every illegal means to leave Iraq for good and that others have already left Iraq illegally. As the presence of subjects of this description, forced to stay in the country and obliged to keep their Iraqi nationality would inevitably lead to results affecting Iraqi security and give rise to social and economic problems, it has been found advisable not to prevent those wishing to do so from leaving Iraq for good, forfeiting their Iraqi nationality. This law has been promulgated to that end.

The bill, which became law with the regent's signature a mere week later, carried a simple message to Iraq's Jews: You are free to go, so long as you

give up your citizenship and never return. In effect, it was carte blanche
for an exodus to Israel.

The so-called Denaturalization Law was a stunning reversal in policy.
A year earlier, Iraq had cast itself as Israel's fiercest opponent. After the
ceasefire with Israel in January 1949, it was the only Arab country to
reject an armistice and the first to float the idea of a new offensive. Iraqi
leaders knew full well that legalizing emigration would make Iraq com-
plicit in supplying Israel — the Arab world's nemesis — with the Middle
East's most populous and affluent Jewish population. Not to mention the
economic havoc it would cause at home. "Responsible [Iraqi] leaders," the
American Embassy in Baghdad said in a secret airgram to Washington in
1949, "recognize the fact that a mass exodus of the Jews, who play such a
prominent role in financial and business circles in Iraq, would seriously
disrupt the economy of the country, further endangering its precarious
stability."

But a lot had changed since then. In recent months, Iraqi bravado had
given way to confusion and retreat. Despite raids on Jewish homes and
the torture of activists, the Iraqi security forces had made little headway
against the well-organized Zionist underground. When martial law was
lifted, in December 1949, Jews flocked south to Basra and made illegal
crossings into Iran, where they eventually boarded flights for Palestine.
Once skittish Arab and Kurdish smugglers, seeing the growing incompe-
tence and corruption of Iraqi police, came forward to guide Jews through
unfamiliar lands. Emboldened Mossad agents shifted into high gear and
put into a place a well-oiled network of smugglers and escape routes.
From January to March 1950, some four thousand Jews illegally fled Iraq
for Palestine. At that pace, Iraq stood to lose as many Jews to Palestine in
six months as it had in the preceding three decades.

The flood of illegal emigration had turned into an internal political
crisis and an international embarrassment. "Jews Leaving Iraq in a Steady
Flow," the New York Times, which had dispatched a reporter to Khor-
ramshahr, on the Iranian border, declared in a February 1950 headline.
"Most are Zionists." Smugglers were having no trouble bribing their way
past border checkpoints, and Iranian leaders rebuffed Iraqi requests to
deny Jews entry.

Backed into a corner and desperate to save face, the Iraqis caved. It was a case of the tail wagging the dog. By legalizing an exodus they had been powerless to stop, Iraqi leaders could claim that they were still in control. They consoled themselves with the thought that perhaps just a few thousand Jews — the poorest and most undesirable — would leave. But that was just their latest miscalculation. The raids on Jewish homes, the Iraqi death toll in the Arab war on Israel, and the determination of Zionist operatives to uproot Iraq's massive Jewish community had turned the tables irrevocably. All too soon, some 120,000 people — nearly the whole of Iraqi Jewry — were preparing to vacate.

On a warm day in March 1950, Yona Beh Sabagha, then eleven, was marching single-file back to town with his classmates, his knuckles smarting from another rapping for mixing up his right and left feet. He had just crossed the bridge over the engorged Habur when he saw his father's Muslim business partner with his hand raised in greeting.

"Have you heard, *ma'alme butchuk?*" Have you heard, little rabbi? Hajji Ibrahim was a rangy-limbed and gentle-mannered textile dealer. People called him by the honorific Hajji because he was said to have left Zakho once to travel to some holy Islamic site. Yona admired him because his store was one of the few in town that had a telephone: a fantastic bramble of wires, bells, and odd plugs reachable by dialing a single number: 8. Or so he claimed. Yona and his father had spent hours in the man's store, but not once did it ring.

"Did they tell you at school?"

"What, Hajji? You mean to watch out for the flash floods?" Yona said.

Ibrahim laughed. "That is one way of putting it," he said. "But no, ma'alme butchuk. My news is more like the story of your Moses, when he parted the sea for the Israelites."

No sooner had Yona and his friends run to the Jewish quarter to confirm the hajji's story than they shimmied off their book bags and tossed them into the afternoon air. It was as if someone had just announced that school had been cancelled, forever.

WHEN I ASKED my father about the Denaturalization Law a few years back, I was working as a staff writer at the *Baltimore Sun* and covering the U.S. Naval Academy in Annapolis. My father said that if I wanted a parallel for the scene among Zakho's Jewish schoolchildren the day the law was announced, I should picture the midshipmen at Annapolis tossing their caps skyward on graduation day.

"We celebrated like that," my father told me. "We threw our book bags into the air, like 'To hell with these books.'"

Among the adults, however, news of the denaturalization law exposed long-buried fault lines. The penniless felt they had nothing to lose. Israel was terra incognita, but the privations couldn't be much worse than they were in Zakho. At least one thing was certain: They would no longer be the least powerful class (the poor) of a minority religious group (the Jews) among a minority ethnic group (the Kurds), in an Arab country (Iraq) that, as at least some people saw it, had all but told its Jews to get lost.

The small but powerful class of well-to-do merchants took a different view. They owned homes, stores, and land in Zakho. To leave would be to give up everything in a gamble against bad odds. They had heard enough about Israel to know that a procession of boats carrying educated Europeans had gotten there years before. They wondered about their chances of ever achieving the same levels of wealth and prestige.

It was true that the Jews lacked power in Zakho. They depended for their security on the agas' of the Sindi, Gulli, and Slivani tribes. They had to seek the agas' blessing and pay a "fee" for every Jewish marriage. They were expected to volunteer their labor when the aga undertook the occasional public works project. But was that really too high a price for freedom of trade and religion? In light of the stories some were only now hearing about the Holocaust in Europe, many Kurdish Jews felt they had it good.

Even after the 1950 Denaturalization Law made the Jewish exodus a fait accompli, Zionism was rarely more than a way to dress up more practical impulses: hopes for a better life; unease over the breakdown in traditional Muslim–Jewish relations; a new generation's alienation from its parents; a thirst for adventure; and perhaps most important, the growing awareness that Zakho could no longer count on its isolation to beat back the wider world.

My grandfather Rahamim was thirty-three years old, and before long, when his father passed away, he would be the family's eldest male and its head. Zakho had not failed him.

In the family's general store one simmering day in the summer of 1950, eleven-year-old Yona sat on a stool in the corner and listened while his father and another Jewish storekeeper mulled over the future. Yona had brought Kocho, a little lamb Rahamim had bought for him a few months earlier, and was stroking the animal's oily wool as the adults talked.

"Let the poor go to Israel," Rahamim said, with a dismissive sweep of the hand. "They may find a better life there. If they do, good for them."

"I'm sure Israel would rather have people like us," the other storekeeper said.

"Israel will have people like us, only here in Iraq."

The merchant returned a confused look.

"I mean," Rahamim said, "that we may be of greater use to Israel as its representatives here. We could import products from Israel and sell them to Iraqis. We could be Israeli sales agents, as it were."

His friend and business partner, Hajji Ibrahim, had walked in unnoticed a few minutes earlier and had been quietly eavesdropping. Hearing this, he let out a snort.

"Yes, Rahamim," Ibrahim said, with mock solemnity. "I will start painting the sign now: 'Special discount: Delicious Israeli oranges, grown on soil freshly fertilized with Arab blood.' The Iraqis will be lining up in the street to help the struggling Israeli farmers."

"To hell with you, Hajji," Rahamim said, glaring at his friend. "What would you have me do?"

"I think you will have a hard time in Israel," Ibrahim said, soberly now. "Here, there are just a few Jews. No problem. You get together, hatch your schemes, and then make a nice living off the rest of us. But in Israel, there are only Jews. So who will you cheat?"

"Leave my store if you want to insult me," Rahamim said, though he didn't look him in the eye. "You don't know what you're talking about."

Ibrahim turned to Yona in the corner and winked. "What do you think, ma'alme butchuk? Let's ask the little rabbi. Am I right or not?"

Yona blushed. "Kocho is tired, Babba," he said, getting up. "I'm going to take him home." Yona knew better than to tangle with adults. But what Ibrahim said to his father that day would stay with him for a very long time.

That night Ephraim could only beam. Whenever anyone was listening and even when they weren't, he rhapsodized that God had at last answered the prayers of the wandering tribes. When Yona told him about the fracas in Rahamim's store, Ephraim's look of beatified contentment did not change.

"Your father is too practical, too much in the world," Ephraim said. "But you, Yona, you have been reading the Book of Psalms. You may one day understand more." The old man was lying on his back on a creaking bedframe on the roof, studying the stars. The only cushion between his tired bones and the rusted metal springs was a sheet of cardboard. His grandson sat cross-legged at his side.

"What do you mean, Babba Ephraim?" Yona said.

"Your father will one day see that the Beh Sabaghas are going to the Garden of Eden," Ephraim said, as a tear streaked down his temple. "No longer will I be the only Jew in the temple at midnight. In the Land of Israel, there will be synagogues on every corner. We will visit the tombs of the kings of Israel. We will drink the nectar of Torah in the streets and in the fields and on the mountaintops and in the valleys. The words of the sages will be the air we breathe. The grit between our toes will be the sand Abraham, Isaac, and Jacob walked on. The water — "

"And oranges!" A woman's voice broke in from the courtyard below. Yona crept to the roof's edge and saw his grandmother step over his sleeping lamb as she put away cooking pots from the night's dinner.

"What, woman?" Ephraim cried, his tranquility finally ruffled.

"Oranges!" Hazale chirped. "Torah, big deal. Sages, very nice for you. But I hear the oranges in Israel are sent from heaven. As big as watermelons, they are. The color of gold, and sweet, like honey. If I eat just one Israel orange a day, I will need nothing else to be happy. So the women say."

"Silence, *gejibaneh!*" Ephraim said, propping up on his elbow and scowling. Blabbermouth! "The men of the house are speaking." He turned to Yona, lowering his voice to a stage whisper. "A shy man is worth a penny, they say. A shy woman, a million."

Like a lizard caught between two predators, Yona slithered, low on his belly, back to his grandfather's side.

"I heard there are no scorpions in Israel, " Yona said, recalling something he had read in a book of his grandfather's called *Legends of Palestine*. "But are there demons, like the Yimid Maya?" Yona asked, wondering whether the Water Mother who drowned children in the Habur would follow them abroad.

"The walls of Jerusalem are strong enough to keep out all of Zakho's demons," Ephraim said.

"But, Babba Ephraim," Yona said, "Hajji Ibrahim said we won't make any money in Jerusalem because there are only Jews and no one to cheat."

"Hajji is an ass," Ephraim said. "His telephone won't save him. Without our suppliers in Turkey, he would have only piss cotton from the villages and his business would fail. He says what he says because he wants your father to stay. But believe Babba Ephraim, the hajji is worried only about himself."

"But what job will you have in the Land of Israel? Do they need dyeing men there?"

Ephraim grinned at the stars. "In Paradise," he said, closing his eyes, "God will provide."

21 ❖ Let My People Go

"You shall be gathered together one by one, O ye children of Israel."

—ISAIAH 27:12

On a crisp day in late October 1950, seventy Jews left Zakho. Bureaucrats from Mosul had set up desks in the synagogue to fill out the paperwork. The departees were the town's have-nots: the small-time peddlers, the porters, the beggars, nearly all of them illiterate. Most carried only the rags on their backs and perhaps a single clay bowl or half-melted candle. Clinging to their children, they crowded onto chartered buses and rolled south toward Mosul and the unknown.

"Let them go," Rahamim sniffed. What did 70 Jews amount to in a community of 1,850?

But those seventy were like the loose thread that unravels the blanket. Fixtures of the Jewish market — the cobbler, the blacksmith, the baker — were now gone. The houses of famously boisterous families were empty and dark. The singing in the synagogue was a little quieter. In the teahouse by the river, each day brought fresh radio reports of the mushrooming exodus: eleven hundred Jews left Iraq in May; twenty-seven hundred in June; nearly forty-five hundred in October.

Later that fall, haggard-looking bureaucrats from Mosul again set up tables in Zakho's large synagogue. The line of people wound past the *gniza* cellar where Jews buried old Torah scrolls, and out the rough-cut stone entryway into the dirt alleys. Here was the bedrock of Zakho's middle class: its storekeepers and farmers, small landowners and kosher butchers, its weavers and blacksmiths and schoolteachers. They were Rahamim's customers. They were the people he prayed with. They were the people he sipped tea with in the evening after the market closed. What would remain for him once they left?

The line inched forward. In the afternoon, when a rain started to fall, Rahamim closed his shop and joined it. Inside the synagogue at last, Rahamim saw a row of low tables stacked with papers and bulging files. There was a commotion in the corner. An old widow, known for her fondness for home-distilled arak, was grousing that she could not understand the Arabic-speaking bureaucrats.

"I will speak slowly," the young clerk said, running out of patience. "Once again, grandma, do you want to leave Iraq? And if you leave, do you promise never to return?"

"Sir," she began, slurring her words, "You must have good spies, for it is true, I loved arak."

A low rumble of suppressed laughter echoed through the sanctuary, and the old woman looked momentarily confused. But she was deter-

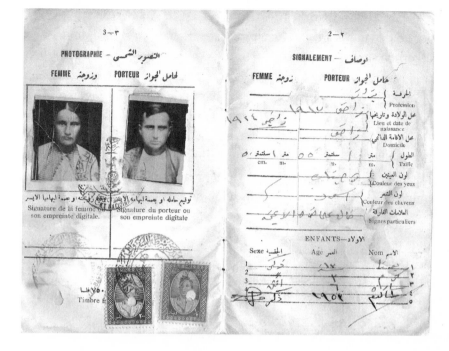

Miryam and Rahamim Beh Sabagha, Ariel's grandparents,
Iraqi passport, 1950 or 1951.

mined to give the young official a full answer. "But let me assure you — all of you," she said, her voice quavering with genuine emotion, "that as of next Saturday, mark my words, I will be leaving arak for good. And no, young sir, I will never go back."

This time, Rachamim and the other men, despite their presence in Zakho's holiest building, could not hold back. They gave in to a cruel fit of laughter, which vented feelings held inside for too long, things that had nothing to do with a foolish old widow.

At the front of the line, Rahamim took a form and wrote down the names and ages of all the Beh Sabaghas: his parents, his wife, his three children, and his brothers and sisters-in-law and their children. The unsmiling clerk looked up the names in the Iraqi citizenship rolls and drew

a black line through them. Then he copied the names into a new ledger, under the heading "Denaturalized." Rahamim signed another set
of forms with a trembling fist. The clerk marked the top page with three
stamps and handed it back.

"Take this to the passport desk," the clerk said, pointing across the
room. "In fifteen days, you and your family cease to be citizens of this
country." The Zakho man the government had hired to shoot the passport
photos, Rahamim saw, was a Beh Dahlika. The same family of Jewish
raftsmen that legend credited with the rebirth of Zakho's Jewish community was now documenting its undoing.

22 ❖ A Suitable Level of Civilization

The Beh Sabaghas' last year in Zakho was the year the government
school began English lessons. "We will start with a song," the
teacher said.

Yona sat up straight. He vowed never to bunk this particular class.
The British spoke English. A few words in the language of those soldiers
would help him stand out in Israel — he was sure of it — just as his sports
jacket and tennis ball had in Zakho.

"Oh my dahrrh-LEENG, Oh my dahrrh-LEENG — " the teacher's voice
was a baritone tremolo, and he swayed a little on his chubby legs " — Oh
my dahrrh-leeng, Cleh-men-tayne!" The children followed along halt-
ingly — Kurdish mountain boys singing about an American mountain
man, a California forty-niner, whose darling daughter drowns in the
"fohmeeng brayne."

After the singalong, the teacher asked the class in what countries, other
than England, English was spoken.

There was a long silence. Then Yona tentatively raised his hand.

"America," he said.

"And what, little scholar, do you know about America?" the teacher replied, taking no small delight in pressing his charges against the limits of their knowledge. "Do you even know where America is?" he teased. The students snickered. "Do you know *anything* about it at all?"

Suddenly something his father once said came back to him. "Yes, Habib Effendi," Yona said, straightening in his chair and looking his squat teacher straight in the eye. "I do know that when it is dark in Zakho, it is light in America."

Like the rest of the Jewish boys in his class, Yona had stopped learning Hebrew some six years before, when he graduated from the synagogue's rudimentary school. But now Zakho's wealthier families saw Hebrew as a link, not just to a distant religious past, but to the future. It was the language of Israel. They would need it not only to study the Torah, but to find the bathroom. So Rahamim and a half dozen other fathers soon hired a sightless violinist and Kabbalist to teach their children modern Hebrew. In those last days in Zakho, Hebrew and English were the only subjects Yona studied with any relish. Language, he saw even then, was the bridge to whatever waited beyond Iraq.

Days passed, and then weeks. More than half of Zakho's 1,850 Jews, from a total of 315 families, had registered to leave, but there was no word on when the next buses would come. Under new Iraqi laws, which gave Jews just fifteen days to depart, many Zakho Jews were now technically stateless. A vague dread settled over the mahala Juheeya, the Jewish neighborhood. Conspiracy theories swirled.

Growing uncertainty over the departure led to a housing glut as Jews dumped their homes on the market en masse. In normal times, the Beh Sabaghas might have expected some 300 dinars for their house. But when they finally sold it in early 1951, to a young Kurdish couple, they got 27 dinars. And they did better than some.

Eventually a delegation of Jews confronted Moshe Gabbay, the owner of a gas station, scores of stores, large tracts of land in the villages, and two small shopping malls. They accused him of holding ordinary Zakholis hostage for personal gain. He was postponing their departure, they charged, to buy time to dispose of his expansive holdings. Gabbay, who had always looked out for the poorest Jews, was incensed by the accusations.

In the end, whether his accusers were correct or not, waiting got him nowhere. In early March 1951, a year after the Denaturalization Law went into effect, Iraqi legislators met in emergency session and ordered the state to freeze all assets and property of denaturalized Jews. Departing Jews would now have to surrender not just their citizenship but their wealth, valued at as much as $2 billion to $3 billion in today's dollars. Moshe Gabbay lost almost everything, as did many of Zakho's Jewish landowners.

"Can it be," Iraqi prime minister Nuri as-Said asked in early 1951, according to the historian Moshe Gat, "that no retribution and punishment will be meted out to people who have enjoyed the wealth of our country, but have extended monetary aid to the enemies of the homeland against whom we have fought?"

In a Robin Hood twist, the poor Zakholis who raced onto that first bus got a better return on their houses than the well-to-do families who waited, only to watch their homes become state property.

HAD ZAKHO'S JEWS known the real reasons for the state of limbo since the poor departed in October, they might have been in less of a hurry to leave. The truth was that Israel had enough housing and building supplies to absorb only so many immigrants at a time, and its largely European cast of leaders was giving priority to their countrymen.

As early as 1949, Yitzhak Rafael, the immigration chief for the Jewish Agency, had said that if Israel wanted to find "better human material," it would have to seek Jews outside of the Arab world. The journalist Aryeh Gelblum, writing in the major Israeli daily *Haaretz* that same year, was blunter, according to a translation by the Middle East analyst Meyrav Wurmser:

> This is the immigration of a race we have not yet known in the country. We are dealing with people whose primitivism is at a peak, whose level of knowledge is one of virtually absolute ignorance and, worse, who have little talent for understanding anything intellectual. . . . These Jews also lack roots in Judaism, as they are totally subordinated to savage and primitive instincts. As with Africans you will find among them gambling,

drunkenness and prostitution, . . . chronic laziness and hatred for work; there is nothing safe about this asocial element. [Even] the kibbutzim will not hear of their absorption."

By November 1950 roughly eighty-three thousand Iraqi Jews had registered to leave, but Israel had managed to fly out just eighteen thousand. Many had left their hometowns only to be crammed into Baghdad synagogues that served as makeshift holding pens for flights that never departed. Reports poured in of clashes with Arab rioters in Basra. Fears of a typhoid epidemic were spreading. The swelling ranks of stateless Jews stirred political unrest. Prime Minister Nuri as-Said threatened to halt the airlifts and expel the Jews to Syria, Jordan, or Kuwait or lock them up in concentration camps.

Israel, however, did not increase its quota for Iraqi immigrants. Instead, it made room for a flood of immigrants from Poland and Romania. The decision was not without reason: Poland had set a deadline for Jews to leave, and Israel feared Romania might do the same. Jews in both countries had already suffered the horrors of the Holocaust.

But another, more subtle reason involved calculations about the relative merits of Jewish immigrants. Zionism had always been a European solution to a European problem. Its growth can be traced across a narrow band of Europe: the rash of mob attacks on Jewish districts across Russia in 1881 and the wave of anti-Semitic legislation known as the May Laws; the conviction in 1895 of French Captain Alfred Dreyfus on bogus charges of passing secrets to the Germans; another wave of pogroms across Russia from 1903 to 1905, which left hundreds of Jews dead; the economic restrictions placed on Polish Jews in the mid-1920s; and ultimately, the rise of Nazism in Germany and the atrocities of the Holocaust.

Not surprisingly, the crusaders for a Jewish state were European intellectuals embittered by failed dreams of assimilation. Budapest-born Theodor Herzl, the father of modern Zionism, wrote his manifesto *Der Judenstaat* (*The Jewish State*) after covering the Dreyfus trial as a correspondent for a Vienna newspaper. Chaim Weizmann, who picked up the reins after Herzl's death, escaped Russian poverty to become a renowned biochemistry professor in England, where his assistance to the British munitions industry won him access to the politicians who would pass the 1917 "Balfour Declaration" pledging Her Majesty's support for a Jewish homeland in Palestine. (Weizmann would go on to become Israel's first president.) David Ben-Gurion, the son of a Zionist leader in small-town Poland, moved to Palestine with nationalist fantasies as a twenty-year-old and joined the British army's Jewish legion. He founded the Zionist labor movement and was chosen in 1935 to lead the Jewish Agency, the executive branch of the world Zionist movement. (He would later become Israel's first prime minister.)

Of the 480,000 Jews who immigrated to Palestine during the twenty-eight-year British Mandate, some 90 percent were European. Herzl envisioned the future state of Israel as a kind of Vienna on the Jordan, complete with circuses, theaters, opera houses, and café-lined boulevards. The ideas of these early leaders, however resonant in Eastern Europe, would have struck the Jews of Zakho as outright bizarre.

The wider welcome mat for European Jews was not simply the result of fraternity among countrymen. Behind it lurked the belief that the Mizrahi Jews, the ones from Islamic lands, detracted from dreams of a Viennese-style Paradise. What to do with them was debated at the highest levels of academia and politics.

Wurmser, writing in 2005 in the *Middle East Quarterly*, offers a sample of views common to the era:

Prime Minister David Ben-Gurion described the Mizrahi immigrants as lacking even "the most elementary knowledge" or "a trace of Jewish or human education." Furthermore, he said, "We do not want Israelis to become Arabs. We are bound by duty to fight against the spirit of the Levant that corrupts individuals and society." Likewise, Abba Eban, one of Israel's most eloquent diplomats, noted that "one of the great apprehensions which afflict us is the danger of the predominance of immigrants of Oriental origin forcing Israel to equalize its cultural level with that of the neighboring world." . . . Israeli Prime Minister Golda Meir once asked, "Shall we be able to elevate these immigrants to a suitable level of civilization?"

Jews from across the Arab world suffered discrimination in Israel. Very occasionally, however, someone took the bolder step of distinguishing among nationalities. "A Jew from Eastern Europe," Nahum Goldmann, a Lithuanian-born publisher who rose in the 1950s to presidency of the World Zionist Organization and chairman's seat at the Jewish Agency, once said, "is worth twice as much as a Jew from Kurdistan."

While Israeli politicians looked down their noses, Mossad agents in Iraq began to panic. By late 1950 they were sending frantic cables to their superiors, urging immediate action to evacuate Iraq's Jews and warning of the dire consequences of further delays. "Why did you permit us to deceive the Jews here?" Mordechai Ben-Porat, an Israeli immigration operative in Iraq, wrote to superiors back home. A few months later, his exasperation reached the boiling point. "This course of action has caused the Jews here to believe sincerely that Israel does not want them. . . . We cannot feed people Zionism instead of bread."

No one in Israel paid much heed until the evening of January 14, 1951, when someone tossed an army hand grenade into the crowded Mas'uda Shemtov synagogue in Baghdad. Three people were killed and more than twenty were injured. Iraqi Jews in Israel staged demonstrations. The U.S. State Department at last stepped in and urged Israel to act; tens of thousands of denaturalized Jews in Iraq were mired in a "delicate and hazardous situation." Finally, two weeks later, Ben-Gurion overcame the objections of the Jewish Agency and Golda Meir, his own minister of labor, and raised the quotas. "There is nothing else to be done," he said.

The flights from Iraq would be one of the largest human airlifts in history, ferrying some 120,000 Iraqi Jews to Israel in less than year. Code-named Operation Ezra and Nehemiah, after the biblical figures who returned hundreds of exiled Babylonian Jews to Jerusalem in the fifth century B.C., the exodus was a marvel of logistics, diplomacy, and con artistry. The Israelis made a show of awarding the travel charter to a hitherto unknown American airline known as Near East Transport Company, putatively run by James Wooten, the president of Alaska Airlines. In reality, it was run by El Al and the Mossad. Wooten, who had earlier assisted with evacuation of Yemen's Jews, had agreed only to serve as its public face. It was a ruse designed to fool only the Iraqi people, who would have been outraged by any official Israeli airlift of Jews to the hated Jewish state.

Iraqi leaders knew the truth but looked the other way. Eager now to be rid of their Jews, they demanded only that the flights stop somewhere before continuing to Israel. (American diplomats persuaded the British to allow brief touchdowns in the crown colony of Cyprus.) A few prominent Iraqis even sought a cut of the action. One of Near East's secret partners was the travel firm Iraq Tours, whose board chairman was none other than the former Iraqi prime minister, Tawfiq al-Suwaidi.

23 ◈ God Will Provide

On an early March evening in 1951, Rahamim gazed for the last time at the barren shelves of his fabrics store and took a ragged breath. Most of the other Jewish shopkeepers had cleaned out days before, selling their goods in large lots to Muslim Kurds for a fraction of their cost. But Rahamim had waited until the end, never quite believing that the buses would come.

His youngest brother, Israel, came up the eerily vacant alley with a cart and loaded the last of their unsold merchandise. He had recently married one of Zakho's beauties, Naima, an angel with turquoise eyes and waves of hair in shades of barley. For a moment, in the evening's fading light, Rahamim could picture his brother, tall and darkly handsome, as one of the *halutzim* he had heard about, the strapping mustachioed pioneers cast in Zionist mythology as the archetypal settler.

"Let's go home and eat," Israel said, brushing the dirt off his sleeves. "Enough work today."

"In Israel, we'll still work together?" Rahamim said. "As brothers?"

"Is that what you're worrying about now?"

"We'll be nothing if we're not together."

Israel was too punchy with hunger to indulge another of his brother's recent moods. "'God will provide,'" he said, drawing out the words to sound like their father.

"And if he doesn't?" Rahamim said.

24 ❧ Iraqi Stamps

Yona Bir Rahamim Bir Ephraim Beh Sabagha was the last boy bar mitzvahed in Zakho. There was hardly time for it. Like the other Jews, the Beh Sabaghas had a hundred details to sweat in the week before the buses came. As if that weren't enough, the house was now shot through with the cries of a newborn boy, Shalom, to whom Miryam had given birth just days before. It was March 1951, and Yona's thirteenth birthday was still nine months away. Why not wait until their arrival in the Holy Land? What better setting than Jerusalem for the ritual that made Jewish boys into men?

But Rahamim would not wait. For reasons that can only be guessed at, he hastily threw together a bar mitzvah celebration for his son on a Thursday and invited Zakho's poor to share a meal at their home. Most of the Jews were too busy with their departure preparations to attend. At a synagogue that hardly looked like one anymore, Yona wrapped his arms in the leather straps of tefillin and read from Exodus. Afterward, the family repaired to the house, where perhaps a dozen of the poorest Muslim and Jewish townspeople, drawn by word of the free food, had lined up for a cup of raisin drink and plate of *rizza bpisra*, peppered rice and meat.

No sooner had Yona sat down than he noticed something amiss. Kocho, his pet lamb, was not at his usual spot. He had hoped to show the lamb off to his guests during the dancing after the meal. But when he got up and ran out to the courtyard, all he found was the tether in a loose coil on the ground.

"Where is Kocho?" Yona asked his mother, who was ladling food for the guests.

"Oh, kurbanokh," she said, dropping her hands limply at her side. "Your father didn't tell you?"

Yona was frantic. He ran through the house until he found his father at the entry to the courtyard, sipping a glass of arak with some friends from the market.

"Where is Kocho?" Yona asked, breathing hard. "Didn't Babba Ephraim say he could go to Israel with us? If you sold him, we have to get him back. I have some money left from my job. Please, Babba. I will pay."

He was shaking.

"I didn't sell him, *Broni*," Rahamim said. "I took him to the butcher's this morning. There was no way to take him to Israel. So we make a mitzvah. We feed him to our Muslim friends, whom we won't see for a very long time. Being a man means making sacrifices."

Yona remembered the lumps of meat in the rizza bpisra. He felt sick. "But, Babba, why?" he sobbed, his knees buckling in grief. "Kocho was my friend! You didn't even tell me! Why? Why!"

Rahamim cursed himself for not waiting until Israel. A Bar Mitzvah was supposed to be a triumphant passage into manhood. But his son, he saw now, was still just a boy.

THE END ARRIVED SUDDENLY. A line of motor coaches rolled into town early one April morning, and word went out that the time had come. Under a sky still full of stars, Jewish families, anxious and bleary, dragged suitcases and children out front doors and into the cramped alleys that led to the main street.

As they crossed the bridge to the bus stop, they saw that another crowd had gotten there first: Hundreds of Muslims had lined the streets to bid their neighbors farewell. Old women raised cries of *li-li-li-li-li-li*, ululating as if a loved one had died. A troupe of child musicians played drums and flute. Teenage boys stepped forward to help with suitcases. One beggar — beloved of the townspeople, though he was slightly mad — pounded his head against a newly erected electric pole. "Where are my brothers going?" he shrieked, until people crowded in to console him. "Why are they forsaking us?"

Yona had never seen anything like it. He threaded frantically through the throng. He studied the tear-stained faces and listened to the hoarse cries. The swarm of well-wishers pressed in around him. He was jostled and tripped over the train of a woman's robe. Getting up, he realized he had lost his parents.

"Ha-ha! Little Yona! My son!" a man's voice called from behind. Yona wheeled around. Looking at him with a sad smile was the old grocer who had given him his first job, as a bookkeeper. "I was hoping I'd see you."

The man, whose beard was grayer than the last time Yona saw him, reached into his pocket and pulled out a small box of Turkish delights. "For the journey," he said. "They may not have these where you're going. So eat them slowly, to remind you of Zakho." The man had no children of his own. Looking like he might cry, he knelt to hug the boy.

Yona wanted to tell him what he had been thinking about for the last few days: that he would come back here someday soon as an Israeli fighter pilot. He would land a gleaming jet right in the center of town, and all the Kurds would pour from their houses to cheer his return. Instead he just stood there in the old man's embrace, his arms slack at his side, tears streaming.

Buses carried the Jews to Mosul, and trains carried them to Baghdad. At the airport, angry mobs pressed against the barricades, hurling curses.

"Die, kilab yahud!"

"Rot in hell!"

"Be gone!"

It was April 16, 1951. Miryam flinched at the ugly words and pulled her children against her skirt as crowds of departing Jews pressed in from all sides. A few hours later, the Beh Sabaghas reached the checkpoint where guards searched bodies and baggage for contraband.

"Boy, are you carrying anything of value?" a policeman asked Yona.

"N-n-no, sir," Yona stuttered. The man's gruff voice reminded him of the officers who had humiliated his father on their last trip to Baghdad.

"No money, no jewelry, no precious metals?" Jews were allowed to take only 50 dinars out of the country.

"No, sir," Yona said, shaking as he tried to remember his Arabic. "Nothing."

"Turn around, Jew dog," said the officer, "I don't know that I believe you."

Yona stiffened as the man's fingers crawled over his thighs and ankles, under his arms and crotch, and, then, suddenly, into his pants pockets.

"What did my son do?" Miryam asked meekly.

"Shut it, woman," the officer barked. The man withdrew three small squares of colored paper from Yona's pocket: postage stamps bearing a portrait of Iraq's handsome boy king, Faisal II. Each one was worth 1 fil, a single penny.

"What are these?" the officer growled, his face reddening.

"Sir, it was an accident. I . . . I forgot I even had them."

"Lying Jew. How dare you try to steal property from the Kingdom of Iraq?"

Miryam put her hands to the side of her head and shrieked as the officer raised his palm. "No," she shouted. "He is a boy." But she might have been talking to a wall.

The officer slapped Yona's face three times. "One smack," he said, "for each stamp."

ISRAEL

A Kurdish family arrives in Israel, Lydda Airport, near Tel Aviv, 1951.

25 ❖ Kissing the Ground

The moment his foot touched the ground at Israel's Lod Airport, near Tel Aviv, my great-grandfather Ephraim began to cry. He dropped to his knees, bent forward, and kissed the tarmac.

In front of the family, the old world was meeting the new. The Kurds stepping off the Near East Transport planes in their hand-spun jimidani head coverings looked as dazed and disoriented as if a time-travel machine had just deposited them in a distant future. Parents descended the steps to the brightly lit tarmac with wary gazes and armfuls of children. Tired bodies clanked, with teapots slung to belt loops and demon-banishing amulets bunched at necks and wrists. Few had ever before seen an airplane, let alone traveled on one.

Receiving the unwashed hordes were fair-skinned giants in rakish felt berets — Samsons, Yona thought. The immigration agents studied the arrivals as if they were a mammalian subspecies hitherto unknown to science, gawking at their slightly ridiculous costumes and herding them as quickly as possible toward the disinfection chamber.

Never before had so many people from so many countries gathered so quickly. Between the declaration of statehood on May 14, 1948, and the end of 1951, some 684,201 Jews from across the globe flew, sailed, rode — and even walked — to Israel, more than doubling the Jewish population. Israel's leaders gave the unprecedented migration a lyrical name: "the ingathering of exiles." Much like the airlift from Iraq, Operation Ezra and Nehemiah, the one from Yemen, for instance, was dubbed Operation Magic Carpet. The phrases evoked soft-focus images of biblical redemption, of Jews from the farthest reaches of creation dropping everything for a homecoming ordained by the Messiah. The truth was more complicated. In large measure, the influx was the result of a deliberate political strategy to make the Jewish state a fact on the ground, in the face of continuing questions about its legitimacy and the immediate threat of military attack.

No sooner had the United Nations' plan for the partition of Palestine come to light in 1947 than Ben-Gurion pointed out a fundamental problem: The Promised Land lacked Jews. U.N. recognition, a constitution, and a government were fine. But without a population in place, the new Jewish state would be a paper tiger vulnerable to both ideological critics and foreign armies. "So long as this lack [of population] is not made up for, at least minimally," he said in a political speech that year, according to the historian Dvora Hacohen, "there is no guarantee that the state will continue to exist beyond its establishment." Ben-Gurion later put it more pointedly: "For thousands of years we have been a people without a state. The great danger now is that we shall be a state without a people." Zionist agents fanned out across Europe, Asia, and North Africa to negotiate for — or, failing that, secretly plot — the transplant of entire Jewish communities. The new state lifted the mandate-era restrictions on immigration and, with the landmark 1950 Law of Return, declared immigration to Israel the birthright of every Jew.

Enraptured by heady images of boats disgorging thousands of soon-to-be citizens at Haifa's ports, Israeli leaders miscalculated the infant state's capacity to absorb so colossal a tidal wave. The newcomers spoke a babel of languages. They could not understand one another, let alone the Israelis, who conversed in a tongue many had never heard outside the formal rituals of synagogue. Many were sick, disabled, or elderly, and in need of immediate health care. People trained as businessmen, teachers, and professionals in their home countries struggled to adapt to jobs as road pavers, construction workers, and farm hands.

The rate of absorption was staggering. From May to December 1948, more than 100,000 Jews washed up on Israel's shores, many of them ragged Holocaust survivors who had been living in squalid displaced-persons camps in Germany, Italy, and Austria. The next three years saw the arrival of 22,000 Jews from Bulgaria; 30,000 from Libya; 30,000 from Turkey; 45,000 from Yemen; 75,000 from Poland; 101,000 from Romania; 121,000 from Iraq; and tens of thousands more from other places. Of the 25,000 Kurdish Jews, some 18,000 were from Iraq and the rest mainly from Iran and Syria.

26 ❧ Where Are the Jewish Synagogues?

Ephraim's visions of a modern-day Garden of Eden dried up as fast as a mirage on the Sinai. Zakho's master dyer thought at first that there had been some mistake. At daybreak on his first Saturday in Israel, he untangled his beard with his fingertips and set off on foot for the heart of Jerusalem. Those first few steps, he might as well have been treading air. He had dreamed of the moment almost from the day word came of the Iraqi exodus to Israel. He had pictured gilded synagogues peopled by luminaries of Torah and Mishnah. He had imagined streets full of holy wizards with beards so long they swept the ground.

Instead, as he cleared the gates of the squalid immigrant tent city, he was assaulted by the stench of auto exhaust and the sounds of purgatory. Car horns. Grinding brakes. A motorist with a blown tire cursing the Almighty between puffs on a cigarette as he fumbled with a jack. It was unfathomable. *I must have the wrong day,* he thought. *Perhaps the week is different here in Israel.* But his eyes did not deceive: Israelis were driving on the Sabbath and working. Even Zakho's Muslims knew to snuff their cigarettes on the Sabbath. Here the Jews themselves were smoking. And where were the great houses of prayer? In none of the neighborhood temples he poked his head into did he recognize the chants, the prayer books, or even, it seemed, the language. He had heard there were Christians in Israel. Perhaps these were churches, not synagogues. But then where were the crosses? And why were they full on Saturday? The worshippers, whoever they were, stared at the droll peasant, a fairy-tale apparition in clownish pants and an Ali Baba turban. Some asked him why he didn't sit, waving him to open chairs. Self-conscious and unsure of his spoken Hebrew, Ephraim bowed in what he hoped would be taken as an act of courtesy and slunk back into the street. He spent the better part of the morning shuffling from one house of worship to the next, eager for some familiar sight or sound. At lunchtime, when his belly groaned with hunger, he turned back, heartbroken.

"Please, tell me," he begged his son Rahamim when he returned to the family's shack. "Is there any way to tell from the outside which are Israel's *Jewish* synagogues?"

So much defied his expectations. No sooner had he landed in the country than Israeli officials lopped off parts of the family's last name, the part that marked him as a Kurd. Beh Sabagha, Aramaic for "House of the Dyer," would have been nonsensical in Israel. So when they registered with immigration officials, his son Rahamim simply put down "Sabagh." That was Arabic for "dyer" and a common name among Middle Eastern Jews. But Ephraim hadn't lived among Arabs, and Arabic had never been his language.

The Israeli absorption agency had settled the Sabaghs in Talpiot, a sprawling *ma'abara*, or immigrant shanty town, on the outskirts of Jerusalem. The *ma'abarot* were Israel's solution to its immigrant housing crisis and would soon become an embarrassing symbol of the state's lack of preparation for its heavily trumpeted "ingathering of exiles." Row after unrelieved row of tents — and later, corrugated tin sheds — was erected atop bare ground on more than one hundred hardscrabble tracts from the Galilee region in the north to the Negev desert in the south. The teeming settlements were often at a remove from the town and city centers where the new immigrants might actually find jobs, integrate into neighborhoods, or even catch a regularly scheduled bus. Isolated in wastelands of flimsy housing far from the institutions that had lured the immigrants to Israel in the first place, the ma'abarot became fertile ground for sudden epidemics, vermin, illicit markets for stolen goods, and sometimes explosive tensions among groups of immigrants with differing customs and languages.

Zaki Levi, the neighbor from Zakho, recalled a melee in the fall of 1951 over access to one of the outdoor taps where residents with pails waited in lines for drinking water. Levi said that a young Moroccan Jew stole some water from the pail of Levi's eight-year-old niece, and the girl screamed.

Ephraim Beh Sabagha, Ariel's great-grandfather,
state ID issued on arrival in Israel, early 1950s.

In a flash, rival mobs of young Moroccans and Kurds — including Levi
and Ephraim's son Israel — gathered. Accusations flew. The young men
moved in and pounded one another with rocks and wooden dowels.
When it was over, several men and a pregnant woman were seriously
injured and a tin shack had been looted and ripped to the ground.

The police officer who eventually arrived just shrugged. "He took one
look, went back to his car, and left," Levi recalled. "He said, 'This is not a
police matter — politicians should take care of it.'"

THE ENTIRE FAMILY could see Ephraim's misery. The daily
scenes of impiety, suffering, and violence lay on his spirit like wet wool.
The right ingredients for kubeh and yaprach were hard to come by at
the Talpiot canteen where the family redeemed their food coupons.
Rain clattered against the tin roof and turned the dirt streets to soup.
Rats skulked among the dimly lit public latrines. American tourists

in shamefully short skirts traipsed through the ma'abarot. A group of Christian missionaries had the gall to visit the camps one day and take Ephraim's little granddaughter Sara to a well-groomed Jerusalem neighborhood to ply her with chocolate and tell her about God's son, Yehoshua.

Ephraim must have sensed early on that this state of Israel was not the Land of Israel he had daydreamed about in Zakho. He must have quickly grasped that though the Land of Israel may have had room for his kind, the state did not. That must have been why, two months after arrival, he felt compelled to lie about his age. He told the official taking down information for his official state ID card that he was fifty-four years old. He worried that declaring his true age of seventy-seven would make him useless in this land of young pioneers, these "Samsons," as his grandson Yona was fond of calling them. The ruse fooled no one. In the next line, the one for "occupation," the official wrote *zaken*, old man.

One night he wandered out under the starlight after everyone was asleep, in search of what he had heard was a synagogue in Bethlehem that was open all night. It was a walk of several miles into the ancient city of meadows, olive groves, and pastures. The next morning, a warm day, the family found him shivering in his bed.

"Did you find it?" Hazale asked, shaking his emaciated body.

"I made it to Bethlehem," he said, coughing violently. "But not to the synagogue."

Rahamim knew that Bethlehem was under Jordanian rule in those days. A Jew could not just casually visit. But he did not have the heart to question his father.

"Was the synagogue closed?" Hazale asked.

"How should I know?" Ephraim said. "I turned around before I got there."

Upon further questioning, Ephraim told a story of a fruitless search. He said that he was passing the fez-shaped dome of Rachel's Tomb in Bethlehem when none other than the matriarch herself appeared before him with a word of caution.

"She floated before me, and I trembled. Then she looked at me right in the eye and said, 'Don't look for any synagogues here,'" he said, as his grandchildren kneeled beside him, riveted. "'This is an Arab neighborhood now.' She said it just like that. 'It is not safe. Go back to the ma'abara.'"

"You could have at least seen the temple," Hazale interjected. "Seen if it was there, after all that walking."

"Woman, are you mad?" he snapped. "Who am I to argue with Mother Rachel?"

For a while, Ephraim tried to keep up a version of his Zakho vigils. He waited until the family was asleep and, so as not to wake anyone, whispered to Rafael, Elijah, and the other sprites who were his nightly companions in Kurdistan. In return came only silence. "Where are you, my old friends?" Ephraim cried one morning. What he told his grandson in Zakho had turned out to be true: the town's jinne — its demons — had not followed them to Jerusalem. But neither, he saw now, had its angels.

Ephraim shared the fifteen-foot by twenty-foot living quarters with his wife and with Rahamim, Miryam, and their five children (the fifth, Uri, was born in 1953). The sleeping pads covered every square inch of floor. In the morning, the children stacked them all in a corner just so people could get up and leave. But not even his daughter-in-law, accustomed, he knew, to all manner of toil, could negotiate the small room. One morning, while cooking eggs on a small propane burner, she lost her balance and tipped the pan. Hot oil spattered. Her newborn, Uri, was at her feet, and the oil scalded his cheeks. An ambulance was summoned.

Then, at last, came a way out. A ma'abara official had noticed their overcrowded shack and came one day to offer Ephraim and Hazale their own place. A cabin had opened up, he said, on the other side of the camp. They were elderly, he explained, and entitled to more comfortable accommodations. In other ma'abarot, residents had actually staged angry demonstrations over access to open cabins. To have a ma'abara official actually offer one unsolicited was unheard of. Maybe God really did have a soft spot for his father, Rahamim thought.

"Go, Babba," Rahamim said. "You and *Ima* need the room."

Ephraim planted his bony hands on his son's shoulders and kissed him tearfully on each cheek.

He dabbed his eyes and turned back to the official. "Thank you, kind man," he said. "But my wife and I will stay right here, with our son and grandchildren."

The man shook his head and left. But Rahamim understood: Family was all Ephraim had left.

In the mid-1950s the Israeli government allotted permanent apartments to families according to the number of shacks they had occupied in the ma'abara. If Ephraim had accepted his own shack, he and Hazale would have been given their own apartment in Katamonim, Jerusalem's Kurdish slums. But he hadn't, so each of his three sons, with growing families of their own, took turns housing their parents. Because the Katamonim apartments were so tiny, Ephraim often lived with one of his sons' families while Hazale lived with another's. The arrangements made the family patriarch feel more like a millstone.

Ephraim was once ebullient and generous, a mystic who saw life through messianic eyes and believed in the ultimate sanctity of family. In Israel, beset by disappointment, his light dimmed. My aunts and uncles remember him in his last years as a picture of defeat. He sat in his Kurdish robes in unlit hallways of his son Eliyahu's apartment, his turbaned head drooping over his lap, trying to stay out of the way of a generation he would never understand.

"He sat in the corridor in the darkest part of the apartment," Uri, my father's youngest brother, told me one day. "It was his way to be polite. He didn't want to disturb you. He didn't used to talk to us. I couldn't speak Aramaic to him. He was just an old man, sitting in a dark corner."

One Saturday night, after eating nothing all day, he asked Eliyahu to call an ambulance. The doctor at the hospital found no physical symptoms, but, given Ephraim's advanced age, admitted him for observation. Word raced through Katamonim, and within hours a group of Kurdish rabbis, younger men who had coaxed a few one-room synagogues into existence in the neighborhood, had gathered at his bedside. Some knew him from Zakho. Others had heard the legend of the dyer with the direct line to God.

"Hakham Zachariah, Hakham Shmuel Baruch, Hakham Yosef . . . all the hakhamim, all these old-time rabbis, all came to the hospital," Eli-

yahu told me when I went to see him in his Katamonim apartment in
2005.

Three days later, Ephraim was dead. Two months and five days after
that, Hazale was buried beside him.

27 ❖ Herzl's Beard

Construction. Jerusalem in the mid-1950s was a one-industry town.
Everywhere the Sabagh brothers looked, bulldozers spitting billows
of dust were flattening rocky hillsides for another corner mall, school,
road, or apartment building. The logic was as pure as the sun beating on
the gold-hued ramparts of the Old City: Mass immigration had doubled
the new state's Jewish population in just three years. More than six hundred thousand immigrants needed places to live, shop, work, and play.
With the ma'abarot becoming a national embarrassment, Israel had nothing but encouragement for men with eyes on the building trades. The Sabagh brothers had a head start: enough cash to start their own company.

Before their flight from Iraq, Rahamim's Baghdadi business partner,
Ezra, had introduced him to a cast of shadowy figures with elaborate
schemes to sneak money past the airport police. One smuggler explained
how he tucked bills inside hollowed-out soap bars or shoe heels. Another
said he could melt gold into suitcase linings. In the end, Rahamim passed
them over for a young man with an earnest face and a fine suit whose fabric Rahamim could tell was of British provenance and expensive. "I am a
rabbi," the man said. "I will find you at the camps in Israel, with God as
my witness." That was all Rahamim needed to hear.

A few weeks into their stay at the Talpiot camp, the rabbi turned up
at their cabin with a cloth sack containing the family's 10,000 dinars.
The impressive vestments Rahamim remembered in Baghdad were gone,
replaced by shorts and a sun visor. Sitting cross-legged on the dirt floor,
the man counted the bills with an expert's swiftness and stuffed a handful
into his own shirt pocket.

"But rabbi —" Rahamim said.

"Two thousand for my services," the man said, getting up to leave. "What? You think I work for free?"

In Zakho, Eliyahu had raised the delicate question of how to divvy up the proceeds from the liquidation of their stores. "We made this money together, Rahamim, and in Zakho, we spent it together," he told his older brother the week before they left. "But in Israel, who knows if we'll even live near each other." Eliyahu, like many others, imagined that in Israel he would step clear of the tripwires of Zakho's social order. With a little money of his own, he could work for himself, not his elder brother, and maybe run his own business. "Let's divide it three ways here," he had urged, clapping his hands as if to wipe them clean.

But Rahamim made it clear that such an arrangement was unacceptable. The three brothers were a unit. It was impossible to say who had earned what share of the money and, as a result, ridiculous to venture a calculation of each one's due. True, he believed his stewardship of the family business entitled him to a greater share of the profits, should there ever be a split. But another reason for his objections to Eliyahu's proposal was something he could admit only to himself: the suspicion that without control of the Sabagh fortune, his family might respect him a little less.

RAHAMIM HADN'T BEEN able to shed his smile after a teller at Bank Leumi converted the 8,000 dinars (about $174,000 in today's dollars) to Israeli *lirot* and deposited them in what she said was a special small-business account. He squared his shoulders and left the bank feeling two inches taller. He knew Baghdadi traders with bank accounts. Now he, too, could toss around words like *holdings* and *assets* with the air of a big-city businessman. It was an enviable sum for an Israeli Kurd: enough to buy an apartment in one of Jerusalem's leafier neighborhoods. But money sunk in an apartment did no one any good. So the younger Sabagh brothers entrusted Rahamim, as the eldest and most experienced, with finding a way into Israel's booming construction trade. A break, or so it seemed at first, came faster than anyone expected.

A distant relative, Saleh, was part of a small wave of impoverished Kurds who had migrated to Palestine in the 1930s and settled around the

Mahane Yehuda bazaar. When he heard of the arrival of his long-lost cousins, the Beh Sabaghas, he paid a visit. He was now a manager in a big construction company, he told Rahamim; he knew a man who needed to get rid of an air compressor and some jackhammers cheap. If Rahamim laid out the capital, Saleh said, filling his cousin's glass with arak from a hip flask, they could form a partnership profitable to them both: "I do this because we're family."

If Eliyahu or Israel had any reservations as their big brother signed the purchase contract, they held their tongues. "I didn't object because we always listened to your grandfather in Kurdistan," Eliyahu said, when I visited him a few years ago. "But we should have known better."

The jackhammers broke the second week. The Sabaghs sank hundreds of lirot into costly repairs, but to no avail; the construction equipment Saleh had brokered for them were lemons. Builders angered by the delays cancelled contracts. The more money Rahamim lost, the more consuming his obsession with making things right. He still believed, as he had in Zakho, that one good turn would bring another. He worked jobs below cost in hopes of winning back unhappy customers. He impliclty trusted the contracts that builders handed him, realizing only when it was too late that they imposed financial penalties for deadlines missed by so much as a day.

After two years of mounting losses, the Sabagh brothers closed the business. They sold the faulty compressor and jackhammers for one tenth of their cost. The three brothers — as inseparable in Zakho as the arms of the Habur River — never worked together again.

For Eliyahu, bitterness over the breakup ran particularly deep. "May shit fall on Herzl's beard for bringing us here," he would say, as though the Budapest-born founder of Zionism were personally to blame for the family's misfortunes.

"How can you say that?" Miryam protested one day, ashamed at her brother-in-law's profanity. She had seen photographs of the Zionist leader and had assumed his beard was rabbinical. "Herzl was pious."

"He and his piety can go to hell," Eliyahu said.

After the breakup, Eliyahu and Israel followed the tracks of so many other Kurds into jobs as construction laborers. It was back-breaking and mostly mindless work. It calloused their hands and lent them the rugged air of men they once saw as beneath them. But it was a living. With their illustrious father dead and their eldest brother adrift, they saw no reason to persist in the dangerous delusion of superiority. They lowered their expectations and stayed afloat, earning steady paychecks for three decades and eventually retiring with good pensions.

But Rahamim was unmoved by his brothers' abdication. He clung to the belief that the Sabaghs could do better.

"What about school, Abba?" Yona said, when his father asked him to find work to help support the family. (*Babba* had given way to *Abba* with the move to Israel.)

"You'll go at night. The unions run schools for working boys."

"But, Abba, can a working boy still become a doctor?"

28 ❧ *Ana Kurdi*

When the man tossed the stacks of bound newspapers from the loading docks of the printing plant, the boys pounced like mountain lions on an unsuspecting sheep.

"Move!"

"That's mine!"

Loose pages of *Ma'ariv* and *Yediot Ahronot* flew in every direction, spiking the air with the smell of fresh ink.

"Get off!"

"Thief! Give me that!"

The first half hour was pivotal. A boy had to grab as many newspapers as he could as quickly as possible and then commandeer a busy Jerusalem intersection before another boy beat him to it. Then came the real test: Shouting headlines, waving the newspapers at passersby, or even, with the ones who wouldn't look at you, tugging at their sleeves and giving them puppy-dog eyes in hopes of a pity purchase. Thursdays, when newspapers published the lottery numbers, were mayhem.

Yona tried to keep up. He leaped into the pyramid of boys tearing at

the stacks of newspapers, but late and without the requisite ferocity. He
called out headlines on street corners, but his voice soon sounded broken
and hollow, like a clarinet with a split reed. He knew he was supposed to
mark his turf at a busy intersection. But if a younger boy began hawking
papers beside him, he let him. It cost him sales, he knew, but he liked the
company. The bravado that had had him flying across Zakho's rooftops
or bragging about some new pair of Baghdad-bought shoes eluded him
in Israel. The boys here were schemers, fast and wily and tough. In their
company, Yona's fearlessness had softened into a quiet, dreamy detachment.

The jobs in Zakho had seemed much more civil. Boys kept stock in
their father's shops, sheared sheep, apprenticed to tailors or cobblers.
Here they did battle. In the book of legends he had read in Zakho, Israel
was a place where the Jews lived together as brothers. It was true that
there were no agas to make you work for free. No roadway bandits to slit
a Kurd's throat. No policemen to slap your face because you were a Jew
and forgot you had three stamps in your pocket.

So why did life seem so much harder in Israel? Or rather, why did it
seem harder for him than for other boys?

When a job opened up at a small, quiet paper factory run out of a Katamonim basement, Yona quit the news business and took it. He clocked in
at seven every morning for the factory's dirtiest work: cleaning out used
cement bags. He scrubbed the loose cement particles from the insides of
the bags, sliced the bags in half with a hand-cranked cutting machine,
then brushed a fresh coat of glue over the seams so they could begin new
lives as grocery bags. By the time his shift ended, nine hours later, he was
coughing up wads of dust and felt weak in the knees. He went home to
change, so he wouldn't itch during the next four hours at night school.

The factory was run on such a shoestring that the owner, Zacharia
Shmaya, had to contract out basic operations. One day he asked Yona to
walk a stack of papers to the printer. "I want them to get started on this
job," Zacharia told Yona. "Don't answer any of their questions. Just tell
them I'll be there later today with more specific instructions."

When Yona arrived at the print shop, the printer, who was missing two
front teeth, looked confused.

"What is this?"

"It's from Zacharia's paper shop. He wanted me to give it to you."

"Well, what am I supposed to do with it?" the printer said.

"I don't know anything more. I'm just doing what he asked me to."

"Just doing what he asked?" the printer said, mimicking the boy. "Ana Kurdi?" If Yona heard correctly, the man had just spoken Aramaic. *Ana Kurdi* means "I'm a Kurd," but the printer made it sound like an accusation, more like, "What, are you a Kurd?"

When Yona returned to the store, Zacharia was out. So he approached his sons, Tzion and Reuven, who were several years older than he.

"How did the printer know I was a Kurd?" Yona asked, after relaying the story and the printer's strange remark. The brothers burst into laughter.

"Why is that funny?" asked Yona, somewhere between amusement and alarm.

"I guess he hasn't been here long enough to know," Tzion, regaining his composure, said to his brother.

"Know *what*?" Yona asked.

"Man, you mean you really haven't heard? Let's see: The Romanians are thieves. The Polish are unclean. The Yemenites — that's our family — are peasants. The Moroccans are brutes. And the Kurds have it worst of all: They're just morons."

"Rubes," Reuven said.

"Dumb fucks," Tzion added, helpfully, and Yona blushed. "Can't think for themselves. Do whatever they're told. Ana Kurdi!"

"Get it now, Kurdi?" Reuven said. "The printer didn't know you were a Kurd. He just said you were acting like one."

"Nice place, this Israel?" Tzion said. "You'd think we Jews, of all people, would know better than to call each other names."

"Oh," Yona said, wrinkling his brow into a look of innocent curiosity. "That's interesting."

TZION WAS SEVENTY-FIVE YEARS old when I tracked him down by phone in Toronto, but he had not forgotten his first impressions of my father. When the brothers explained the Kurdish stereotype to

Yona, Tzion recalled, there was understanding but no disquiet. The way they'd been goading him, Tzion would have forgiven Yona for rampaging back to the print shop and socking the gap-toothed twit in the nose. But Yona looked more like a scientist digesting a theorem at odds with current knowledge than he did a teenager whose entire people had just been dragged through the mud.

Back in those days, Tzion, a native Israeli with Yemenite parents, was a long-haired high-school dropout and dilettante, part Beatnik, part self-styled disciple of the Russian anarchist Peter Kropotkin.

Yona wasn't a rebel, exactly. He was too reticent. But Tzion came to see him as a kind of fellow traveler, free enough to rise above the noise of the street and take in life from a quieter vantage nearer the clouds. Their conversations on the shop floor lightened the drudgery. Yona asked Tzion questions about the news of the day: the excavations at Masada that turned up the remains of Herod's palace, the mysterious ancient scrolls that scholars were plucking out of eleven caves along the northwest shore of the Dead Sea, the resignation of Prime Minister Ben-Gurion, the merits of the state's decision to abolish the death penalty for murder. Tzion introduced him to the music of Mozart and Beethoven.

On weekends he invited Yona to the small café on Allenby Street where Tzion's circle of bohemian friends gathered for café au lait, *borekas* pastries, and beer. After a few drinks, Tzion took a copy of *Reader's Digest* from his satchel and began to read aloud, running his fingers under the words so Yona could follow. Tzion had never finished high school. But during his stint in the army, he survived ten months in a squalid Jordanian POW camp by memorizing lists of English vocabulary words an officer had prepared for him.

"English is the language of the future," Tzion said to the boy. "Look at the letters and listen to the sound the words make. It's a funny language, man."

Yona tried to impress Tzion with what must have been a one-of-a-kind rendition of "Oh my Darling, Clementine!" But his older friend either didn't know the song or, more likely, couldn't make sense of Yona's garbled pronunciation. "I'm not sure that's the same English the queen speaks, Yona," he said.

So every weekend, they muddled through another issue of *Reader's Digest* or as much as they could before the letters blurred.

"I was too lazy to finish high school," Tzion confessed at the café one autumn day. "I'm still waiting to find my calling. But you've got yours already."

He tapped a finger against the side of his head, then pressed a palm to his heart. "They're going to expect you to drop out or go to some sort of trade school," Tzion said. "That's all Kurds are good for, right? Primitives that you are. But you can do better. Trust in the zodiac to show you the way."

Over two years, Yona's grades in English climbed from satisfactory to very good. When he told Tzion he had scored a nine out of ten on the English portion of the *bagrut*, the national standardized test, Tzion bought him a mug of beer.

Yona took a sip, then asked if it was okay to send it back for tea. Tzion laughed. He was just twenty-five, but he felt toward Yona the way he imagined a father might.

Yona left the print shop in the eleventh grade, after Tzion's father went broke and stopped paying his employees. But his three years in the dusty basement of a Katamonim apartment building had given him something beyond an income: an Israeli who believed in him.

29 ❖ Some of the Best in Zakho

Rahamim scarcely saw his son. The boy was up at 4 A.M., hunching over his homework, then out the ma'abara's cabin door for work at 6:00. He tramped in at dinnertime to eat his mother's cooking, and was gone at 5:30 to classes at the night High School for the Working Youth. Rahamim stayed up late sometimes. He made a show of studying his accounts or reading the evening newspapers. But what he really wanted as the candle sputtered down was a little time with his son, through whose young eyes he hoped Israel's mysteries might seem more clear. He hoped those eyes would reveal something else: his son's continued respect for him. But the boy returned from school at 11:00, so weary that he tumbled onto his mattress like a sack of cantelopes off the back of truck.

"*Lila tov, motek*," Rahamim said, tousling his hair. Good night, sweetheart.

"Lila tov," Yona said. The words came out muffled, because Yona had already tugged the covers over his head to block out the candlelight.

WHEN I CONSIDER the next few years of my grandfather's life, I am struck by his persistence in the face of disappointment. For most of us, experience grinds down dreams. Time clarifies our aptitudes. We scale back our expectations. Setting the bar lower is a basic human defense. It lets us celebrate small triumphs. It protects us from the realization that some hopes are forever out of reach. It is a trade-off all immigrants make, sacrificing what we were for what our children might be.

So what do we make of a man who stubbornly presses on? Do we applaud his determination or pity his bullheadedness? No one would have blamed Rahamim for lowering his sights. But he never really did. When he finally humbled himself enough to work for someone else, he promised himself it would be temporary. The bosses, he was sure, would take note of his business acumen and put him in charge of other people. If he played it right, he might soon be running the company.

But it never worked out that way. After the excavation business failed, he took a job as a manual laborer at a book bindery that printed official forms and leaflets for the Israeli bureaucracy, work that left his back sore and his fingers filleted with paper cuts. At quitting time he foraged wastebaskets for loose scraps of paper to take home for toilet tissue.

He knew it could be worse. All he had to do was look at the Kurdish day laborers on the street corner beyond the bindery door, the sad souls who waited half a day to earn a few lirot by hoisting pianos and beds and god-knows-what up narrow staircases. Rahamim at least handled printed materials, not baggage. As he shuttled stacks of paper from machine to machine, he saw ways to institute efficiencies, to get more out of the workers. He could run a place like this one day, he thought, if only he could get the owner's attention.

Rahamim was in awe of Mr. Rothberg, a well-dressed German Jew with sandy hair and a silver tongue. If he could shed some of his Kurdishness and reinvent himself in something like Rothberg's mold, Rahamim thought, Rahamim might just make it in Israel. One day he asked for a word with his boss.

"You're a good man, an honest man," Rothberg said, slapping him on the back as he directed him to a seat in his office. "I wish we had more like you, believe me, *habibi*."

Feeling encouraged, Rahamim launched into a description of his family's stores in Kurdistan. "Some of the best-run and most profitable in Zakho," he crowed to Rothberg. He said he was still waiting for the right business to invest in here in Israel. "If you need a new partner—"

Rothberg cut him off with a belly laugh. It was an audacious proposal from a low-wage manual laborer. "You are a kind man, Rahamim," he said. "But keep your money in the bank. With all those children, it's better not to take risks."

But a year later, when the company fell on hard times and creditors started calling, Rothberg came to Rahamim. He said he would take his money as a loan and make Rahamim a shop foreman, with opportunities for further advancement if he proved himself. "We're expanding," Rothberg lied. "This may be your chance."

Rahamim loaned Rothberg nearly all that remained of his savings.

30 ❦ John Savage

The night of Sushan Purim 1954 found Yona Sabagh and his high-school friends at their Saturday lair: a third-floor balcony in a narrow alley a few steps from the corner of Ben Yehuda and Yaffo streets, the pulsing heart of Jerusalem. Yona's friend Shlomo, an aspiring troubadour, lived in the three-room apartment with his parents, three brothers, one sister, and an aunt. They were from southern Iraq and somewhat better off than their Kurdish friends, who lived a few miles away in Katamonim. On Saturdays they pushed the beds against the walls and remade the apartment into a ballroom. The guests were an assortment of squares, nerds, and oddballs from Middle Eastern countries, never stylish or confident enough to be seen at the high-stepping parties of their counterparts in private day schools. Still, from the balcony of Shlomo's house, the group had a view any teenager would envy: the cafés and bars on Ben Yehuda, the guests who occasionally disrobed at the windows of the hotel across the street, the chic patrons of the Café Vienna, and the flashing marquee of the Zion movie theater.

On the night of the Purim party, Yona and his friends weren't looking at the street or the hotel windows. They had their eyes on the apartment door and the influx of Queen Esthers in dime-store tiaras and shimmering gowns their mothers had hastily sewn together from old silk scarves.

"I wonder if any of them need a royal escort," Yona said, sliding the King Achashveyrosh mask over his face and tightening the elastic bands around the whipped-up effusion of dark waves that one might have called a pompadour if it had been intentional.

"What do you think?" Yona asked Shlomo, elbowing him in the ribs.

Shlomo made a convincing Haman, even if he had fashioned the wicked courtier's three-cornered hat from that afternoon's newspaper.

"Divide and conquer, your majesty."

It was *Beyt Ha Sefer Shel Ha Noar Ha Oved*, Jerusalem's labor union–run night High School for the Working Youth, that had brought the boys together. Some twenty kids gathered every night after work for four hours of classes: Hebrew literature, Hebrew grammar, composition, Bible, English, history, math, physics, chemistry, Israeli geography, civics, and, it being a union school, labor history. Most of the students paid the annual tuition of 90 lirot a year from their own meager earnings. Nearly all had destitute parents. Nearly all were from Muslim lands: Iraq, Iran, Morocco. The Iraqi boys quickly found one another.

Shlomo Bar-Nissim, the son of a customs agent and the brother of three activists in the Zionist underground, was from Basra, in the far south. He had watched through cracked shutters as a funeral procession bore the body of Shafiq Adès, the wealthy Iraqi Jew executed in 1948 after a show trial, past his house on the way to the Jewish cemetery. A little over a year later, his parents decided it was no longer safe for their children to stay in Iraq.

"School had started in September, but every day more and more students were missing," Bar-Nissim recalled over coffee when I went to visit him at his house in northern New Jersey. "One day I came home and saw my mother crying. 'You don't have to go to school anymore,' she said. My father gave me jackets and suits. A guy from the underground was there. 'You're leaving tonight,' he said."

His parents had business affairs to wrap up before leaving, so they sent Shlomo, just eleven, with a group of other Basra Jews on a dangerous and illegal journey over rivers and desert to Tehran, where, with forged identity papers, they boarded a flight to Israel.

Another of Yona's high-school friends, Abraham Zilkha from Baghdad, was the youngest of a thrift-store owner's seven children. Nerdy but a little reckless, he sent a handwritten letter to the Iraqi government before his family's departure, asking for official permission to take a few things with him to Israel: some geography books, an Arabic-English dictionary, a first-place award certificate from an Arabic handwriting competition, plus his coin collection. Maybe some bureacrat was moved by his childish scrawl; in any case, a letter bearing official stamps arrived, granting his request.

Only one thing came before his studies at the French-run Alliance Israelite Universelle school in Baghdad. "I'd tell my mom I was going to a friend's house to do homework, then I'd cross the bridge over the Tigris to go see any movie with Esther Williams," Zilkha recalled recently. "I was crazy about her. I'd buy Egyptian magazines and look for her picture."

Yosi Elati was the group's quiet one. He was the fifth child of a Baghdadi textile merchant. His earliest memory was of hiding, terrified, in the attic during the Farhud, while a mob slaughtered a Jewish family a few doors down. In Israel, his parents penniless, he went to work as a mechanic's assistant, showing up at night school speckled with motor oil and axle grease.

"After eight hours of work, we were very tired, and it was hard to concentrate in school," Elati said, when I spoke with him at a hotel café in Jerusalem. He might well have been speaking for the bunch, all of whom worked menial day jobs — washing clothes, planting trees — that wrung them of strength and spirit. "Sometimes I'd fall asleep in my book. And then I had to go back to the ma'abara. You'd walk from the bus station in mud for twenty-five minutes. Even when you got home, you couldn't wash yourself, because to boil water at that hour was impossible. So you would go to sleep filthy."

Yosef Sagi, from Kirkuk, was the contrarian, a my-way-or-the-highway scrapper who liked to pick fights and fan arguments. He didn't go to school with the rest but had known several of the boys from the ma'abara.

The wild man was Baruch Givati, the only boy besides Yona from Zakho, or from Kurdistan, for that matter. His father, a tailor, died in 1952, just two years after the family's arrival in Israel. At fourteen, Givati, the second oldest of six children, became the family's breadwinner and leader, selling newspapers and working as an office gofer.

Yona stood out for his intellectual curiosity and a chameleonlike ability to transform from good-natured friend to academic isolate. One week he might be going out to movies and eating kabob with friends. The next, if an exam was looming, he would vanish. When I visited Zilkha at his house near the University of Texas at Austin, where he is a Hebrew professor, he clicked through a series of black-and-white photos from the 1950s that he had scanned into his computer. A grainy image of their high-school classroom appeared. A bespectacled teacher at the head of rows of dark-haired students is gesturing with his right hand, and apparently saying something funny or engaging, because half the kids are either smiling or looking up at him. Not my father. He is seated in the first row, right in front of the teacher. He is hunched so low over his notebook that his nose is almost touching the page. He is inscribing something with a pen or pencil with one hand, and tamping down the page with the bunched fingers of the other. He looks like a surgeon making a tricky incision. "That's your father," Zilkha said to me, as we studied the photo. "Writing down every word."

The lines of language, social class, and education that separated these boys in Iraq blurred in Israel, where they were lumped together as backwater Jews in need of civilization. "In Baghdad, I never saw any Jewish Kurds and didn't know any Muslim Kurds," Zilkha told me. "The only Kurds I saw were street cleaners, sewer cleaners, porters. I could recognize them by their headdress. The prejudice was that they were uneducated, primitive. I shared that prejudice as a child. The Baghdadis were the elite, so they looked down on everyone else. In Iraq we had two different worlds. But in Israel the worlds met."

AS THEIR PARENTS withdrew into their shells, clinging to memories of days when money and honor came easier, the boys raced into Israel's incandescent future. Yona sent away for a "youth phonograph" he saw advertised in the newspaper *Yediot Ahronot*. He paid for the ungainly tangle of wires in monthly installments. He had too little loose money to buy records, so he and his friends visited the free library at the American consulate. They checked out an eighteen-volume history of jazz collection, concertos by Beethoven, Dvořak, Ravel, musicals by Rogers and Hammerstein. They practiced their English with the library staff. Then they lay on the floors of Katamonim apartments, listening to the soaring melodies, taking turns reading liner notes and memorizing music trivia. On weekends they headed to the cinema for Broadway musicals: *Seven Brides for Seven Brothers, West Side Story, The Pajama Game.* They pitched in for a joint membership in an album-a-month record club and entered a music knowledge competition.

On weekends Yona grazed in used bookstores. He bought books of English and French cartoons or beat-up copies of adventure books like *The Three Musketeers, White Fang,* and *Robinson Crusoe.* He even had a place to read in peace: the bathroom. In the mid-1950s, Israel transplanted poverty-stricken Kurds from tin shacks in the ma'abarot to publicly subsidized apartment blocks in Katamonim. The Sabaghs' one-bedroom apartment on Rashbag Street was tight for a family with five children and soon a sixth. But it had its own toilet—no more outdoor latrines—and Yona quickly discovered it could be latched shut: a private library.

Yona and his friends were undergoing a wholesale reinvention. They were shedding one layer of skin and growing another. Their parents were their only link to the past. And what exactly was that past worth in Israel?

My father's friends told me that their parents did not fit the American stereotype of the whip-cracking immigrant couple who, though poor, demand straight *A*s and check every scrap of homework. Emasculated by their new culture, most fathers — and mothers — were too lost in depression or the exigencies of daily survival to play more than a spectator's role in their children's lives.

"We were self-made," Bar-Nissim said. "Nobody told us to go to school and learn and after that go to university."

Baruch Givati added, "Our group was a lucky group. It was a very small difference as to who fell on this side and who fell on the other. We happened to fall on this side. Many of the others we knew didn't go to school." That "very small difference" was critical: All of my father's group would grow up to be educated and successful. Givati, Elati, and Sagi would become lawyers; Bar-Nissim, a cantor; and Zilkha and my father, professors. What accounted for that very small difference was some elusive calculus of ambition, self-confidence, and an ancestor — like Ephraim — who believed in the life of the mind.

"My father was one of very, very few in Zakho who learned at his age to write in Arabic," the language of the educated Middle East, Givati said. "And he could listen to radio and understand and explain things to others in a teahouse. He influenced me about education. Most of our friends didn't study, didn't go to university. Many were jealous of us. They thought we were proud because we studied."

Mostly, though, they weren't thought about at all.

"We were all kind of wimps," Abraham Zilkha said.

My father agreed: "We were total squares."

They were dark-skinned, of unremarkable height, with hair that spumed like whipped fudge. Photos show a group of lean young men in neat slacks and dress shirts with sleeves rolled in neat square folds above the elbow: Baghdadi Beatniks, Kurdish Kerouacs. Bar-Nissim told me they were simply *yaldut ashuka*, deprived children. Deprived not just of wealth but also of place. Yona Sabagh was one of the few Kurds of his generation to enroll in high school in Israel. Some of his former friends began to see him as proud and aloof. He was abandoning his people, shaming them with his achievements. Kurds in Israel were supposed to hang together, not outdo one another. And yet if he wasn't one of them, who was he?

On Saturday evenings, he and his friends would stroll Jerusalem's crowded promenades and see a world forever out of reach: the well-dressed sons and daughters of the Ashkenazi elite, who went to private schools during the day and had every night to do as they pleased. The "salon crowd," the *hevra salonit*, the Iraqi boys called them. The salon crowd had money in their pockets. They drank at fashionable cafés. They laughed and flirted. And, as Yona noticed, some of their college boys wore a remarkable furrowed fabric: corduroy, he heard it called. He had seen nothing like it in his father's stores. *Beautiful*, Yona thought. *Like the robes of King Arthur.*

"We sat there, and it felt totally beyond us," my father told me. "Sometimes we envied them. They had so much, could be so free."

Only later would my father and his friends realize they had something far more precious: one another. On my trip to Israel in 2005, Givati, Elati, and Sagi invited me to a Jerusalem restaurant one night to reminisce about their childhoods. They told me that the group had met there for coffee and dessert every Thursday night now for decades. (The three in America, Bar-Nissim, Zilkha, and my father, go when they're in Israel.) Five decades after high school had cemented their friendship, with parents long dead and families scattered across the globe, it was impossible to pry this group of deprived children apart.

AT THE PURIM PARTY that spring evening in 1954, the celebration was soon in full swing. Shlomo was singing tenor, as usual, by the balcony, gesturing theatrically as he ran through a song list that ranged from "O Sole Mio" to "Hava Nagila." A backup band had assembled and were passably keeping up: a blind boy from their school (Chaim Tzur, who would go on to write the famous Israeli folk song "Al Shlosha Devarim") on accordion, a Russian neighbor on mandolin, and a newly arrived American on guitar.

Yona hadn't touched the gin and tonic a friend tried to press on him, but his head was whirling. He wished he could freeze all this sound and feeling and live inside it forever. "Hey, Sabagh." It was Avigdor Shemesh, grinning as usual. He was one of those kids who was always laughing to himself, as though he's just dying to share some inside joke. "I was think-ing I might go to Hollywood and become a famous actor."

"Really?"

"Yeah, man, look at me in this Haman costume. I have style, don't you think?"

"Your name, though," Yona shouted over the music. "I haven't seen a name like Avigdor Shemesh in any credits."

"All these big movie people have fake names. Marilyn Monroe. John Wayne. Boris Karloff. All of them were born Avigdor Shemesh, or some-thing like it. When you become a star, you get to make up a new name that looks better in all those big letters."

"Yes, yes," Yona said. "Peter Lorre, I think, was really László Löwenstein."

"That's what I'm telling you. They're all really Jews."

"So what will you call yourself when you go to Hollywood?" Yona asked.

"Easy. Avigdor Shemesh becomes, da-da-da-taaa, Victor James."

"Bravo."

"See? It even sounds like Avigdor Shemesh. It's good not to forget where you came from. Magazines will show me in a limousine with all fifteen of my girlfriends. But my friends in Israel will know that Avigdor has not abandoned them."

"So what would my name be, if I went to Hollywood?"

"*Not* Yona Sabagh."

If Yona weren't still wearing the King Achashveyrosh mask, Avigdor might have noticed he was blushing.

"Let's see," Avigdor went on. "'Yona' is no problem. That would be become John. But Sabagh. *Eeechs.*"

"I got it!" Yona said, tugging off his mask so Avigdor could see the inspiration flash in his eyes. "Twentieth-Century Fox presents . . . da-da-da-taaa, John Savage."

"Perfect," Avigdor said, nodding wildly. "You're brilliant, Savage."

Reborn as John Savage, Yona threaded through the clots of revelers in search of a Queen Esther who had caught his eye earlier in the evening.

Her name was Ofra, the girl from a dream he'd told Tzion about. Reddish blond ringlets cascaded around an angel's face that was as white as dove feathers. He put his mask back on and steeled his courage. "Twentieth-Century Fox presents . . . John Savage," he kept saying to himself.

She was standing with a girlfriend near the door, and he felt he had to act before it was too late. "Pardon me, your highness," he said at last, sweeping toward her as though across a stage. "May I have the last dance?" He had always looked down on dancers in Zakho. But now he was John Savage, not Yona Sabagh. She giggled and then locked eyes with her friend, a Queen Vashti, before turning back to him.

"That's sweet," she said, tilting her head coquettishly to one side. "But I'm sorry. You see, I'm taken."

"By whom?" he said.

She winked, then headed with her friend for the door.

"I'm saving myself for Gregory Peck," she quipped, before vanishing down the hallway.

31 ❖ Sleepwalking out Windows

Yona was a boy in motion. No more inhaling cement dust in a dumpy paper shop, for a boss who paid only occasionally. His new job gave him the run of all Jerusalem: from the busy markets of Mahane Yehuda to the industrial wasteland of Romema, from the working-class back alleys of Makor Baruch to the hills of Givat Shaul, the streets of the city were his office. Leather tanneries. Jewelry factories. Print shops. Diamond polishers. Metallurgy plants. And the closest he had to come to the dirty work was the front office, where he'd trade a few pieces of paper with one of the pretty secretaries and then board a bus or hoof it to his next assignment.

It had been the dumbest of luck. In eleventh grade, after the bankrupt owner of the print shop stopped paying his workers, Yona took a bus to the youth employment office of Israel's largest union. The Histadrut, as it was called, was a sprawling and powerful organization with tentacles that stretched into every recess of Israeli life. Most important to the brigades of young Israelis in search of paychecks, it held proprietary lists of job vacancies across the country, including those in the union's own massive construction firms and steel factories.

"If you can work with numbers, I may have a job for you right here in the Histadrut offices," said the young clerk, an apple-cheeked Belgian with a handsome tousle of blond hair.

Yona's heart began to race: a job inside a real office, where people sat at desks and answered phones and clicked away at typewriters. Not only that. He knew even then that the Histadrut equaled power. It was the circulatory system of Israel's vigorous labor movement. It dispensed health care, defended workers' rights, ran a network of schools (including the night high schools), and wielded enormous sway through the Socialist parties that dominated Israeli politics in the late 1950s. Histadrut membership even entitled you to a week of paid vacation at beachside resorts in Neharia and Netanya. If the man had asked him to scrub toilets, the answer would have been yes.

"We need a dues collector," the clerk said. "Nothing too glamorous. You'd have to travel to factories around Jerusalem and get lists from the bosses showing which workers have paid their union dues and which haven't. You'll also spend a little time in the office, helping set up payment plans for workers behind on their dues."

Yona looked over his shoulder, to make sure the man was actually addressing this string of impressive words at him.

"How old are you?"

"Sixteen, sir."

"You're on the young side. But we're — how did my boss put it this morning? — desperate." The clerk cracked a nervous smile, as though he had second thoughts about his choice of words. "Let me rephrase: This job isn't for everybody. You have to be good with numbers *and* a real nudnik. Forget the capitalist bosses. Even good union members will come up with a million stories about why they're behind on dues: The kid's got tuberculosis and is on a breathing tube in the hospital. Grandma needs airfare to Minsk to comfort dear, dear Guta, her dying sister, who the doctor says has just a few more months to live. Et cetera, et cetera. You get what I'm saying? You're going to need to be a pain in the tussick. Is this something you think you can do?"

Nothing could have been further from Yona's natural talents.

"Yes, sir," he said. "When would you like me to start?

"Tomorrow, eight A.M. Go to the *lishkat hamas*—" the union taxation office "—and ask for a guy named Palgi. Nice man. He'll send you on your first assignment. Probably to some capitalist bloodsucker who runs a very nice chemical plant whose fumes are slowly poisoning his workforce. Have fun."

Yona thanked the clerk several times and turned to go. His chest felt like an inflating balloon. He would be a Histadrut clerk, or something nearly like it, at sixteen. It wasn't being a movie star, exactly. But he suspected that even Avigdor Shemesh—that is, Victor James—would look at him a little differently. Or better still, that Ofra would break off her movie-house romance with Gregory Peck.

"One last thing," the clerk called. Yona, who was halfway out the door, spun around and saw the man giving him a once-over from hairdo to shoe leather. "Put on a nice shirt. I would suggest white, and, ahem, ironed."

YONA AND HIS FRIEND Abraham Zilkha, the Esther Williams fan, had been neck and neck all fours years at the night High School for the Working Youth. Their final grade-point averages were so close that the principal, Moshe Hillman, named them both valedictorian.

Hillman, a martinet who had once wrestled an unruly student to the ground, stunned the two boys with a rare act of kindness: a gift of 12 lirot apiece. "Buy yourself something nice," he said to the boys, gruffly.

"Thank you, Mr. Hillman," Yona said, blushing. He ran to a bookstore and spent it all on a finely printed set of volumes on French Impressionism.

The official graduation party was a low-key affair at a union hall, where the spread comprised a pitcher of orange juice and a few bowls of nuts and cookies. The newly minted graduates didn't stay long. Most had to be at work in the morning.

Everyone who knew my father then spoke of him as a boy wonder, a prodigy with blinding promise. But when I found my father's twelfth-grade report card in a file cabinet in my parents' house in Los Angeles a few years ago, I saw a student far more down to earth. Yona Sabagh's grades were those of a reasonably talented student, not a wiz. He had no marks of "excellent." He scored a "very good" in just two subjects, Israeli geography and English. The remaining eight subjects were evenly divided between "good" and "nearly good." Affixed to the bottom of the tattered report was a violet tax stamp (everything in Israel in those days was plastered with them) bearing the likeness of Albert Einstein. The white-haired embodiment of genius, his forehead in full crease, is leaning in a semibored pose against the fingers of his right hand, as though decidedly unimpressed.

This was why Yona had not gotten into medical school — why he never even applied. Even then, my father told me during that visit to Los Angeles, he knew that his marks, from a mere night school, were nowhere near strong enough for admission to Israel's one medical school.

My father began mandatory army service a month after graduation. Because of a litany of physical defects, from flat feet to a perforated eardrum, he was assigned a low-level desk job in the signal corps.

ON DAYS WHEN his dreams felt like they were slipping away, he came home. And on Rashbag Street in Katamonim, they greeted him like a returning hero.

Little girls in threadbare dresses and boys in hand-me-down shorts came running the moment Private Sabagh, nineteen and dashing in his uniform, turned down the street. "Yona's here! Yona's here!" they cried, swarming behind him.

In the small patios strewn with watermelon rinds and pistachio shells, plump Kurdish matrons in frocks and flip-flops looked up from their laundry lines to bless him.

"The great student! High school graduate!" someone might cry.

"Not student! Soldier now! Why do you say student?"

Unshaven men draining small glasses of tea summoned him with a jerk of the chin for small favors. Could he help them fill out a government form? Could he draft a proper letter to the principal of their daughter's

*Yona and his siblings. Small photo: from left, Sara, Yona,
and Avram, 1951, Zakho, Iraq. Large photo: from left, Shalom,
Ayala, Yona, and Uri, 1960, Jerusalem.*

school? And a letter to the man at the credit union, too? Could he take a
minute to explain long division to their son?

"I'll try to come by later, *mamo*, I promise," Yona would say, tousling
some boy's hair. "But if I'm one more minute late to eat my mom's kubeh,
my father may not let me out of the house alive."

Three siblings were waiting for him on the landing to the tiny second-
floor apartment at the end of the street.

"Yona!"

"Ima, Yona's here!"

"I want to show you something, Yona."

"Sara got all As on her report card, did you hear?"

"Come see the baby!"

Yona was surprised by how much his siblings had changed. Sara,
wrapped in a stained apron, was already fourteen, a blossoming young
woman with shining coal-black hair. Her eyes, uncrossed by surgery,
seemed to understand more about you than you did about yourself. Avram

was square jawed, lanky, and handsome, a precursor, even at eleven, of the strapping army parachutist he would one day become. Five-year-old Uri was a fireplug of raw energy and rascally charm; he held some kind of makeshift slingshot and buzzed about his eldest brother like a hornet.

Yona kneeled to enfold all three in a single hug. "I brought a book for each of you," he said.

"*Yofi!*" Neat!

"Yona, I got that other one you told me about from the library."

"Abba says we don't have room for any more books."

"That's not what he said."

"Yeah it is. 'Does everyone in this house need to have a library card? Soon we'll have so many books we can become a library ourselves.'"

"He was joking, dummy."

"Yona, did you hear what Ima did? You know that Roald Dahl book Avram had? Well, he dropped it in the mud last week. When Ima saw it, she tried to clean every page with a sponge. You should have seen it. Then she hung the book on the laundry line to dry!"

"Yeah, it was right there next to Sara's underwear."

"If you don't shut up, I'll clip your lips."

Yona watched their bickering with the detached fondness of a grandfather. He had forgotten how much he missed home. He entered the apartment, rested his rifle against the wall, and took a deep breath. The scent of seasoned ground meat and lemony broth drifting in from the kitchen cocooned him like warm bathwater.

The newborn, Ayala, was asleep in swaddling on a bassinet on the table. "She looks like you, Ima," Yona called to his mother, who had yet to appear from the kitchen. Yona had begun stroking the girl's forehead with his thumb when he heard a *clop-clop* in the hallway. He looked up at the sorriest sight he had seen in years: his mop-haired brother Shalom in a full leg cast, his shy eyes downcast as he dragged himself forward on a pair of wooden crutches.

"*Oy va voy!*" Yona said. "What happened?"

"He fell," said Uri. "Fell. Fell. Fell."

"Walked out a window," Avram said. "Thought he could fly."

"Ima didn't want to worry you too much," Sara said.

"Slow down, everybody, " Yona said. "I want to hear this from Shalom."

He helped the seven-year-old into a chair by the table. There wasn't much to it, Shalom explained. His sleeping mat was by the window. He got up in the middle of the night and stepped out the window.

"Took a wrong turn on the way to the toilet," Avram said.

"I think I was walking in my sleep," Shalom said, looking as if he had just woken from a long nap. "I don't remember, really."

"He was just lucky for the watermelons." Their downstairs neighbor Salman, a watermelon peddler, had taken to sleeping with his inventory in the front patio ever since a rash of thefts. The thick rinds broke Shalom's fall.

"*Misken*," Yona said, with a sympathetic laugh. Poor thing. He remembered his own tumble from the roof in Zakho, when he landed on his friend Zacharia's plump mother. "So little room in this apartment, the only place for Shalom to go is out the window."

"We don't even have space to study," Sara said. "If I want to read quietly, we hide in the toilet, like you used to."

"Yeah," Avram said. "But someone always has to pee, so we can't hide for long."

Two adults and five children shared one toilet, two bare-walled rooms, and a kitchen they had to turn sideways to fit into. A rocky, trash-strewn embankment behind the double-decker row of apartments served as a communal backyard, and starving stray cats in the alleys squabbled nightly over tins of half-eaten food. The whole street looked as though it had been thrown together overnight. It was better than the ma'abara, but not by much.

Yona helped his tired brother back to the bedroom and down onto a mattress far from the window. When he opened the door to the hall, Sara was waiting on the other side. "Sorry, Yona," she said, fidgeting with her hands. "I just wanted to tell you that I think I want to be a teacher."

"I know, Sara," Yona said. "You told me last time. I brought a book for you." He reached into his satchel for a Hebrew translation of a British book, *Race, Prejudice and Education*.

She paged through it, then gave Yona a hug.

"Sara, what are you still doing out here?" Their mother, droplets of perspiration at her temple, had finally emerged from the kitchen. "I need you in the kitchen. I can't stir the hamusta all by myself. Move, girl."

"Yona gave me a book," Sara said. There was a note of defiance in her voice, but her face was a picture of calm.

"*Shtuyot*," Miryam said. Nonsense. "What do you need with that? Leave the reading to Yona, and leave poor Yona alone."

Sara turned sharply and stamped to the kitchen.

Miryam wiped her hand on her apron, then touched her son's face. "Kurbanokh," she said, looking at him tenderly, as a mother might gaze at a newborn. "Go to the bedroom and sleep a little before Shabbat dinner."

An hour later, he was awakened by his siblings' cheers. Rahamim had burst through the door with his hallmark Friday afternoon haul: a sack of end-of-season cantaloupes; five-pound bags of rice and sugar; a bag of two dozen oranges; various containers of dates and nuts and roasted pumpkin seeds; boxes of cucumbers, tomatoes, and apples; and two braided challahs.

Yona stepped out of the bedroom just in time to watch his mother throw up her hands and press them against the sides of her head.

"What are we going to do with all this food?" Miryam said. "We have no room."

"If you don't like it, go put it on top of the Great Rock of Italy," Rahamim said, equal parts cranky and amused. "Leave me alone."

He saw his eldest son and dropped the bags, leaving the children to sort through their contents. "Shabbat shalom, Broni," he said. Good Sabbath, Son.

"Shabbat shalom, Abba."

Rahamim walked over and fingered the lapels of Yona's army uniform, putting an eye close to examine the way the stitching came together at the corner. "Good fabric," he said. "Not cheap."

"Yes, Abba," Yona said. "They're treating me well."

"Good. Now off with it. Put on a white shirt. It's Shabbat."

"Yes, Abba."

Shabbat dinner was the family's sanctuary. Rahamim needed the familiar rituals of Friday night the way a man overboard needs a lifeline, or a lost sailor the steadying sight of land. His children knew to have their shoes lined up in the hall before he came home from the *shuk*. Even when weary from the afternoon's shopping, he sat on the floor and brushed each pair until they gleamed. The shoe shines were the final touch to preparations that began the day before, when Miryam bathed the children with water warmed on a Primus burner, and once a month, a barber came to trim the children's hair.

At sundown, the family gathered around a small dinner table. So many melons were stored beneath that Avram and Uri treated them like foot rests, stretching their skinny legs over the cool rinds.

Everyone was silent as Rahamim blessed the Kiddush wine and the challah. Then, when Miryam and Sara carried in the first steaming plates of food, the table exploded in sound.

What was the army like? the siblings quizzed Private Yona Sabagh, turning to the elder brother who always seemed to have some new and interesting thing to say. Had he shot anybody? Wouldn't he tell them just a little about the secret codes of the signal corps? Could he get in trouble if he said too much? Would they maybe even put him in jail? When Yona caught his breath, *he* took a turn asking questions. What books were his brothers and sisters reading? he asked. Who remembered who wrote *The Tempest*? What was a prime number? Who composed Symphony No. 9? When it was 7 P.M. in Jerusalem, what time was it in New York?

Yona could sound more like a teacher than a brother sometimes. But his siblings seldom minded. The dinner-table trivia contests were a chance to impress their big brother, and few things were sweeter in those days than his approval.

After dinner, the family—minus the injured Shalom—decamped for their Friday evening constitutional. They had scarcely stepped into the street when Avram and Uri began clapping and hooting at the sight of each passing car.

"Hey, don't be mean," Yona said. "Not everyone has the luxury of observing the Shabbat. Maybe it's a police officer or a doctor who has to work tonight. Did you think about that?"

"A doctor, in this neighborhood?" Avram snickered.

"That's not why they're clapping, Yona," Sara said, leaving her mother cradling Ayala a few steps back and catching up to her brother. "It's just that we don't see a lot of cars in Katamonim. I guess they think it's special. It's not just them. A lot of kids here do it."

"Really?" Yona said, pondering a moment. "The way some of the people here behave, you'd think maybe they never left Zakho."

When a Kurdish family went out for a stroll, they didn't walk in a bunch. They sorted themselves into a single-file line, a moving, horizontal totem pole. The eldest male led, followed by the eldest son, then the wife and the younger children. With Sara ahead of her mother and Yona behind with the youngest siblings, the column had fallen out of alignment. It was not a complete accident. Yona had dreaded joining his father at the front of the line that night. But something about this foolish clapping at cars deepened his feeling that he had to tell his father now, that he had good reasons for his plan of action. He had grown tired of the Ana Kurdi jokes that tarred people from places like Zakho as bumpkins. But there was a grain of truth in them, wasn't there? Walk through Katamonim and you could see for yourself. All you had to do was watch children applauding some jalopy as though it were a rocket to the moon.

He had gone over the talk many times in his head, softening the edges so it would do the least damage when it slid into his father's heart. *I love and honor my family very much, especially you and Saba Ephraim. But I am finishing the army now and preparing for college. I have to think about the future. Many of my friends have wanted to become real Israelis. And the way they have done that is with a new last name, an Israeli name.*

He caught up with his father as they made their way up a winding street. Rahamim grinned and slapped him on the shoulder. "Heh, heh, heh. Ephraim would have been proud to see you finishing the army and getting ready for university. He would have said, 'If it wasn't for me, Yona would not even know how to read.'"

Yona laughed. "He would have loved university."

"I wish I could have done more to help you," Rahamim said.

"What are you talking about, Abba?" Yona said.

"With money. To put you in a better school. To be a doctor."

"Shtuyot," Yona said. Nonsense.

Yona guessed that his father had already sneaked a few glasses of arak — Friday was the only night of the week he allowed himself drink.

"Abba," Yona said, tenderly, as they reached the top of the hill.

"Yes, motek."

"There is something you can do now, or let me do, that will help a little," he said.

"Do you need money? I can give you . . ."

"No, Abba, not money. It's our name, Sabagh. I feel a little funny about it sometimes."

This wasn't coming out right. But something about his father's candor had made him feel he could speak more freely than he had intended. Now, though, fear overtook him and he felt his heart thrashing. Honor. Respect for family. No principles mattered more to his father. How could Yona do this, after all his father had suffered since his arrival here? Would he now rob him of every man's right to see his name passed to his grandchildren? What bigger insult could an eldest son inflict on a father than to reject the family name?

Yona was afraid to lift his gaze from the sidewalk, afraid of what he might see if he met his father's eyes. But then he felt his father's hand on his arm.

"Change it," Rahamim said.

On his next liberty, Yona felt light as he carefully filled in the boxes on the form at the Office of Vital Records. Many new immigrants to Israel gave a Hebrew makeover to their old-world names. David Ben-Gurion had been David Green; Golda Meir, Golda Myerson. It showed patriotism and was a nod to Israel's popular image as a melting pot where a smorgasbord of old identities gave way to a single new one. But where others sought subtlety, Yona reached for a bludgeon. *Sabar* was no less than the Hebrew word for *sabra*: "native-born Israeli." Literally translated, it means "cactus fruit," the *ur*-symbol of the Israeli national character: prickly outside, tender and sweet inside. Jews had never used it as a traditional last name. (There were — and still are — few other Sabars.) Even among the most eager immigrants at Ellis Island, one would have been hard-pressed to find any leaving the name-change counter as John

American. And yet there Yona was, inking its Israeli equivalent onto a government form.

Old name: *tzadik-beyt-gimmel* — Sa-ba-gh.

New name: *tzadik-beyt-reish* — Sa-ba-r.

It was so easy. Change a single Hebrew letter and you were born again. Free.

Rahamim visited the Office of Vital Records a few months later. His brothers, Israel and Eliyahu, would remain Sabaghs for the rest of their lives. But as early as the late 1950s, Rahamim saw no benefit to such mulishness. Rahamim, Miryam, Sara, Avram, Shalom, Uri, and Ayala would all henceforth be Sabars. "Who needs Sabagh?" Rahamim told his family. "A guy at work told me that in Russian it means 'dog.'"

32 ❖ The Brotherhood of Man

"Few of the ethnic ingredients in Israel's sizzling melting pot have been as cruelly maligned as the Kurds. The deprecating image of a hot-tempered illiterate primitive is so deep-seated that for years many Israelis of Kurdish extraction denied their origins and identified with other national backgrounds. . . . The effort to distance themselves from their past had an unfortunate effect. They began to forget their customs and traditions. There was an acute danger that the very existence of Kurdish Jewry would be erased from the annals of history."

— "The Pride of Being Kurdish," Greer Fay Cashman,

Jerusalem Post, August 26, 1983

The early 1950s brought a fresh round of insecurities for Israel. The 1949 armistice had failed to bring peace with her Arab neighbors, who were undergoing their own internal crises. King Abdullah ibn Hussein of Jordan was assassinated in Jerusalem in 1951 for his willingness to negotiate with the young nation. Egypt closed the Suez Canal and the Gulf of Aqaba to Israeli shipping. Syrian forces and Jordanian fedayeen fighters were infiltrating Israel's borders to sabotage and murder, in open violation of the armistice agreements. Israel's responses were occasionally just as brutal; in 1956, Israeli soldiers massacred forty-nine Arab-Israeli civilians as they returned to their village of Kafr Kassem.

Tensions in the region boiled over with the Suez War in late 1956, when in just one hundred hours Israeli air and ground forces routed Egyptian troops from the Sinai desert as they advanced toward the canal. The concessions Israel won as part of its withdrawal in 1957 slowed the fedayeen attacks and reopened shipping lanes. There would not be a major renewal of hostilities with Israel's Arab neighbors until the Six-Day War in 1967.

It was in this decade of relative peace, as the young state caught its breath and turned more of its attention to the home front, that Yona Sabar came of age.

I could see it in a cache of late 1950s photos I found in a mildewed box in the basement of my grandparents' apartment in Katamonim: Sabar in a mock commando stance, in khaki uniform with shirt unbuttoned. Sabar, Zilkha, and Sagi in dark sunglasses, lounging on matching striped lawn chairs under a tree — the picture of cool. Sabar in swim shorts on a beach, stroking the neck of a white horse mounted bareback by two women, one in a dainty white sun hat.

I found myself studying the tiniest details: the laces of my father's shoes, the lenses of his sunglasses, his grin in the photos with young women, a grin whose precise meaning I knew because I'd worn it myself when I knew I was getting away with something.

He was twenty-one, and a new man. With a changed name and a new-found independence, he had cast off the part of his past that felt like a chain tied to a post. He was an Israeli now. Medical school may have been too far a reach. But he had applied to the prestigious Hebrew University, and — by some mistake or miracle, he thought — had been accepted.

FOR A VERY SHORT WHILE, Israel was good to Rahamim, too. He was made foreman at the book bindery, in exchange for his loan to Rothberg. He drew a big enough salary to buy white shoes, a Seiko watch, a new cap. He was appointed *gabbay*, or caretaker, of the one-room Kurdish synagogue down the block.

And he began a campaign of self-improvement. So many library books were piled up around the house — thanks to his children, with their multiple library memberships — that he began picking up some of the simpler ones and reading them. It was a struggle. Israel's language was Hebrew, not Aramaic, which was spoken only among the country's Kurds. Israelis were so confused by the strange tongue that few even knew its official name. Some called it *Kurdit*, Kurdish; others, *Leshon ha Targum*, the language of the famous Aramaic translation of the Bible some two thousand years earlier.

Like most Kurds, Rahamim had never before read secular writings in Hebrew. So most days he set aside a few minutes to become more literate in the language of his new land. Before long, he had muddled through novels by S. Y. Agnon, Chaim Hazaz, Yehuda Burla. His children recalled seeing tears in his eyes as he neared the end of each book, where the protagonist meets his fate and some deeper truth is revealed.

"Every book I brought home, he'd pick up and want to know about," my uncle Uri recalled. "He'd read and then tell me his experience of the book and what he thought about the characters in the novels. This was the only serious thing we'd talk about."

Rahamim felt like a student sometimes, and his young children like his teachers. It was funny in a way, but he began to see his job at the bindery as a way to share in his children's literary ardor. The spines on some of their most pawed-over volumes were crumbling, and Rahamim would sneak them into the bindery for repairs. The Sabar children had collected a couple of years' worth of *Haaretz Shelanu* and *Ma'ariv L'Noar*, the Israeli newspapers' weekly editions for youth. One day Rahamim neatly bound the entire collection between two orange covers. "I would sit for hours and look at it," his youngest child, my aunt Ayala, recalled.

What no one knew then was just how fragile Rahamim's happiness was. He had endured so many small humiliations since his arrival in Israel that his pride had been hollowed out. To shatter it, all a person needed was a feather.

The moment came in the early 1960s, when Rothberg announced that his plant was closing and he'd be unable to pay his debts, among them Rahamim's loan.

"But you said loans were safe," Rahamim pleaded, the blood draining from his face.

"Sorry, habibi," Rothberg replied. "I guess you didn't read the contract. Look at it again."

The loan represented the last of Rahamim's savings, and for one of his coworkers the schadenfreude ran deep. Beefy, dark-skinned, and with a smile full of gold-capped teeth, Nechemya had needled Rahamim from the moment they were assigned adjoining workbenches at the bindery. Nechemya resented the way Rothberg had treated Rahamim, as though he were made of finer stock than himself. They were both ordinary Jews from Zakho, so why should Rahamim be made foreman?

Rahamim, meanwhile, saw Nechemya as a clock watcher, a shirker who put in the minimum effort and still griped about his paycheck. What rankled him even more were Nechemya's romantic boasts. It was unseemly for a married man with children to speak of relations with other women.

"He did things to infuriate my father, like wink at me," Sara recalled of her visits to the factory as an adolescent. "He was tall and fat — the opposite of my dad. All the men my father hated were charmers. And here this guy comes and winks at me. And when he winked, his gold teeth would flash."

The day of Rothberg's announcement, Nechemya couldn't restrain himself. As embittered workers put on their jackets at closing time, Nechemya winked at Rahamim and grinned. "Hey, former foreman," he said, loud enough for the other men to hear. "You hear what they're saying around town, don't you?"

"Go to hell," Rahamim said.

"They're saying that pretty wife of yours has a boyfriend."

Rahamim ran at him, his fist cocked. He felt as though he might finally sock Nechemya and break his ugly teeth. "Do it, little fella," a floor worker said, and when the others laughed, Rahamim lost his nerve and slunk red-faced into the night.

If every life has a turning point, that was my grandfather's. The will to do violence, to bloody Nechemya and every other man who had belittled him, turned to a poison that ran cold through his heart. Gone forever was the part of him — the Kurdish part — that had always believed in the brotherhood of man.

33 ◆ Gold

In the late 1950s, Yona and Shalom took their mother to her first movie, *The Ten Commandments*. When Moses filled the screen in his brown robe, his arms spread before the throngs of Israelites, Miryam rose from her seat. She kissed her fingertips and turned them toward the screen, repeating the gesture until the camera panned away. Tears filled her eyes.

For Miryam, the bearded man who had just said "Love cannot drown truth, Nefertiti!" in dubbed Hebrew was not Charlton Heston fresh out of wardrobe. He was the Law Giver himself, speaking to her, right there in that Jerusalem theater.

My grandmother adapted to Israel the way prehistoric man might adjust to life in modern-day New York City: less than totally. Her relatives bought her a washing machine and stove, but the controls confounded her and she cursed them, often preferring to wash by hand in the tub or cook on a hot plate. She trudged off to night classes to learn Hebrew, but quit in frustration after two years, scarcely able to distinguish the letters of the alphabet. She had never learned to read or write her mother tongue. Why did people think she could now master a second language?

Her isolation left her dependent on her husband. He filled out her voting cards, bought her medicines, set aside *lira* notes so she would know much to pay the sales clerk for the bag of groceries. Still, store prices often confused her and she never knew whether a cashier had given her the right change.

The kitchen was cleaner and had more counter space than the one in Zakho. But the work was just as punishing. Sara remembers her mother fainting from exhaustion while preparing a Passover seder. She always waited until everyone had finished eating before feeding herself. When she finally sat down with a small serving of food, she took a chair alone in the corner, sitting stiffly upright, with the plate on her lap, as if ashamed to take up even that much space.

This minimization of self was a kind of credo. She refused to eat or drink at other people's houses. She carried a cup in her purse in case her hosts insisted on serving tea. She refused gifts to her children from people outside the family. Some afternoons she'd leave her children and walk a half hour to the fashionable Rehavia neighborhood, where she cleaned the houses of Hebrew University professors and sold some of the free eggs she received with food stamps. She scrubbed their floors and boiled their children's diapers. One professional couple paid her to make a meal for their son upon his return each day from school. "It killed her that her children were alone while she was taking care of this only child," Ayala told me.

At every turn she deflected attention from herself and toward others. She brought plates of fresh-cooked food to the bereaved. ("You go to too many funerals," Rahamim complained.) She took hot drinks to the Arab vendors who pushed fruit carts through Katamonim. If she saw a scrap of bread in the street while taking a walk, she'd pick it up, kiss it, and put it on a ledge where a bird might find it.

People saw in her silence, devotion, and hard work a kind of monastic self-denial. "She was a woman of gold," a woman who had known her since their childhood in Zakho told me. But her asceticism was also a product of a life that had made her feel small: her mother's death, her stepmother's cruelty, the loss of Rifqa, the deaths of five babies, the move to a mystifying new country.

A couple of her father's children had gone mad in Israel, and some days she wondered if the evil eye on that Zakho mountaintop was still following her family. Salim, a half brother, was in his forties when he suffered a psychotic break on his wedding night. Her brother and childhood protector Shmuel, who fled Zakho for Israel in the 1930s, was diagnosed with clinical depression and hospitalized for more than thirty years. Both died in mental institutions. Every now and then, Miryam's children drove her to visit her brothers in the hospital in Holon, just south of Tel Aviv. She returned each time with a knot in her chest. This is who my grandmother was when my grandfather returned from the bindery on the day of its closure, with no savings, no job, and the conviction that his last scrap of dignity — his wife's faithfulness — had also been stolen from him.

IN THE SECOND-FLOOR apartment on Rashbag Street, the children raised their books to their faces, like shields against a spray of arrows.

"They're calling you a whore at the factory, did you know that?" Rahamim said, confronting Miryam in the kitchen as she prepared dinner. "A dirty whore."

Miryam was so startled by his language that her knees buckled. She thought she might collapse. She did not know what to say. Was he drunk?

"You're not leaving this apartment, you understand?" he said.

"Please. Please, husband. Someone has put a spell on you."

"These funerals you go to. The sick people you say you visit. You think I am stupid?"

"What do you mean? I haven't — "

He pushed her against the countertop. When she reached behind to brace herself, her arm clipped a pot of soup, and the bubbling liquid streaked across the floor. "Who is he, you whore? Tell me now. Who is he?"

MY GRANDPARENTS ARE DEAD now, as are many of their closest friends and even Nechemya. But the relatives and family acquaintances I tracked down in Israel, some of whom had done their own investigations, said the story of Miryam's affair was no more than an ugly fabrication. Nechemya resented my grandfather's status at the factory and knew where to strike for blood. But my grandfather, his ego ground down by too many disappointments, never accepted his wife's innocence, and Miryam silently endured his accusations for the rest of his life.

ARAMAIC

"Mamo" (Uncle) Yona Gabbay, Zakho's master storyteller,
Jerusalem, 1967.

34 ❖ Lishana Deni

To look at Professor Chaim Menachem Rabin, a dwarfish man with kind eyes and a gentle voice, you would have never guessed his stature in the field of modern-Hebrew education. He spoke to the freshmen in his history of the Hebrew language class as though they were shipmates of the same rank, on the same giddy voyage of discovery.

Gripping his chin in his right hand and lecturing in that sonorous voice, the German-born Rabin radiated a self-effacing European courtliness that stood out against the rougher-edged personas and outsized egos then on the faculty at Hebrew University. Not that his credentials were any less impressive: He was educated at London University and Oxford, where he also lectured, and had turned out an impressive number of textbooks on Hebrew and Arabic. Yet he was perhaps the only professor who didn't hesitate to back up a point by quoting from one of his own students' work. "As Rafi Cohen said in his brilliant term paper for this class last year, . . ."

Such graciousness was remarkable for a man whose family had seen so much dislocation and suffering. His grandparents were murdered in the Ukranian pogroms, and his father, also a university linguist, fled Nazi Germany in 1935 for an elementary-school job in Haifa.

Yona had sat through just three or four of the man's lectures on the history of Hebrew when he felt a strange new current drawing him away from the things he had thought he had wanted. He had scarcely thought about language as such. Language was like air: essential, ubiquitous, and uninteresting. But Rabin, in his easy-going way, showed his students how to look at language as a dynamic organism. Language lives. It inhales culture and history. It sprouts new limbs, sloughs off old ones. It goes through cycles of rapid growth, unremarkable periods of stable maturity, decay, and sometimes, as with Hebrew, miraculous rebirth.

You wouldn't know a language's life story simply by browsing through, say, a modern Hebrew dictionary. "In its pages," Rabin once wrote, "words over three thousand years old rub shoulders with words created a mere thousand years ago, and others which entered the language only a few years ago." Words from the Bible and the Mishnah mingle with medieval innovations. Thousands of Aramaic words from the Talmud and Kabbalistic *Zohar* vie with the nearly fifteen thousand new coinages invented by the cast of Jews who revived Hebrew, strictly a written language for sixteen centuries, as the spoken language of twentieth-century Israel. "Hebrew ... thus grew in layers, each corresponding to a period of the language," he wrote. "In the Hebrew of today, all these elements are combined into a new organic unity."

He made the study of language look like an archaeological dig, a forensic investigation, or better still, an autopsy. Rabin was an expert on homing in on a student's strengths. He prodded those with unusual backgrounds to turn their life stories into tools for linguistic investigation. Yona Sabar was a particularly fascinating specimen: He was, Rabin had heard, a native speaker of Aramaic. It was as if a teacher of South American anthropology had a Yanamamo in tribal garb sitting right there in his class, taking notes on what the brightest European scholars had discerned about his people. A little awkard, maybe. But bewitching, all the same.

"Yona," Rabin said, calling him aside one day after class. "For your midterm paper, I'd like you to take a close look at your mother tongue."

Yona's cheeks flushed crimson. "How do you mean?"

"Travel back through your memory. Run through the words you spoke with your mother and father in Kurdistan and write down all the Aramaic words that you can think of that sound like they might have come from Hebrew."

Rabin looked at him with the grave air of a squadron commander sending his best pilot, the one he thought of as his own son, on a risky mission.

"I mean, I can, if you want," Yona said. This was supposed to be a class in the language of the new Israel; that's partly why he'd signed up. But this guy wanted him to make lists in the language he spoke as a boy in Zakho? He had hoped to be assigned a more ... well, modern topic.

"I mean, that's all I have to do for my midterm?" Yona said, dubiously. "It will take maybe five minutes."

"Maybe you can make the list in five minutes," Rabin said, wearing that grave look again. "But then I want you to compare those Aramaic words with their homonyms in modern Hebrew. See what you find. Are the meanings the same? If not, tell me what you think happened. How is it that the same word can mean one thing when spoken by a Jew in Kurdistan and another when spoken by a Jew in Israel."

"Okay," Yona said, doubtfully.

"This is just a guess, because I have never myself done such a comparison: I suspect you'll be surprised by what you find," he said. "You may even surprise me."

YONA'S ROOMMATE HAD already gone to sleep. The room was dark, except for the cone of light cast by the dim bulb over his own desk. He recalled that among the Jews of Zakho, there was no awareness of language as an object independent of its speakers. On the rare occasions when someone asked his parents what language they spoke, Yona remembered, they'd think for a moment and just say, "*Lishana Deni.*" Our Language.

The Aramaic he spoke as a boy was like a toy treasure chest made from a single extrusion of plastic. A keyhole was molded into the front, but only for show, for the chest was a single mass and did not open. Now someone was telling him the chest was real, not pretend, and that there were jewels inside. Now someone was asking him to jimmy the lock and sort the contents into neat stacks. He had to transform Aramaic from "Our Language" to a language in the Northwest Semitic family, a relative of Hebrew and Arabic, with its own alphabet and history and highly specific rules of grammar and morphology.

He closed his eyes and thought of the synagogue in Zakho. He imagined his grandfather on his rug, crying out to the heavens. Words fluttered in and out of memory: *Bracha*, prayer. *Mitzvah*, blessing. *Kettubah*, marriage contract. *Matzot*, Passover bread. A trickle, but enough to start his list. But what was Rabin getting at? Those words meant the same thing in Zakho as they did here in Israel. You couldn't even call them Aramaic words. They were just Hebrew religious words the Jews of Zakho had picked up from prayer books and the Bible.

Figure it out, Sabar. Professor Rabin believes you can do this. What will he think if you can't?

So much for the five-minute list. An hour and a half had passed, and all he had were four unremarkable words. He went to the toilets to pee, splashed his face with cold water, went back to his desk, and promptly fell asleep. Fever dreams: Late spring, Zakho. The sloping hillsides sprinkled with wild cereal grains and red and yellow flowers. His mother scrubbing laundry at the edge of the swollen Habur River and losing a blouse to the raging currents. "So much water," she had said when she got home. "*Kha olam did maya.*"

Yona's eyes snapped open, and he peeled his cheek, moist from sweat, off the stack of dictionaries. *Olam.* In Hebrew it meant "world." In Aramaic it meant "so much" or "a lot of." There must be a connection. He wrote it down.

I have to think sideways, he thought. *Not like a mathematician doing equations, but like a poet searching for* — What were the words he had just learned in his class on verse? — *metaphor, metonymy, synecdoche.*

Then another word came. The Hebrew *atzamot* meant "bones." *Asamoth* in Aramaic meant "a stubborn person." Someone who was *unbending* . . . someone who was bonelike! He wrote it down.

He stood up now and paced the narrow passage between the two single beds, the ball-point pen clutched between his fingers like a scalpel. His roommate was still snoring softly, but dawn was now streaking violet across the sky outside his window.

In Zakho, Yona remembered now, the Jews called any foul-mouthed malcontent a *wa-zikhro.* The old blowhards in the teahouses; the bitter fishwives with an unkind word for every passerby — these were Zakho's *wa-zikhro*s. Could there be any connection to the Hebrew expression *yimmach shmo veh zichro?* Just the other day, he had heard a classmate use that phrase, meaning "May his name be erased from our memories," after someone had mentioned Hitler. In Israel, it was a stock phrase invoked whenever an odious name came up in conversation. Could there be link between *veh zichro* and *wa-zikhro?* He wasn't sure, but he wrote it down.

As soon as he lifted his pen, another word flowered in his mind: *shamati*. In Hebrew it was a conjugated verb meaning "I heard." In Aramaic it was a noun: an obedient wife. Yona shook his head and muffled a laugh. There had to be a connection. He wrote it down and tried to imagine the look on Professor Rabin's face.

35 ❖ Cleft Sentences

In college, Yona returned to the day job he'd left when he joined the army: union dues collector. He looked around the office those first weeks back and noticed things he'd somehow missed as a teenager. Like the young guy with red hair in charge of collections, the one who so mercilessly browbeat workers who were late on their dues that they'd come in, a few *agorot* in hand, looking like whipped dogs. After humiliating them, he'd kick his feet up on his desk and read the newspaper for the rest of the day. Other men with nebulous job descriptions seemed to break every half hour for coffee, then spend the rest of their workday in chitchat about their romantic exploits. As summer approached, the teenage sons of the union bosses were put on the payroll and sometimes actually showed up. They were assigned do-nothing jobs that, as best Yona could tell, involved shuffling sheets of paper from one pile to another and then back again.

On his rounds at the factories, Yona saw Iraqis with high-school degrees consigned to menial jobs. He saw hard-working Kurds toiling for small paychecks, while the sons of privileged European Jews landed sinecures in comfortable union offices. He looked into the sad eyes of the men on the job sites and recognized his father: They all had the same look of defeat, of surrender to lives they had never imagined possible in this holy city.

Some days he felt like a turncoat. What exactly had he done to deserve his job, his life? What dispensation did he have to spend his evenings in the classrooms of an elite university, contemplating ideas? Had he been born with a different temperament, his self-reproach and sense of injustice might have turned outward. He might have run for office, become a leader of protest movements. But he came from people who survived by keeping their heads down, and he journeyed inward. He wanted to give his people a voice, but in another way, a quieter way, a way he hoped would still count.

Before leaving the union office for his morning rounds at the factories, Yona started now to paw through the trash bin by his desk. He fished out discarded scrap paper and stuffed a fistful in his pocket. Old ledgers, pay stubs, half-addressed envelopes — it didn't matter, so long as at least one side was blank. Later, on a bus in traffic or in waiting rooms at the factories, he drew out the slips, pulled a pen from his vest pocket, and wrote down words he had spoken as a boy. A feverishness infected the work. The words came in random streams; some days were devoted to animals, some to household objects, others to colors, feelings. He had never written in Aramaic. Almost no one in Zakho did — it was a spoken language. So he used Hebrew script, and noted, as best as he could remember, the pronunciation and meaning. Each day, the piles of scrap paper on his dorm-room desk grew.

Professor Rabin handed back the midterm papers at the start of class. Yona's hands trembled as he turned the pages, looking at the dozens of questions and "suggestions for follow-up" that Rabin had frantically, it appeared, scribbled in the margins. It was a blood bath of red ink. When Yona saw his grade on the last page, "Very Good +" he let out a long breath. "You are in virgin territory here, Yona," Rabin had written. "I have not seen some of these connections before. You don't yet have all the tools to grasp the bigger meaning. You need to work harder on what these links tell us about the evolution of Aramaic and its borrowings from Hebrew. Have you thought about furthering your studies in linguistics? As a native speaker of Aramaic, you could make significant contributions to a field that few have been able to penetrate. In the meantime, I would like you to take this paper to Polotsky. I have already told him to expect you."

If Chaim Rabin was every student's best friend, Hans Jacob Polotsky was a deity who looked down on the world from a heavenly throne. In obituaries after his death in 1991, colleagues in the field of linguistics spared no superlatives: "The world of Egyptology, Semitic scholarship and general linguistics lost one of the greatest philologists these subjects

have ever known, a scholar of massive learning, penetration and origi-
nality, who towered, Colossus-like, over the rest of his generation," one
academic journal rhapsodized. A lengthy obituary in the 160-year-old
Journal of the Royal Asiatic Society, published by Cambridge University,
was titled simply: "H. J. Polotsky (1905–1991): Linguistic Genius."

Polotsky was a puff-chested man whose walrus mustache invited com-
parisons to Stalin's — not, one suspected, exclusively for its design. He
brutally dressed down witless undergraduates, and he was visibly dis-
comfited by small talk and stingy with praise. Friends took to calling
him HJP, as though he were less man than machine. When one of his
best students was preparing to leave Hebrew University for Oxford, he
wrote a two sentence recommendation. "Mr. E. Ullendorff was my pupil
from __ to __. I have no complaints against him."

Ullendorff, who eventually became a professor and Ethiopic expert at
the University of London, later chalked up his mentor's lack of social
graces to simple self-effacement and shyness. Most students, however,
saw him as arrogant. Even Polotsky's letters to friends often carried a
whiff of pomposity. "My inclination for Egyptology and indifference towards Assyriology is decidedly connected with the fact that hieroglyphs
appeal to my aesthetic sense, while cuneiform repels me aesthetically," he
wrote in a letter quoted in Ullendorff's obituary of his mentor.

Neo-Aramaic was the sort of virgin territory that Polotsky relished.
That was what scholars had termed the language's final historical stage.
First had come Old Aramaic (1000 B.C. to 700 B.C., the period when the
first written records were found), then Official (700 B.C. to 200 B.C., when
it came to dominate the Near East), Middle (200 B.C. to A.D. 200, covering
the birth of Christ), and Late (which began in A.D. 200 with an explosion
in Aramaic literature and ended abruptly in A.D. 700 with the Middle
East's conquest by Arabic-speaking Muslims.) Neo-Aramaic was what
remained after the Islamic conquest, the language's moribund phase, spoken by impoverished groups of mountain-dwelling Jews and Christians
who were generally too poorly educated to write it.

Neo-Aramaic's relationship to the Aramaic of Jesus' day is roughly
that of modern English to Old English: Spelling, vocabulary, and pronunciation evolved over time, yet it is fundamentally the same language.

But the analogy ends there. For modern English to be a true correlate of Neo-Aramaic, the United States would have to have come under the rule of a foreign power that imposed its own language; English's only surviving speakers would have to be hillbillies in Appalachian villages so cut off from civilization that the new power's language failed to penetrate, even after hundreds of years.

With Kurdistan's twenty-five thousand Jews transplanted to Israel, Polotsky had one of the main groups of speakers squarely in his crosshairs. Neo-Aramaic was an unexplored frontier in Semitic linguistics, a perfect target, it seemed, for Polotsky's avid intellect and one that stood to bring him even greater glory. But much of the Neo-Aramaic material he collected — recordings of native speakers, shoe boxes of vocabulary words, notes on grammar — remains unpublished. As some of his disciples see it, this stage of the language was so uncharted that even the great Polotsky, a notorious perfectionist, was daunted.

DESPITE RABIN'S ENCOURAGEMENT, Yona did not have the daring to approach HJP directly. He was too shy and had heard the stories of Polotsky's take-downs of overeager undergraduates. Yona thought it better to watch the master from a distance, in hopes that it would reduce him to a human scale, so he signed up for a Polotsky class on Arabic syntax. The lectures were marvels of erudition. Drawing from a dozen languages, all of which he seemed to know fluently, Polotsky illustrated how syntax could unlock hidden links between seemingly unrelated languages. Sifting through a welter of disparate tongues, Polotsky could tease out overlapping patterns and unspoken grammatical rules, like a cryptographer spying a secret code where others saw only random strings of letters.

"If I might, an example of a cleft sentence in Neo-Aramaic," he said one day.

"'It is this man whose wife is sick.' Is that right, Mr. Sabar?"

Yona stiffened in his chair and found he couldn't speak. Polotsky almost never called on undergraduates.

"Mr. Sabar?" Polotsky asked, his voice edged with impatience. "This is your language, isn't it? You can't tell me anything about 'it is this man whose wife is sick'?"

A few students let out coughs that sounded like half-muffled laughs. Several heads turned toward him, and he felt the blood drain from his face.

"I mean, if you say it's right, sir, it . . . it must be okay."

A queasy silence settled over the room. No one so much as turned a page in their notebooks, for fear of becoming Polotsky's next target. The professor licked his finger and slowly leafed through some paper on the rostrum, as if he had suddenly forgotten that he was supposed to be giving a lecture. More time passed.

Then he cleared his throat. "See me in my office at one, Mr. Sabar," Polotsky barked, without so much as a glance at the rows of desks in the lecture hall.

Yona ran back to his dorm room to put on a tie. At precisely one o'clock, he knocked on the door in the Sprinzak building marked H. J. POLOTSKY.

"Yes?" croaked a voice inside.

Yona cracked the door just enough to see the corner of a large desk. "You asked me to see you, sir," Yona said.

"Who is it? How can you see me if I can't see you?

He opened the door. The man was scarcely visible behind the ziggurats of paper on his desk. But Yona could make out the silvery hair slicked over to one side, the eyes drooping beneath shaggy salt-and-pepper eyebrows.

"I'm sorry about today in class," Yona stammered. "I, I checked with my father. You were right about 'It is this man whose wife is sick.' People in Zakho split sentences that way, and so I think it's okay, as far as my father knows."

"Enough," Polotsky said, rapping his knuckles against the tabletop. "You can't have thought I really needed your help."

"I'm sorry, sir."

"I asked you to come because there is some work for you," Polotsky said. "I have so many research grants I don't know how to spend all the money. So if you'll help me."

"I'm not sure if you know, sir, but I have a job during the day, at the union."

"Okay, here's what you do," Polotsky cut in, as if he hadn't heard Yona.

"You go find some Kurdish informants in Jerusalem. Aramaic speakers. People in your parents' neighborhood. Bring them here to the language lab. Get them talking. Folk tales. The lullabies their mamas sang them. Their favorite recipe for — what is it called? — chi-mush-ta?"

"Hamusta."

"It doesn't matter what it's called. Just get them talking, keep them talking, until they beg to go. Use the reel-to-reels. And come back to me with transcripts. I'll see you in a month."

"Thank you very much. But with my other job, it's full time, I mean, and a month, with schoolwork, it's . . ."

"Good-bye, Mr. Sabar." Polotsky lifted a stack of manuscripts off the top of one pile and let them fall on his desk with a thump. "I have other things to do now."

36 ❧ It's All God's World

"Very few hand-written works in Neo-Aramaic have ever been found. No doubt related to this lack of written tradition is the fact that the oral tradition was very highly developed and the Kurdish Jews possess an oral literature which is remarkable in its abundance and high quality."

—"Family Conflict and Cooperation in Folksongs
of Kurdish Jews," by Donna Shai, 1974

A bba," Yona said, coming home to his parents' apartment that afternoon with an urgent question. "Who were the best storytellers in Zakho?"

"Leave it alone," Rahamim said, chewing roasted pumpkin seeds and spitting the shells into an ashtray. "Everyone in Zakho was full of long stories."

Yona nodded and laughed.

"What would you want with them anyway?" Rahamim asked. "They're old men now, poor, sick. Leave them alone." He spat.

"Someone at the university, a professor, wants me to find one," said Yona, sitting down next to his father.

Now Rahamim laughed, throwing him a doubtful glance. "Shtuyot. What for?"

"Research," Yona said, shrugging. "Something about the language."

"Nonsense. What language?" he said, irritated, as usual. "Why did they ask you?"

"The professor must have heard I was from Zakho."

"Leave it alone," Rahamim said. "You are an Israeli now. *Sabar.* Don't tell your professor too much. Shtuyot. The language!"

"They're going to pay me," Yona said. "Five lirot."

A clanking sound came from the kitchen — Yona hadn't realized anyone else was home. He turned and saw his mother poking her head into the doorway.

"Yona Gabbay," she said. "The one they called Mamo Yona." Uncle Yona.

"Get back to your washing, woman!" Rahamim thundered.

"Abba, please," Yona said.

A long silence followed, punctuated only by the sound of children trading profanities in the street below.

"Five lirot?" Rahamim said.

"An hour," Yona said. "If I can find someone."

"Mamo Yona was the best," Rahamim said, clearing his throat and pushing aside the ashtray, now overflowing with shattered husks. "He could tell stories until morning."

"Where does this Uncle Yona live?"

"In the neighborhood. The building across from Uncle Israel."

Mamo Yona was not just Zakho's best storyteller. He was also one of its wiliest con men. Possessed of a charm unburdened by shame, Mamo Yona could spin sob stories that had pity-struck agas handing over food, money, and property. At least, that is, in his own telling. All I have to go on are the transcripts of the tapes my father eventually recorded.

Mamo Yona's storytelling skill was a product, it seems, of necessity. He was still a child when his father, a peddler, died, and his older brother fell ill. The timing couldn't have been worse. The family was drowning in debt, leaving his mother helpless. Little Yona Gabbay pulled off his first con shortly thereafter.

He hoodwinked a visiting Turkish officer into buying him a donkey. He thumbed scales while trading wool in tribal villages. He palmed off a useless old "Damascene she-ass" to one of his creditors, on the pretext that she was a favorite of "the lords of Mosul."

Then there was the time an aga refused to pay for a set of clothes, and Mamo Yona picked up a rifle, begging the man to shoot him.

"I say, 'Shoot me with the gun! Kill me!'" Mamo Yona recalled. "The property you took is not mine, it belongs to other people. It is more proper for you to kill me here than for me to return without these people's property." Unnerved by Mamo Yona's bizarre conduct, the aga paid full price for the clothes, plus a little extra.

Mamo Yona returned a few days later, when the aga was out, and retailed the same pitiful story to the aga's unwitting wife. She loaded his saddlebags with enough wheat to feed his family for a month. "I felt content," Mamo Yona chuckled. "My soul was restored."

Israel leveled him the way it did so many other Jews from Zakho. Like other Kurds, he had tried to get into the biggest game in town: construction. But employers turned him away, saying that at eighty he was too old for manual labor.

"Master of the universe," he pleaded, "what shall I do now?"

An answer to his prayers seemed to arrive one day in the form of a carload of young Hebrew University scholars who had heard he was a native speaker of Aramaic. They were there, it seems, on an early mission of Professor Polotsky's. They said they'd pay him two lirot an hour, plus bus fare to the university's language lab, if he told them stories in his mother tongue. But it was a fiasco. As far as anyone knew then, Aramaic in its latest phase was exclusively a spoken language, and none of these young scholars spoke it. For outsiders to map it out, they would have to transliterate every sound from a speaker's mouth. Then, to figure out the meaning and structure, they'd have to guess at spelling and try to correlate the words with ones in related Semitic languages or in the one or two missionary dictionaries compiled a century earlier. Or they might have to ask the subjects to translate their own Neo-Aramaic into

Hebrew, a laborious and scientifically dubious approach that would try the patience of speakers and probably introduce a messy array of errors into transcripts.

Mamo Yona knew a scam when he saw one. And he soon began to feel he was on the receiving end. "There were six people, all of them looking like agas, their notebooks in their hands, sitting in a room," he recalled in those long-ago tape recordings. "I sat down, began telling them a story. I would say a word or two, and one of them says, 'Say it one more time!'"

Mamo Yona came back the next day and the next, and he could scarcely get a word out before the linguists begged him to slow down and repeat himself. For a storyteller accustomed to the effects of unbroken narration on a bewitched audience, it was hell: "I said to myself, 'This is giving me a headache! No more! I had taken twenty liras from them and said to myself, 'What will I do with more money?'"

It was probably the only time in his life he had felt that way.

When the linguists sent for him again, he told them he was done.

When my father first found Mamo Yona, he thought he had stumbled upon a very lost extra from one of the biblical epics he had recently seen in the Jerusalem theaters. Mamo Yona's daughter-in-law had set aside a corner of her tiny apartment for him, and when my father walked in, he was lying on his side on a rickety cot, facing a blank wall and stuffing powdered tobacco up his nose.

"It's turning all the sheets yellow." His daughter-in-law grimaced, shaking her head. "He doesn't listen."

"How old is he now?" my father asked in a low voice, looking at the creaky collection of bones on the cot and wondering whether it was advisable even to move him.

"He thinks he's twenty-five," she said, letting out a tired laugh.

At the commotion, Mamo Yona stirred and shot bolt upright on the bed. He reached for a curved wooden cane to steady himself as he threw his legs over the side and propped himself into a sitting position.

"Who's twenty-five?" he croaked happily, stamping the butt of the cane against the floor and brightening at the sound of some young visitor speaking Aramaic.

The full effect of the man hit my father like a broadside. Mamo Yona had screwed his toothless mouth into a childlike grin. Mirth lines ran from candlelit eyes to the fringes of a wiry white beard. The beard stretched in a foamy mass to the bottom of his breastbone, then split suddenly, like tongues of flame. A tasseled white jimidani spilled out from under his black cap and down both sides of his face, all the way to his waist, as if he had elephant ears.

"Mamo Yona?" my father said.

"*Mayla, kassid mamo?*" the old man said sweetly, in an Aramaic as honeyed and pure as Yona's grandfather's. What is it, uncle's dear?

"I am Yona Beh Sabagha of Zakho," my father replied, in his best Aramaic, "the son of Rahamim and the grandson of Ephraim."

"Ephraim Beh Sabagha's grandson?" Mamo Yona said, with a look of delight. "Sit, kassid mamo. Anything you want, I will give you."

In his billowy sherwal trousers and headdress, Mamo Yona was a walking anachronism as he shambled past Hebrew University's gleaming new buildings and the students in blue jeans and sunglasses. When he approached the humanities building, a modernist structure of glass and white stone, he slowed his step at the sight of the armed guard at the door. In Zakho, Mamo Yona knew, men at the entrances to grand buildings were most likely their owners or perhaps even agas. So Mamo Yona stopped, swept aside his robes with a flourish, and folded his torso in a bow of deep respect.

"Who is this guy?" the young guard, a recent Hungarian immigrant, sputtered, casting an annoyed look at my father. "What does he want from me?"

Once inside, my father explained to Mamo Yona that such courtesies were not necessary in Israel. Then he led his informant to a windowless room with soundproofed walls and set a chunky microphone on the table. In an adjoining room, he tested the sound inputs and then switched on a reel-to-reel recorder the size of an orange crate.

"Okay, Mamo, tell me a story," my father said.

"Which one?"

"Any one."

Mamo Yona had never learned to read or write any language. But beneath that jimidani lay centuries of Kurdish-Jewish folklore. There were thrillers, love stories, and comedies, each of which could fill an hour or two on a summer afternoon. There were epics and sagas meant for performance over a week of winter nights.

Back in Zakho he had sat cross-legged by a fire, as comfortable in front of a single family as before dozens of villagers in the outlying tribal regions. His eyes glinting against the night like embers, he wove stories about heroes and demons, doomed lovers and money-drunk swindlers. In an era before multiplexes and surround sound, he was a one-man entertainment complex. He imitated voices. He mimicked animals. He became the murmuring forest, the rushing river, the hooves of donkeys sloshing through mud.

In the adjoining booth where my father sat, the narrow brown strip of magnetic tape made a dry, crinkling sound as it wound through the recorder's switchbacking spindles and onto the other reel. In an instant, centuries of silence gave way to sound.

During a break from several hours of recording, Mamo Yona said he needed a restroom. My father pointed him down the hall. A half hour passed with no sign of him, and my father grew alarmed. Mamo Yona was an old man. Maybe he had fallen or gotten lost. My father went to look. What he saw, at end of the hall, took his breath away. There, bracing himself in the frame of an open window, was Mamo Yona. My father could tell from his posture that he had parted his robe, for between the man's legs a stream of liquid arced onto what my father remembered was a garden two stories below.

"What are you doing?" my father inquired. "Didn't you find the restroom?"

"Yeah, yeah," Mamo Yona said, without turning around. "But I pushed and pushed and the door wouldn't open."

The sign on the door, my father saw later, said PULL. True, Mamo Yona couldn't read. But he was always bragging about his daring escapes from all manner of calamity. And, what? He couldn't figure out how to enter an unlocked restroom? "Why didn't you just come back and ask me?" my father asked. "I could have helped."

"Kassid mamo," he told my father, buttoning his fly and turning around with a boyish smile. "It's all God's world. He doesn't care where you pee."

*Yona, right, recording "Mamo" (Uncle) Yona Gabbay's stories,
Hebrew University, Jerusalem, circa 1963.*

PROFESSOR POLOTSKY'S INTEREST was linguistics: what an
informant's words could reveal about Neo-Aramaic grammar, syntax,
and its ties to other languages. Content was virtually irrelevant, the
speaker's toileting habits beside the point. What drew a linguist to storytellers wasn't their stories but their long-windedness, their ability to
rattle on for hours. But how could my father listen to this bearer of his
own culture and not be drawn in deeper?

Last year, at the Israeli National Archives, I was leafing through a
1964–65 Hebrew University catalog and found a black-and-white photo
of my father and Mamo Yona in the recording booth, over the caption
"Research in Ethnic Dialects." Mamo Yona, looking as if he had just
emerged from forty years' wandering in the desert, is speaking into the
microphone and gesturing with the bunched fingers of his right hand.
My father, buzz cut, and in a crisp white dress shirt and slacks, has his
back to him as he works the reel-to-reel. You would never know they once
breathed the same air or drank the same river water.

But keeping up appearances was harder than my father expected. One day in the early 1960s, he clicked on the recorder and made an unusual request of the old man. "None of the usual fables today, Mamo," my father said. "Please, just tell me, if you would, the story of your life."

There was a long pause, and then a deep breath.

"Dear audience," Mamo Yona began, "once, when we were very poor . . ."

Mamo Yona didn't stop until his autobiography reached the very day my father entered his life. "One day, I look, I see this Yona come looking for me, saying, 'Uncle Yona.' I said, 'What is it, uncle's dear?' He says, 'Get up, let us go, quick!' 'Where?' He says, 'Get up! Let us go to the language lab. Tell us a story, we'll pay you five liras per hour.' "

It was soon clear that Mamo Yona had lost none of his wiles: "One time I told stories, and Yona gave me my earnings," he said, well aware that my father was listening through a headset in the next room. "Another time, I told stories for four or five days, and he gave me my earnings. Lately, I've been telling stories for a few days, but he hasn't yet paid me. We'll see. Whatever he wishes, we'll take him at his word."

My father had to smile: Mamo Yona was back at his old game, a hustler softening up another mark.

Mamo Yona was 103 when he died, in Israel, in 1970. He lived until the end in a corner of his son's apartment. The recordings would win Mamo Yona a small kind of fame, at least within the world of Semitic linguists and folklorists. A photograph my mother took of him would grace the jacket cover of my father's 1982 book on the folk literature of the Kurdistani Jews. A few years ago, my father translated Mamo Yona's story into English for a 2005 issue of the *Mediterranean Language Review*. Among highly technical articles on "Late Samaritan Hebrew" and "Morphologically derived animate nouns in Judezmo and Yiddish" was one titled "Yona Gabbay: A Jewish Peddler's Life Story from Iraqi Kurdistan; As Narrated by Him in His Jewish Neo-Aramaic Dialect of Zakho."

Mamo Yona let my father tape him because they were both Zakholis fluent in the ancient language of Kurdish Jews. With my father, he could tell stories as he always had: in marathon sessions, without interruption. Still, Mamo Yona was never completely at ease inside that windowless recording booth. Where were all the villagers? he asked my father. Where were the saucer-eyed children? There could be no stories, he said, without an audience.

"In the old days," he said, "the whole village would be listening."

Now Mamo Yona had an audience of one. "If I didn't know you were there," he whispered to my father through the microphone, "I don't think I could do it."

37 ⁕ *Hets and 'Ayins*

On April 12, 1962, a letter arrived at Student Housing Building Number 7, addressed to Yona Sabar and Abraham Zilkha. The envelope bore the insiginia of *Yeda-'Am*, the *Journal of the Israeli Folkore Society*.

Yona and his Baghdadi friend, roommates now, had written to the journal's editor a few months before, asking if they might write an article on some aspect of Kurdish Jewry. It was an audacious pitch for a couple of undergrads, but they felt they had nothing to lose. If nothing else, it would give the two a chance to work together. And that might help mend fences after the recent weeks of squabbling over Yona's tendency to transcribe Mamo Yona recordings in the apartment at, say, 3 A.M.

("It was quite a bother to me," Zilkha recalled when I saw him in Texas in 2005. "I'd be trying to sleep and he'd be playing the tapes back and forth. Mamo Yona even kept my girlfriend from coming over. I brought her once or twice, then no more." When I shared Zilkha's four-decade-old gripe with my father, my father showed uncharacteristic pique. "What, he was annoyed?" he said. "Well, I remember the smell of his feet when he took off his socks." There was a pause. "*And* he snored.")

Yona slipped a finger under the envelope flap, and Zilkha peered over his shoulder as they read.

"Dear Sirs," Yona read. They looked at each other and laughed. "We will be very happy if you'll honor us with an essay or longer article on the folkore of Kurdistan or Iraq. Sincerely, Shlomo, the secretary."

As he had with his paper for Rabin, Yona spent an evening or two scouring his memory. Could people really be interested in the ghost stories of his childhood? the stories of the howling jinne who stalked his dreams? the stories of the Yimid Maya, who drowned hapless children in the Habur and still sent chills up his legs every time he got near water? If he wanted to be taken seriously, he would have to drain his memories of their emotional content and then examine them under a magnifying glass. He would have to test his memories against those of his parents, of adults who might interpret Zakho's ghost stories in a different light.

Zilkha got distracted by other projects. But Yona polished draft after draft, and finally dropped one into the mailbox. In autumn of 1962, *Yeda-'Am* published his first article, a two-page piece titled "Beliefs in Demons and Evil Doers among the Jews of Kurdistan."

YONA'S SIBLINGS HAD LIVED up to his expectations in almost every way. Sara had graduated from high school and was eager to leave the strictures of home. She was soon off to a teachers' college and an army hitch teaching immigrant school kids in Kiryat Gat, an hour and a half from Jerusalem. Avram was blossoming into the strapping young man who would one day join the Israeli Army's elite paratroopers, a crack unit made up almost entirely of European-born Jews. Shalom won a citywide academic contest and, as his reward, a Hebrew translation of Louis E. Lomax's *The Negro Revolt*. Dazzled by The Beatles, he decorated his bedroom walls with magazine photos of John, Paul, George, and Ringo. At age twelve, Uri took first place in a literature knowledge contest and represented the city of Jerusalem in the national finals. He would soon win a spot in Jerusalem's most prestigious high school, operated by Hebrew University, where he would study in the same classroom as the sons and daughters of Israel's upper crust of intellectuals and businessmen. Ayala, the youngest, was the precocious doll with black ringlets, a chatterbox with dimples who inspired the family's hairdresser to write amusing children's songs just for her.

All five left the neighborhood in the mornings to attend better schools. They immersed themselves in Western music and literature. They mingled with well-to-do schoolmates who opened windows to new worlds. They turned denial of the past into an art form, just as they thought their eldest brother had.

"For years we could not say we were Kurds," my aunt Sara told me recently. "We had to lie. The message was that there was a hierarchy. The Ashkenazis there were gods. Then came the Morrocans or the Iraqis, and the Kurds were at the bottom. Kurds were treated like the scum of the earth. Even among Middle Eastern Jews there were hierarchies, and the Kurds were the worst."

Their next-door neighbor in Katamonim, a middle-aged woman with an Ashkenazi-sounding last name, flung ethnic slurs when the Sabar children committed one offense or another against her delicate sensibilities. "She called us *Kurdia masricha, primitivit*," stinking Kurd, primitive, Sara recalled. "We found out later that she herself was half Kurdish."

That is why everyone was startled when Yona turned on Ayala one day. She was talking to her mother in Aramaic, but her pronunciations, Yona noticed, were full of Ashkenazi inflections. Her *mirra*, the word for "she said," came out as "mee-gha." It grated on the ears, like the twangy Hebrew of Americans at the Wailing Wall, asking for directions to the nearest "bait shee-mush," the bathroom.

"Why are you talking like that?" Yona asked, irritated.

"Like what, Yona?" she said, giggling and dancing in circles around him.

"I don't know, like the kids from Rehavia. What happened to your *hets* and '*ayins*?" He was referring to the Hebrew letters whose deep-throated pronunciations were markers of Middle Eastern ancestry.

"Eeeechs!" Ayala said. "No one I know talks that way."

Yona looked at his little sister, then at the rest of his siblings, and saw that each step toward the West was a step away from the East. Was this really what he wanted for them? Was it what he wanted for himself?

38 ❖ Abandoning the Fountainhead

"[David Ben-Gurion] perceived the immigrants as objects that required shaping.
... For those involved in absorption, the rich cultural heritage of the newcomers
meant nothing." —DVORA HACOHEN, *Immigrants in Turmoil*, 2003

Itzhak Ben-Zvi and David Ben-Gurion were sometimes called "the twins": They had studied law together in Constantinople, undertaken similar literary projects, and cofounded the Hashomer militia before eventually serving side by side at the highest levels of government, Ben-Gurion as prime minister, Ben-Zvi as president. Yet, on the question of Israel's Middle Eastern immigrants, they never saw eye to eye.

To Ben-Gurion, Israel was a "melting pot." Newcomers were encouraged to let the cultures of their native lands dissolve into a bubbling gumbo, so that a new Israeli identity could be constituted from the congealed gray mass. In Ben-Gurion's view, the traditions that Jews had acquired in far-flung lands over two millenia were like viruses threatening the integrity of the new state. And some immigrants were more in need of reconstruction than others. "Those from Morocco had no education," he has been quoted as saying in the 1960s. "Their customs are those of Arabs. They love their wives, but beat them. . . . Maybe in the third generation something will appear from the Oriental Jew that is a little different. But I don't see it yet." On another occasion, he was quoted as saying, "We do not want Israelis to become Arabs. We are duty bound to fight against the spirit of the Levant [the Arab Middle East], which corrupts individuals and societies."

Ben-Zvi, whose quiet humility contrasted with Ben-Gurion's fist-pounding belligerence, was perhaps the only man in Israel with the stripes to challenge the melting-pot theory. Long before he became Israel's second president and served alongside Ben-Gurion in the Mapai party, the Ukranian-born Ben-Zvi had developed a fascination for the history of obscure and unsung Jewish communities and sects. He was a self-styled historian without formal training, who turned out engaging books and pamphlets on Samaritans, Karaites, Shabbateans, and the Jews of Yemen, Egypt, Ethiopia, Persia, India, Afghanistan, and Kurdistan. (Ben-Zvi rhapsodized the Kurds as a "forlorn Jewish tribe" of "hardy mountaineers," who "may well be regarded as a faint shadow of the Jewish people as it was at the end of the period of the First Temple.") His crowning work was *The Exiled and the Redeemed,* an anthology of his writings on the Jews of the East that was translated into six languages.

For Ben-Zvi, the truth about Jews' common past could best be glimpsed, not through an erasure of differences, but through the light refracted by its many subcultures. In what must have been a particularly courageous stance for a statesman of his era, he cast European influence as a threat to the vitality of Middle Eastern Jewry, not its salvation. "As long as these countries were untouched by European influence and their Jewish inhabitants remained rooted in their own cultural tradition, their creativeness was unimpaired and they continued to make considerable contributions to Jewish culture," he wrote in 1960. "However, with the penetration of European culture, to which Jews, owing to their difficult economic and political situation, were particularly attached, this creativeness came to an end during the last century. [Middle Eastern Jews] abandoned the fountainhead of their own tradition without acquiring a deeper understanding of European culture; their contact with the latter remained superficial and consequently their general cultural level dropped. In the absence of a sound, genuine culture, they were influenced by their Levantine environment and they adopted ways of life equally foreign to Judaism and to enlightened Gentile civilization." A close study of the Jews of Islamic lands "should yield a better understanding of the historic past common to the entire nation prior to its exile." The work was of the utmost urgency, he said, because every day the distinct identities of these Jews were dissolving into Israel's new culture.

Ben-Zvi tried to live as simply as the downtrodden people he wrote about, making himself an example of the humility often missing among his Ashkenazi peers. He and his wife, Rahel Yanait Ben-Zvi, "lived for many years in a tar-papered wooden shack in the Rehavia district of Jerusalem," the *New York Times* stated in his obituary. "Their official residence when he became President of Israel was a three-room prefabricated bungalow of the type erected for immigrant families in villages."

In 1947, under the auspices of Hebrew University, Ben-Zvi founded the Institute for Research on Jewish Communities in the Middle East. Six years later it was renamed the Ben-Zvi Institute. The institute, housed on campus, set three goals: Amass the world's largest collection of documents relating to the history of "Oriental Jewish communities"; promote the publication of articles based on those documents; and "encourage young scholars to enter this field of research by giving guidance and enabling publication of their works." These were radical proposals for their time. In 1956 one of the institute's senior officials noted that "in our higher institutions of learning there are still no courses offered pertaining to the Eastern communities, although their contributions to Judaism and to the world at large were of great importance."

By the 1960s the institute's staff had scoured major libraries from New York and England to Holland and Russia, making copies of everything from biblical commentary and messianic poems to lists of addresses, speeches, and business letters. They soon compiled nearly half a million pages on microfilm and thousands of rare books and original manuscripts.

Buried in the piles were a set of ancient manuscripts that had confounded the institute's academic director. Meir Benayahu was a hot-tempered autocrat who viewed the institute as his personal fiefdom and no area of Middle Eastern Jewish history as beyond his ken. And yet here was a large sheaf of papers, apparently written in the 1600s in a tiny village in Kurdish Iraq, that he simply couldn't crack. What in God's name were they? Hundreds of pages of Hebrew characters that didn't make Hebrew words. A rich trove of apparently Jewish writing from a part of Iraq where Jews — peasants and peddlers, mainly — were thought to be illiterate. Some form of Aramaic, perhaps? But Aramaic was said to have vanished from the planet, at least as a written language, hundreds of years before the 1600s.

It didn't make any sense.

"WHERE'S THE KURD?"

It was 1963, Yona's senior year. Meir Benayahu had sidled into Polotsky's classes one afternoon and waited in a seat by the rear door. When Polotsky dismissed the class, Benayahu, in a stiffly pressed suit, fedora tucked under his arm, elbowed a path through the currents of departing students. He greeted Polotsky with a curt nod of the head.

"Which?"

By way of an answer, Polotsky lifted his red face and let his gaze rest for just long enough on the skinny undergraduate in the second row: the one who always tarried for a few minutes after class, seemingly to review his notes.

As quietly as a ghost, Benayahu slipped into the seat next to Yona and pulled a few pages of runic writing from a leather valise. He slid the pages over Yona's open notebook so stealthily that Yona turned with a start.

"I have a homework assignment for you," Benayahu said, cracking a weak smile that turned his pencil-thin mustache up at the ends. "Can you read this?"

"I can try," Yona said, not sure who the man was.

Staring at the same pages a few days later, at a long table in the library at the Ben-Zvi Institute, Yona felt as though he were peering through the lens of an out-of-focus camera. He wanted crisp outlines and primary colors, but all he saw were blobs and smudgy pastels. The Neo-Aramaic of his people in Zakho was a spoken language. Rarely was it spelled out. If you read or wrote in Zakho, which wasn't that often, it was in Arabic or Hebrew. But what if someone were to write Neo-Aramaic? He had to admit that it might well look like the words on those pages.

In the coming days his vision grew sharper. The ancient texts, he now saw, must have been an older form of the language he spoke as a boy. Some words, if you sounded them out, were the same. Others had seemingly superfluous letters. If you pronounced those letters, you had different words. If you didn't, you might have the same word or something very close to it. It reminded him of the English in the Shakespeare he had read: extra letters, whiplashing syntax, the occasional word you couldn't find in your English-Hebrew dictionary, allusions to unfamiliar people and places — but still, when you stripped it all away, English.

As page after page piled up on his desk, he realized he was looking at legends, homilies, and commentary on the Book of Exodus. A strong Kabbalistic strain ran through the writings: there were mentions of the celestial wheel, the great prophecy, the holy spirit, the banners of the chariot, the Explicit Name.

Scholars had long suspected that the rabbis of Kurdistan in the second half of the 1500s had come under the influence of the Spanish Kabbalists; now there was written proof. The writings were most likely Neo-Aramaic translations of Hebrew, Old Aramaic, or even Judeo-Arabic texts. What was remarkable was that these weren't verbatim Neo-Aramaic knockoffs of the well-known writings of Rashi, Radak, or the other olympians of biblical commentary. As Yona would later discover, one could not link the texts to any single source. The authors of the manuscripts appeared to have drawn inspiration from a raft of texts and then refashioned them into entirely new stories. A few homilies appeared wholly original, while others were the 1600s equivalent of Hollywood adaptations.

One author undertaking a translation of the Talmudic Legend of On- kelos snipped out a tedious description of the Roman army's command structure — "The *Agripa* carries the lamp for the *Apifyora*, and the *Api- fyora* for the *Ducas,* and the *Ducas* for the *Hegemon*, and the *Hegemon* for the *Koma* . . ." — and whipped up this arresting exchange of dialogue, which appears nowhere in the Talmud: "O you stupid men of Caesar, have you any idea of the benefit of the mezuzah?" "No!" "O you fools."

These revisions baffled Yona. Why would a translator of biblical com- mentary take such liberties? Weren't they cheapening the original? Wasn't it sacrilege? Then, one day, Yona came to an inscription from the author — a one-sentence mission statement — at the top of a page: "One reads this in the everyday language so that the people may understand."

Midrash for the People. When Yona thought about it, it made perfect sense. Aramaic had all but vanished from the world some eight centuries earlier, replaced by Greek in the west and Arabic in the east. But this author wanted to bring the wisdom of the Bible's great interpreters to the Jews of Kurdistan, however small their number and far-flung their homes. The peasants and peddlers in the mountains of northern Iraq didn't have the learning to understand the original texts in Hebrew or

Old Aramaic. They would have known as little about the Roman military as about Galileo's laws of motion. So the authors wrote in the everyday vernacular, axing dull passages and injecting drama.

It may have been a kind of dumbing down. But God loved all creation, didn't He?

When Yona reached the last page of the first manuscript, he felt his fingertips go numb: The author had left a personal notation. Not just the date, 1647, and his name, but also some family history and even a little intrigue. The author had signed off as "The Lowly Abdallah the son of Sibar, May he Rest in Peace. This was completed three days after Shabbat, the 11th day of the month in which Yitzhak was born, and in which our forefathers were redeemed from the slavery of Egypt."

Behind all these words, Yona now saw, was a soul, a heartbeat, a man bent over these pages for months or years, forsaking sleep and family to complete this sacred labor. Yitzhak must have been Abdallah's son. And look at the way his birth was tied to the Torah portion traditionally read that month. Yona's father, Rahamim, had marked Yona's birth the very same way, in the pages of the tattered prayer book he carried with him in Zakho.

The evidence of a human hand at work so stirred Yona that he grabbed the next manuscript and turned directly to the last page. Sure enough, there was another inscription, or "colophon," as his professors called them, and this time the year was 1669: "This commentary on Beshal-lah — " the passage in Exodus on the parting of the Red Sea " — was finished two days after the Sabbath, thirteen of the month of Ilul. Here, Nerwa, I finished it — I, Yitzhok, the son of Abdal, May he seed and live long, Amen."

The sequence of dates and the similarities between the names in the two manuscripts raised tantalizing questions. Could this Yitzhok, the son of Abdal, have been the same Yitzhak whom Abdallah mentions as his son in the earlier manuscript? Twenty-two years after Abdallah's handi-work, had his son heeded the same calling? The spellings were a little dif-ferent, and the Ben Zvi Institute had found the manuscripts in different places: One at Columbia University in New York, the other at the Israeli National Library in Jerusalem. But it certainly looked like more than coincidence.

Page from a Neo-Aramaic midrash, or commentary, on the Book of Exodus,
written in Nerwa, northern Iraq, 1669.

And what about "Nerwa"? Yona had never heard of it. He went to the university's cartographic collection and ran his finger over the dots that marked tiny villages across southeastern Turkey, northeastern Syria, and northwestern Iran. No luck. He had left behind the map of northern Iraq; if a place called Nerwa was there, he thought, he would have already known about it. But when he went back for it, he found he was wrong: The village of Nerwa was just seventy miles southeast of Zakho. They were almost neighbors.

Yitzhok closes the colophon with a dedication: "For Shamso ben Sapto. May God grant him the fortune to study it, and a thousand like it." Yona laughed when he read the name. He had known a half dozen Shamsos and Saptos in Zakho. They were folksy names, the equivalents of Jack or Tommy in the United States. It was funny how something that at first looked so strange and inscrutable could so suddenly feel familiar.

Then came the third text, dated 1670, just one year after the second. If Yitzhok had not signed his name to it, Yona would never have guessed he was reading the same author. In the second manuscript, Yitzhok had written in a neat hand, faithfully copying stories from known texts and rarely erring in his spelling. The third was a mess. The handwriting was sloppy, the spellings off, the original texts butchered. What happened that year? Had Yitzhok been drinking too much arak? The colophon suggested a more somber reason. Instead of wishing his father a long life and many children, as he had just done a year earlier, he was in mourning for a man who had apparently just died: "Yitzhok, the son of Abdal, May he rest in Eden." It must have been an abrupt death, perhaps an accident or sudden illness.

When you put them together, Yona saw now, the colophons told a story. A father in a small Mesopotamian village in the early 1600s translates biblical commentary into the Aramaic vernacular, weaving gripping tales with characters the local townspeople can relate to. His son follows in the footsteps of his father, a man he appears to revere. Then, with little warning, the father dies. The son tries to go on with the translations, but he can't. One theory, Yona thought, was that grief poisoned the son's work, miring the last manuscript in misreadings and misspellings. Another, perhaps more plausible, was that the father had helped his son with the second manuscript, proofreading or even ghostwriting. With his father gone, the son was rudderless.

"When I first looked at those texts, it was a spiritual experience of communing with a distant past," my father told me not long ago. "I thought of a man in some hole somewhere writing out these little inscriptions and dedications. Would he have thought that three hundred years later someone would be looking at it?" Later I asked him to tell me more about his feelings as the manuscripts finally revealed their secrets. "It was," he said, "like meeting your great-great-grandparents."

39 ❧ Exiled and Redeemed

Itzhak Ben-Zvi died in office on April 23, 1963, at the age of seventy-eight. In several obituaries, writers took a measure of the man from a small episode in his final days. The Knesset had proposed a presidential pay raise, to $6,000, but Ben-Zvi objected. When they pushed the raise through anyway, Ben-Zvi announced that he would donate half his salary to research. He wanted to set aside the money for a fellowship, to be awarded each year to a single young scholar.

"Have you ever written a speech?" Benayahu, the Institute's academic director, asked one day. Yona looked up from the old manuscripts, slipped off his black-rimmed glasses, and slowly shook his head. "Well, start writing one."

On the afternoon of May 7, 1964, in a conference room at the institute, Yona walked to the rostrum and looked out over the small crowd. Standing in a semicircle before him were intellectual heavyweights from the university's linguistics and Judaic studies departments. Some were on the committee that had named Yona Sabar, then twenty-five, the first recipient of the research grant established by the late president. A little past his left elbow was Ben-Zvi's widow, Rahel Yanait Ben-Zvi, a flinty first lady in the mold of Eleanor Roosevelt, who with her pointy eyeglass frames and mop of dark hair managed to look at once professorial and grandmotherly. In the corner by the door were Yona's mother, dressed in her finest silk dress, and his father, in the dark wool suit he normally saved for Shabbat. Miryam was standing on her tiptoes to see over the shoulders of the professors; she was holding his father's hand, for the first time in as long as Yona could remember.

The speech Yona had prepared the night before was folded in eighths and stuffed in the pocket of his white dress shirt. He unfolded the crinkling page now and, clearing his throat, began. "The Honorable Rahel Yanait Ben-Zvi, the Honorable rector, the head of the academic committee, and the honorable guests and my teachers and masters, with your permission I will say a few words about the work I undertook and for which the committee was kind enough to grant me the prize on behalf of President Itzhak Ben-Zvi, of blessed memory."

The biblical commentaries he had started to translate, he explained, were meant not for fancy people or scholars, but for common folk, the illiterate lumberjacks and dyers who gathered in mountain synagogues on Saturday afternoons to be lifted above their circumstances by the words of rabbis. Yona assayed a brief technical description of the material, then shifted to the cultural values at stake in rescuing the history of this forgotten community. He did not say that these were his own people — people like the shy Kurdish couple standing nervously, with hands clasped, in the far corner of the conference room. He didn't have to.

"Our fathers and mothers were lost in the land of Assyria," he said, feeling something catch in his throat. "We need to recover the light inside them.

"We need to dig up the buried treasures of the Jewish community so that we can study not just the center but also what lies at the edges."

At his dorm room later that night, he opened the gift Rahel Ben-Zvi had given him at the ceremony: a copy of her husband's opus, *The Exiled and the Redeemed*, with an inscription inside the front cover: "To Mr. Yona Sabar. The first young scholar deserving the research award from the Itzhak Ben-Zvi Fund. Bravo and Best of Wishes."

In his pocket was another gift: A check for 3,000 lirot, nearly $7,000 in today's dollars, more money than his father made in a year.

IN THEIR DORM room a week after the ceremony, Yona was nap-ping when Abraham Zilkha burst in and lobbed a newspaper at Yona's bunk. The tabloid traced a perfect parabola before landing on Yona's bare chest. Yona leapt from the bed with the panic of a man suddenly realizing that he is being nibbled by a scorpion.

"So," Zilkha asked, removing his sunglasses and leering, "did you get any dates out of this thing, you bastard?"

"What thing?" Yona said. "You scared me half to death."

"Page six," Zilkha said. "Habibi, the girls will be lining up outside your room tonight, just to see your so-called 'envy-inspiring' Brahms collection."

Yona opened the newspaper. A journalist from *Pi Ha'aton*, the Israeli student newspaper, had stopped by to interview him a few days before, after seeing a short article about Yona's award in the daily *Ma'ariv*. Now here was the student article, in the upper right-hand corner of page six, with a big photo and a decorative border to set the piece apart.

He looked good in the picture, even handsome, if a little stiff. Then the two-word headline caught his eye: ANA KURDI! Block letters, with an ex-clamation point. Ana Kurdi! I'm a Kurd! The shopworn epithet. The one Israelis tossed around to tar people as dolts, buffoons. If it was meant as a playful gesture, a co-optation of the common insult, it was pretty ham-handed. Kind of like Spick Gets into College. Or What, Me, Stupid? says High School's Polack Valedictorian.

"I can't read this," Yona said, lowering the newspaper, his stomach churning.

"Forget the headline, John Savage," Zilkha said, leaping onto the bed and throwing his arm around his roommate. "You got to get to the good parts. Here, I'll read it to you." So he picked up the paper and, under the creak of the ceiling fan, read:

They're writing about him, this Yona Sabar, in every newspaper. . . . Despite his name, Sabar is not a Sabra. He was born 25 years ago in Iraqi Kurdistan and . . . he's not ashamed of it at all. On the contrary. From the Kurdish shtetel to the last year of his master's program in Hebrew and Semitic Lan-guages, Yona has come a long, long way. . . .

The article recounted his schooling, his day jobs in high school, his discovery of classical music.

Yona, do you love Brahms?

"Also Brahms? Why not," he answers with a mischievous smile. For Yona is not only "mad" about classical music, but he has a collection of records of Western music that inspires envy. Western civilization won out in Yona's life. Is that so?

"In today's way of life" — Yona says quietly, quietly, choosing carefully the right words — "there is a preference for the Western culture (he smiles), the . . . Ashkenaz. The verb *Le-hitashkenez* [to make Ashkenazi] has an emotional charge, and therefore it's not good to use. But the move toward blending into Western culture has to come. And this, by the way, is not a process that marks only Israel. This process is evolving for us, but" — and here comes the famous 'but' that is usually more important — "not enough is being done, despite all the talk, to help us really adjust. It starts with the fact that our living conditions aren't fair. True, when a family from Europe comes to Israel, and a 'Sephardic' family, they both get the same housing. But the European family has two children, and the Eastern family has 7 or 8. . . . To have a level of cleanliness in these conditions. . . ."

It's clear that this point is very sensitive for Yona.

"Such a sensitive boy," Zilkha interjected when he reached this line, blubbering mockingly.

"Get your arm off of me," Yona said, wriggling free. "I can read by myself now, thank you very much."

"Even here, in the university among the students, all my friends after five years are from the East. And you know the percentage of mixed marriage? 0.0. You tell me that it depends on the person, in every case, and every individual? Not true. Also, all my other 'Sephardic' acquaintances have no real Ashkenazi friends. Why? Are they all anti-social?!

"I once had a female friend" — he emphasizes the once. "As soon her parents heard that I was 'Sephardi,' they objected to the friendship without even knowing me."

But to overcome the bigotry, Yona had told the reporter, young Kurds needed not revolution but hard work and willpower. "You don't need a rich father to study at a university. What you need is the determination to study and progress, even if you have to support a whole family by selling newspapers."

All this ink sent a trickle of anxiety up his back. Politicians, famous artists, army generals: These were the people newspapers wrote about. Not Kurds, not unless they had robbed somebody or committed a murder. The headline said one thing; but in the article itself, the writer had turned him into some kind of spokesman for his people. *I sound so righteous*, he thought. *It's like I'm talking out of both sides of my mouth: Listen to Brahms, but don't throw out those recipes for kubeh.* It looked awful there in black and white.

It was time, he felt, to lie low for a while, maybe even forever. He had climbed high enough, hadn't he? He was about to get a teaching certificate that all but guaranteed lifetime employment in one of Israel's high schools. He had been saving for a decade to make a down payment on a hilltop apartment in Katamonim. One day soon, he might marry a girl — maybe Hadassah, the Brazilian exchange student he was dating — and raise a family there.

A few teachers prodded him to pursue a Ph.D., but Yona balked. He saw the packs of graying postdoctoral students waiting for the likes of Polotsky and Rabin to die, so they could fight like jackals for once-in-a-decade vacancies at Israel's universities. He could not see himself in these men and women — they were sad sacks and toadies whose lives were forever in limbo. "I guess I was being realistic," he told me many years later.

He wanted to be useful. Or, more precisely, he could not afford to wait.

Soon after graduation, he took a two-day-a-week job teaching Arabic at Givat Haviva, a Socialist training institute for Kibbutz leaders. The institute was trying to foster ties between Jewish kibbutzniks and the Arabs in neighboring villages. Yona and Zilkha were hired as a pair. But the pay was meager, the chance for advancement grim. His best prospects, he felt, lay in the same job he had held since high school: collecting dues for Israel's largest union.

WHEN MY FATHER first told me this story, I struggled to understand why he had set his sights so low. He was one of the first Kurds of his generation to graduate from college. He had won a prestigious research grant named after an Israeli president. He had impressed some of his university's leading intellectuals. He had decoded ancient Aramaic texts that had confounded established scholars. And that's that? You just throw it all away? You keep your high-school job and plan a life around it?

Up to that point, I had assumed that the path from Kurdish squalor to leather-backed university office chair was a straight line. By will and wiles, I had thought, my father had parlayed each hard-won success into a more unlikely and spectacular one, never looking back. He heard Aramaic's come-hither whisper as a boy and never strayed from destiny. Wasn't that how the story was supposed to go?

What I had not figured on was the way a person's self-estimation could sink dreams. The way one's own culture could slap down hands that reached too high. The way a nation's priorities could whither the ambition of certain of its citizens. My father would never put it this way. He would blame only himself. He would point out his weaknesses, his limitations. But this is what I see.

"I thought that was the highest I could go," my father told me not long ago. "Sometimes you find your abilities and potential as you go. You have to constantly readjust your dreams. Sometimes you have to go higher, sometimes you go lower. I thought, What else can I do with this? I didn't think I could make it in academia."

What about Aramaic? I asked. What about saving his mother tongue? "I felt if I were going to preserve the language of my parents, I'd have to do it on a private basis, as an amateur."

40 ❧ Systematic Description of a Living Dialect

The summer crawled along in a succession of long, sweltering days. Yona beat the hot pavement for his morning union rounds, then caught an afternoon bus to his teaching job at the kibbutz. When he visited his parents, he didn't stay long. He hated being drawn into their squabbles. He often just checked in on his brothers and sisters. But they didn't really need him anymore, or so it seemed. They were flying now under their own power.

And then came fall. A cool wind was gusting across the university's Givat Ram campus, as Yona stepped through the gates for a stroll across the leafy grounds. It felt good to see freshmen bustle about with their new book bags and notebooks. He remembered the time five years before when he was one of them, the way he had to sit down at the edge of the fountain just to keep his head from spinning. No one knew what you could do then, he thought, so the assumption was that you could do anything. But when you left this place, after playing your best hand and coming up short, people stopped using words like *promise* and *potential*. Now they said "Be realistic," "Get a real job," "Find a wife, "Settle down."

The wind rose in the trees. Yona found a spot under a eucalyptus to sit. Lost in thought, he picked blades of grass, unclenched his fingers, and watched the green wisps scatter.

"What, you haven't graduated yet?"

Yona looked up and saw Raphael Kutcher walking toward him, palms up. Kutcher, the brilliant and perennially disheveled son of a Hebrew University Semitic languages professor, was a few years older than he and had also studied under Polotsky. He had been a star student and, the last Yona had heard, was in graduate school somewhere in the United States.

"Rafi!" Yona said, blushing as he stood up and brushed the grass off his lap. "It's been a long time. What are you doing here?"

"Just bringing some books to my father's office," said Rafi, reaching up with his free hand to recenter his yarmulke. "What about you, sitting there all alone under that tree?"

"Feeling a little nostalgic, I guess," Yona said. Suddenly self-conscious, he cocked his head toward a group of girls near the administration building and said, "Plus, the view is pretty good this time of year."

"Oooh, hoo, ladies man," Rafi said.

"So how do you like the United States?"

"If you like beautiful women, none of whom will date you," Rafi said, and they both laughed. "But really, New Haven is a pretty town. The work is hard, but Yale has a very high-level faculty in Near Eastern languages."

"Really?" Yona said. "I thought all the best Semitists were right here."

"Okay, okay," Rafi said, suddenly defensive. "There is no Polotsky. But you must have heard of Franz Rosenthal."

"*He* is at Yale?" Yona asked, suddenly stirred. Rosenthal was only one of the many Semitic scholars whose work he had read in his advanced classes. But a passage in one of Rosenthal's books on the short history of Neo-Aramaic studies had stuck with him: "We do not possess sufficient first-hand knowledge of the language," Rosenthal had written in a landmark 1939 survey of the young field. "The systematic description of a living dialect requires a phonetic and practical understanding of the language."

"Yeah," Rafi said. "I took a class with him."

"I didn't even realize he was still alive," Yona said. "Didn't he write that famous book in the 1930s?"

"You know how old he was when he wrote that? Twenty-five. A wunderkind."

"Sounds even more intimidating than Polotsky."

"The opposite," Rafi said. "Welcoming, humble, a gentleman."

"Wallah," Yona said, looking preoccupied. "Franz Rosenthal!"

"So you still haven't told me what you're doing. I heard you won the Ben-Zvi prize."

"Thanks, for whatever it's worth," Yona said. "I'm looking for high-school teaching jobs, mostly. Lots of applicants, few jobs. Maybe I'll finish my master's, to help me stand out. I'm not sure. I thought I'd look around campus a little today, see if any of the classes looked good."

"I have an idea for you: Why don't you write to Rosenthal?"

"What?"

"Write to Franz Rosenthal."

"And say what?"

"That you know Neo-Aramaic and have spoken it since you were making little poopies in your Kurdistani diapers."

"You mean to go to Yale?"

"Why not? With your background, I'm telling you, Rosenthal would pounce."

"A thousand reasons why not," Yona said. "I mean, I just got an apartment. My parents are here. My friends. My brothers and sisters. My girlfriend. If I go to America I'll never see them again. And anyway, who has the money to study in America?"

"I come back for a few weeks every year. Haven't you heard of airplanes? And when you get your Ph.D., you can come back and teach here and be a big shot like Polotsky. As for money, you get a scholarship. Yale is Ivy League, you know what that means?"

Yona gripped his forehead with his thumb and middle finger, like a man warding off a headache.

"Just write to Rosenthal," Rafi said, adjusting his skullcup again. "Tell him who you are. I mean, what else are you doing now?"

That night, in his dorm room, Yona wrote fifteen drafts of the same letter, carried along by currents of electricity. He described his background, and then asked, timidly, "Do you think I might be the native speaker you once wrote you were looking for?"

For days the letter sat addressed, stamped, and unsent on Yona's desk. After a couple of weeks, Zilkha, who was also applying to graduate schools, got tired of looking at it. "I didn't want him to miss the deadline," he recalled many years later. "So I got on my motor scooter and drove both my application and his to the postal station."

Rosenthal's reply arrived in the mail two weeks later, and soon after, a formal-looking typewritten letter from the admissions office. Behind the letter offering him admission was another from the financial aid office: He had been awarded a full ride.

41 ❖ Getting Lost

On a cloudy September day in 1965, the Sabar family and a few friends piled out of the backs of two borrowed pickup trucks and spread a blanket across a grassy plot across from the airport runways. Miryam unpacked the yaprach, and Rahamim set about carving the two large watermelons. Across the paved road, just past the low-slung terminal, airplanes streaked into the sky. In less than two hours, Yona Sabar, formerly Sabagh and before that Beh Sabagha, would be on one of them, New York bound.

At the good-bye party the night before, a professor had scolded him, asking why he had to go all the way to America and leave his family when the world's best Semitic linguist, Polotsky, was right there in Jerusalem. His friends had needled him about abandoning the Promised Land so soon after his arrival. Israelis had a term for what he was doing: *yer-ida* — stepping down. In the minds of some, it was tantamount to treachery. "For two thousand years, Jews across the world prayed to God for the return to their homeland," his friend Moshe had said. "To have their own state, their own independence. And now that God has listened to us, you get up and leave after just fifteen years. What's wrong with you?"

"Relax, Moshe," Yona said, looking a little hurt. "No one is abandoning anything. I'll be back."

Yet even then, he felt himself pulling away. He looked at his mother bustling about in her house dress and head scarf, at his father in his gray cap, beetling his brows a little too seriously as he handed out half moons of melon. He saw Hadassah, the pixielike girl from a broken home who had clung to him so fiercely these past weeks. They were like characters in a movie now, and he was in one of the theater's rear seats. He heard their voices and watched their movements, but the screen was faint and lifeless, the images already out of focus.

He had begun to fill out an immigration form for Hadassah; she had said she would come live with him after her year at a teachers' college in Jerusalem. But his own father had stopped him, putting his foot down in his son's life for the first time in years. "She'll be a stone around your neck," Rahamim said, with an emotion that surprised his son. "When you go to a new place, it's better not to bring things from the old."

Another airplane roared overhead, leaving a plume of exhaust in its wake. "Eat, kurbanokh," Miryam said, handing Yona another of her famous stuffed grape leaves, her arm trembling. She took a few more out of a satchel and set them beside one of his bags.

"Take these for the journey, broni," she said.

"They will spoil on the plane," he said. "Let the children eat them."

"You will be hungry in America," she said, her voice cracking. "Who will cook for you?"

"Don't worry, Ima," he said. "There's a cafeteria at university."

The tears were flowing now. Miryam looked stricken, paralyzed, the way a mother does when a young child is pried unexpectedly from her arms.

"Why is it so important to go?" she said. "Please tell me, broni."

"To study, Ima, to learn more, so maybe one day I can be a professor in Israel."

"But to study what?" she said, averting her eyes, too shy to look at her own son, whom she hardly recognized anymore. "If Zakho was so special, why did we all leave? May God wipe Zakho off the face of the Earth!"

"Ima, please," Yona said, squeezing her hand, which felt as limp as a rag doll's.

"We'll never see you," she said.

Yona held her hand for a long time. Except for her quiet sobs and the distant engine noise, everything was quiet.

"I'll take the grape leaves, okay, Ima?" Yona said.

She nodded and dabbed her tears with the sleeves of her long dress.

YALE

Yona studying in New Haven, winter 1967.

42 ❖ Aramaic for Dirges

Yale's Hall of Graduate Studies was a sprawling Gothic citadel. The forbidding towers and ramparts looming over York Street seemed designed as both a declaration of high-mindedness and a warning that not every caller was welcome. Yale erected the structure in the 1930s, and its design was purposeful. One dean of the graduate school described the interlocking perimeter of halls, which denied visitors to its central green any view of the outside, as a "moat" that "held the streets at arm's length."

The late-afternoon sun bathed the granite and limestone façade in a dazzling light as Yona walked toward it, passing elderly scholars leaning on canes and packs of tweedy freshmen. The ornate metal handle on the side door reminded him of the medieval castles he had seen in his siblings' story books. He tugged on it, and the heavy oak door swung open to reveal a long, dimly lit hall smelling faintly of old books.

His heart raced when he spotted the door marked REGISTRAR. He reached down to smooth the pants he'd bought in Jerusalem just before he left — a pair of corduroys, like the ones he'd admired as a boy, looking down from his friend Shlomo's balcony at the worldy "salon crowd" on Ben Yehuda Street. Then he dipped into his jacket pocket and ran his fingers over the edges of the letter confirming his spot — and his scholarship — in the Department of Near Eastern Languages and Literatures. The touch of the fine paper infused him with new confidence. Since it arrived at his family's apartment in Jerusalem a few months back, he had committed nearly every word to memory. It was discolored from so much handling. "We very much look forward to seeing you when you arrive in September," it concluded. It was the phrase "look forward to seeing you" that stuck with him. He had not heard it before, and he liked its ring. Yale might be far from home, he thought. But at least there would be a committee to greet him once he stepped through the registrar's door. This was an honor. And out of politeness, he informed the office of every change, big or small, in his travel plans. No, it looked like he'd be arriving on the fifth, not on the fourth. And oh, yes, the plane would be stopping in Switzerland now, not Amsterdam. This was only proper, he thought. It would be rude to keep a large group of people — the ones very much looking forward to seeing him — waiting.

Yet when he swung open the heavy wooden door, he saw a nearly empty office, just one secretary with a bouffant hairdo clacking away at a typewriter. Was he in the right place?

"Excuse me," Yona said, making a froglike sound as he fought the growing knot in his throat. "Pardon me."

The secretary looked up. "Yes?"

"My name is Yona Sabar," he said. "I am here."

"How nice," the secretary replied, snapping a wad of chewing gum. "Who are ya?"

"I'm supposed to go to study here," he said. "Please look." He handed her the admissions letter.

Still nothing.

"Your office sent this, I believe, no?" Yona said. "Are there some people waiting here for me?"

"No, honey," the secretary said. "Just a bunch of forms. Take these, go next door, fill out both sides, sign here and here, then come back."

He shuffled to the oak-paneled room and sank into an orange vinyl chair with his stack of forms. There was a clean-cut blond man in a herringbone blazer, perhaps another student, in a similar pose. But the man gave no sign of either hearing or seeing Yona take a seat beside him. So Yona squinted at the endless list of questions and checked boxes about his medical history, meal preferences, and athletic interests, trying to decipher words like *childhood vaccines, vegetarian,* and *table tennis.*

That first year at Yale showed Yona an America he hadn't glimpsed in the Jerusalem movie theaters. Everyone here wanted you to complete questionnaires, rate and rank your likes and dislikes, mince your life into a thousand categories that some school administrator later turned into statistics.

Then, at the cafeteria, people disgorged the most intimate details of their lives to everyone within earshot. "My sister's pregnant. She doesn't know who the dad is," one student had said at dinner, as casually as he might have noted the next day's weather forecast. "Let's just hope she didn't get the clap from the scumbag." Others talked about the prescription drugs they were taking for their "shitty" moods, about the worms the veterinarian had found in their dog's feces, about the guy from the frat house who was arrested for driving drunk.

"They would tell you things which would never occur to me to mention to someone I just met, if ever," my father told me not long ago. "I would think, this guy feels very comfortable with me. I thought we'd be acquaintances or friends forever. So the next day, I would sit next to him again and he wouldn't even remember who I was." The conversations shamed him into silence. One Japanese student thought he had finally figured my father out: Yona's restraint was nothing less than a mark of the nobility. "Sir," the student asked one day, "are you by any chance a Saudi prince?"

America, it seemed, was a land of contradictions. Students could return to the buffet line at the dining hall over and over, piling their plates with multiple helpings of pasta primavera, baked haddock, chicken cordon bleu. But on a visit to New York City, he saw hungry-looking men sleeping in alleyways, as if one foot were already in the grave. "These people are Les Misèrables of America," he wrote to his parents in September 1965. "People that don't make it in America's social race to succeed are simply run over."

A happier revelation was that Jews were everywhere. And everyone was talking about them, even celebrities. "It was interesting to hear Bob Hope hosting the evening and putting Jewish words into his remarks," he wrote in a letter to his parents about the televised Oscar ceremonies in 1966. "For example, bar mitzvah: 'Danny Kaye isn't here yet because he's having a bar mitzvah now . . . ' And here all the actors were bursting with laughter, because they also know it's a little late for Danny Kaye to be of bar mitzvah age." Outside a church on Easter, he added, he had heard two old men arguing about what language Jesus spoke. "One said it was certainly Greek. And the other one said, 'No, no, it was Yiddish. Don't forget that Jesus was Jewish.' Many people think that Yiddish was the eternal language of the Jewish people."

It was an even greater shock to sit in a student clubroom and watch as actors on the hit CBS series *Secret Agent* launched into fluent Hebrew. The story centered on a rogue Israeli agent who commandeers a British spy plane over the Egyptian desert in order to execute a German scientist who performed medical experiments on Jews during the Holocaust. Beside Yona in the clubroom were students from every corner of the globe: physics and economics students from Lebanon, a Saudi studying law, two Pakistanis, a Greek, a student from Taiwan, and a Polish Jew who lost her parents in the Holocaust and was raised by adoptive Catholic parents who converted her. Hearing the agent speak Hebrew was titillating, but a little uncomfortable, he wrote his family. "One of the Hebrew sentences that grated on my ears was, 'Let's destroy him fast because we are in enemy territory and some dirty Arab may come and destroy our whole mission.' I prayed the Arab friends sitting next to me wouldn't understand this sentence, and it was huge luck that the Jordanian Arab who understands Hebrew wasn't there to hear that." Of the evening's cultural incongruities, he wrote, "What happened there could happen only in America."

But he sensed that Judaism's currency in America masked a spiritual shallowness. His Jewish friends at Yale rarely went to synagogue. The children he taught at a Sunday Hebrew school looked as though they'd rather be anyplace else. In Israel, on the harvest holiday of Sukkot, his mother would whip up a feast of fried *kotel pisra* dumplings, lemony rice, and hamusta *kuvi*, "wild hamusta." In New Haven he managed only a sad trip to a diner with a friend for stale blintzes. A low point came on his first Yom Kippur, the somber high holiday of fasting and atonement. He walked to a synagogue near campus and found a seat next to a well-dressed man and his wife, both about forty. As the rabbi began the series of confessions known as *Al Chet*, the couple launched into a discussion of their weekend plans, which as far as Yona could gather involved a trip to a cabin in the Poconos.

"The services are so boring," the man told his wife.

"I know," she said, in a stage whisper. "It's good the kids stayed with the sitter."

"Here," the man said, digging into his pocket and handing his wife a stick of chewing gum. Seeming to suddenly remember his manners, he turned to the lonely-looking young man at his other elbow and held out another stick.

"Like some gum?" the man asked, with a friendly smile.

In Israel teachers gave Yona high marks for his high-toned vocabulary and his recitation of passages from classic works of English literature. In America no one understood him.

One day, at a hole-in-the-wall New Haven deli, he asked for a sandwich.

"What kind?" the gray-haired counter man asked.

In Israel, you took whatever they had made that day. In America, you always had to make decisions. *I guess this is freedom*, Yona concluded.

"Egg?" Yona said, though it sounded more like a question.

"Egg salad, sure. Lettuce tomata?"

"Ehh, yes."

"What kinda bread?"

"Em, do you have the black bread?" Yona said, offering a direct translation of the Hebrew word for pumpernickel.

"Black bread? Never herda it," he said. "But we got some real nice rye."

"Dry bread?" Yona asked, doubtfully.

"Look kiddo, you'll like it. I've been in the business long enough to tell ya that egg salad goes good with rye."

"Okay," Yona said, resignedly, "give me the dry."

In America, Aramaic was not the vibrant language his family had spoken around the dinner table. Here Yona heard it only in the synagogue, as the language of two of Judaism's most plaintive prayers: the Kaddish, the words of mourning for the dead, and Kol Nidre, the release from vows on Yom Kippur, the Day of Atonement. Listening to his mother tongue's long vowels and solemn cadences that first Yom Kippur in New Haven, he thought he finally understood that ancient passage from the Talmud.

"Four great languages have been given to the world," Rabbi Jonathan of Bet Gubrin had said, in the Jerusalem Talmud, completed in the fourth century. Greek, he said, was for poetry. Latin, for war. Hebrew, for speaking. And Aramaic, for dirges.

My father's letters to his family that first year at Yale are a catalog of homesickness and disillusion. I found them in 2005, in a shoe box in the basement of the Katamonim apartment where my grandparents had lived.

The ones to his sister Sara, who had romantic notions of coming to America herself, lifted the lid on his disenchantment.

On November 14, 1965, he wrote:

> The more a society advances in a technical and material way, the more its people grow complicated and distant from one another. Everyone here, and especially the intellectuals, is an individual. The innocent, simple man who accepts things at face value, the nice guy who worries about people and not just himself, that person disappears, Sara.
>
> ... You have no idea how much I miss a simple conversation — natural, without superficial small talk. A conversation like one between Mom and Habe, or between Uncle Eliyahu and his friends. One story of Mamo Yona is worth all the lame entertainment of America. Sara, you have no idea how good it is to have parents, a warm home, brothers and sisters. Most of the people in America are sad, mostly because their family life is wrecked and irreparable.

The months passed, but not the feelings of isolation. In one letter he told his sister that "America is a country of 200 million lonely people." In another he described America as a land of false hopes.

By autumn 1966, his second year at Yale, he had fallen into a kind of existential funk.

> Sara, the older I get, and the more people I know from my stay here (without exaggerations, I've met thousands), I feel life is incomplete and damaged. The people I knew in Israel, and especially the Kurdish people, were an ideal of the complete soul, compared to the complicated souls and the

complex problems of people on this side of the world. Everybody here seems happy and carefree. But after one or two conversations, you discover how many different problems everyone has. How many crises and "*sarbouray*" [Aramaic for "traumas"] people have been through. . . .

In Israel, I myself was divided between two worlds: Zakho and Jerusalem. Now I have a third world, New Haven. Sara, if you knew how many dreams I dream where Zakho, Jerusalem and New Haven mix together in the strangest ways!

43 ❖ To a Deep Well

The smell was worse in the morning. Yona pulled the pillow over his head, but it didn't help. Something in this ant hole of an apartment was giving off an odor halfway between decomposing roast beef and rancid orange juice. Four stories below, on St. Mark's Place in the East Village, fire trucks and police cars rumbled past, sirens wailing. He pulled the pillow tighter around his ears. It was Labor Day weekend, 1966. The apartment was rented by his old friend Shlomo Bar-Nissim, who had hosted those grand high-school Purim parties in Jerusalem and was now trying to make it as a singer in New York. When Bar-Nissim headed out with a few visiting Israelis to a parade on Long Island, Yona had told them to go without him.

"I didn't sleep well last night," he said. The truth was he wanted to be alone with his melancholy.

A year had passed since he arrived in the United States, and all he could think about now was the stream of letters from his family. It was sweet the way his brothers and sisters took turns sharing some bit of news or asking for advice. They wanted his opinion on everything: What did Yale students think about the Soviets' *Luna* 9 moon landing? How do American Jews celebrate Hannukah? Do they even light the Hannukiah? Does he know that Israel banned the James Bond movie *Goldfinger* because the title character was played by Gert Frobe, a onetime Nazi? How did Americans react to the trial of the Soviet dissident authors Yuli

Daniel and Andrei Sinyavsky? Do Americans sit around the table eating seeds the way Kurds do?

The thought of their innocence sent a tear down his cheek. He had thought they no longer needed him, but maybe they still did.

The stench in the apartment was growing more fetid with the warming day. There was no question now: It was coming from the place where Yona had slept. He picked up his pillow case and shook. A stained cushion slipped out, followed by the eviscerated carcass of a mouse. He found himself hyperventilating.

Outside, in the sunlight, he walked and walked. The rabbis of Zakho had an Aramaic saying for people who tried, like Daedelus, to fly too high, and the words came rushing back to him now: *Me-igara rama lebera 'amiqta*. From a high roof to a deep well.

There was a park just ahead. *I'll find a bench and rest there*, he thought. *I'll sit for as long as it takes to collect my thoughts.*

He was walking so fast, his eyes locked on the sidewalk, that he almost bumped into a woman just ahead of him. When she turned from Eighth Street onto Fifth Avenue, he slowed down. She had long, dark hair that was parted in the middle and fell gracefully across an alabaster forehead and down to the middle of her back. She wore a long green raincoat and carried a big camera. He trailed at an inconspicious distance as she walked under a grand arch and into the bustling gypsy camp that was Washington Square Park in the mid-1960s.

His thoughts these days had a way of snowballing into despair, and he was grateful for the distraction of this enigmatic woman.

She must be a tourist. Who else would wear a raincoat on a sunny day?

He watched as she traded a few words with the rag-clad vagrants, the sputtering crazies and the down-on-their-luck musicians, then framed an image of each in her camera. Looking through her lens, she circled these figures like a bee choosing a landing spot on a flower. Then she moved in — close enough, Yona figured, to smell their vinegary sweat, their boozy breath. Close enough to record the sorrowful creases on their brows, the leathery calluses on their fingertips.

He observed her for ten minutes, feeling as paralyzed as he had that day in Baghdad when his father's business partner had invited him to sit for lunch. Then he felt his legs move, despite himself.

"Pardon me," Yona said. He was perhaps too close to her, because she started.

"Yeah?" she said, stepping back with what Yona took to be a suspicious look. He could see her now. She had a slim frame, a slightly aquiline nose, and intelligent brown eyes that held you.

"Em," Yona began, "I wanted to know, eh, are you a tourist?"

She laughed and scrunched her eyebrows. "Why do you say that?"

"Well, like, em, Sherlock Holmes, you know, the process of, how does he say it?"

"Deduction."

"Yes," Yona said. "Deduction."

"Go on."

"I see a camera, so you are probably a tourist. And I see the raincoat, so you live maybe in a place with a lot of rain, like, em, London, England."

"Do I have a British accent?" the woman asked, walking slowly now and turning her head slightly so he knew he had permission to follow.

"Emm, no," he said. "British? No, I don't think so."

"That should be clue," she said, "that maybe you need more clues."

"But why would you wear a raincoat, when there are only, let me see —" he looked up and counted, his finger stabbing the air " — four, five clouds in the sky?"

"To be prepared," she said, stopping abruptly and fixing him with those eyes. She wore a look that said she relished another chance to confound this strange if harmless man. "What if it does rain? Then I'll stay dry, and keep my camera dry, while everyone else gets soaked."

"Ahh," he said, at a loss for words. "I see."

They walked quietly for a minute, circling the sunken plaza and passing the monuments.

"What are you reading, Sherlock?" she finally asked, looking at him again.

He lifted his hand to show her the cover: *Language: An Introduction to the Study of Speech*, by Edward Sapir.

"Light summer reading?"

Yona laughed.

"Are you a student or something?"

"Yes, I am at Yale University, in New Haven."

"Really?" she said, smiling. "I grew up in New Haven."

For the rest of the afternoon, at the park and then over coffee, they talked and talked. She was a Connecticut girl, she said, and Jewish, like him. Her father owned Bayard Shirt Corp., an apparel and resort-wear manufacturer. (Two years later, the better-known Manhattan Shirt Co. would buy the business.) Her parents now lived just over there, on the twenty-fifth floor of a building on East Ninth Street, nearly overlooking the park. He wasn't the only one interested in language, she told him: She had majored in Russian studies at Brown University. She taught Russian in a Stamford, Connecticut, high school for two years, didn't like it. Now she was a case worker at a foster-care agency in Utica, in upstate New York, and was visiting her parents for the weekend. Her name was Stephanie Kruger. Her grandfather, she said, had immigrated to New York City from Lodz, Poland, in 1907.

How old was he? Twenty-seven? She was twenty-eight.

He told her his life story — the short version, anyway — and he noticed how closely she studied his face. He was taken by her directness, the way she said what was on her mind without fear or polite preface. There was none of the empty small talk most Americans were so fond of.

As they walked, she stopped when something caught her eye and took more photographs: old men with tin cups in outstretched hands, sidewalk entertainers, hunchbacked peddlers. He didn't ask why she chose those subjects, but her choices left a profound impression on him.

She sees the image of God in human beings even when they are not at their best, he thought.

MY MOTHER DID NOT tell him the real reason she was in New York. She had moved upstate not for the job, but for a boyfriend she'd met in a photography class who was completing his studies at a local college. Recently, though, the boyfriend had grown unstable and paranoid. Stephanie felt isolated and trapped. A psychiatrist had told her she needed a break. "Go to New York for a week, visit your parents," he said. "Just be alone for a few days."

The Manhattan businessman's daughter would never have met the Kurdish shopkeeper's son were it not for their aloneness in America.

The next morning, Yona called her. He was so relieved when she sounded glad. She said she had longstanding plans to drive up that day to visit a married friend in Ephrata, in rural Pennsylvania. Did he want to come?

"Ehh, yes," he said. His classes at Yale did not begin for another week.

"But before we go," she said, "I want to introduce you to my parents."

She met him in their lobby. "Is it the top floor?" Yona asked in the elevator.

"Almost," she said.

The cables purred outside the small cabin. He was aware of the sound of her breathing.

"Don't worry," she said, squeezing his hand. "They're still out at the NYU club for lunch. When they get back, we'll say a quick good-bye and go."

Stephanie opened the door and led him into an apartment that had nothing — except possibly a zip code — in common with his friend Shlomo's. A thick pile of crimson carpet spread across a vast living room, down a long hall, and into four bedrooms. A crystal chandelier hung over a mahogany dining table. Original paintings — Yona could see the artist's brushstrokes — decorated the walls. Glass display cases were filled with miniature china.

"Look at the view," Stephanie said, pulling him to the balcony and an aerial panorama of Greenwich Village. "That's Washington Square Park. Where you, um, picked me up, remember?"

The traffic was so far below, he could hardly hear it. The city was almost pleasant from this altitude. When they stepped back inside, the front door swung open and Codman and Jeannette Kruger walked in.

"Oh, hello," said the woman, a radiance of golden curls, glinting earrings, and a blouse imprinted with the likeness of some species of jungle flower. "I'm Mrs. Kruger. How do you do?"

"Fine, thank you very much," Yona said, smiling nervously and bowing slightly. "I am Yona Sabar. Nice place you got here." He remembered that line from a movie and was glad to have something so gallantly American to say at a time like this.

"Why, thank you," she said. "That's very kind."

"I'm Stephanie's father," said the tall man in the gray suit and striped suspenders. "We hear you're from Jerusalem."

"Yes, Mr. Kruger," Yona said.

"Shalom," he said, looking Yona right in the eye and giving the distinct impression that it was the only Hebrew word he knew, but a very good word still. "We are big supporters of the Jewish state."

"Em, thank you, Mr. Kruger," Yona said. "Have you been there?"

"Well, no," Mr. Kruger said. "But next month we're on a cruise from Marseille that stops in Tel Aviv. We're looking forward to it."

"I can give you my parents' address, if you like," Yona said. "They could make you lunch, maybe, and show you where to go in Jerusalem."

"Listen to that, Coddy," Mrs. Kruger. "Why, that would be very nice, don't you agree?"

His bona fides — Jewish, Israeli, Yale — made a favorable impression on the Krugers. (Jeannette Kruger's stepmother, Winnie, a devout Catholic, seized on another of the boy's attributes: "Anyone who speaks the language of Jesus," she told her stepdaughter, "is welcome in my house.") And his decency, gentle manners, and devotion to his parents and siblings endeared him to their daughter. Things were moving fast, but it felt right. In their three days in Ephrata, in the idyllic heart of Amish country, Yona fell deeply in love. Any girl who would take him to a place like that, not so unlike Zakho, he thought — had to have values like his.

"I was impressed by all of the biblical names I saw there," my father recalled. "The people looked to me like some Hassidic Jews, the way they were dressed. Some reminded me of people in Zakho. All this simple life. No electricity. People depending on donkeys and horses."

It didn't hurt that she was one of the few American women who laughed at his often-lost-in-translation Israeli jokes. That fall he called every few days from the lobby pay phone in the Hall of Graduate Studies. He visited her in upstate New York, where she cooked lasagna for him and he made an Israeli chopped-cucumber salad. She visited him in New Haven, where she had to sneak into the his dorm room (no overnight visitors) and teased that his wardrobe of heavy, ill-cut jackets could use a makeover.

It was a day's journey by bus, and the trips grew exhausting.

"Why don't you move to New Haven," Yona implored on the phone in late October, watching the leaves blow down York Street. "We can rent an apartment and be together all the time."

"Look, I already moved once to follow a boyfriend who didn't work out," she said. "I won't do that again."

"You are so practical," he said. "What, you don't think it will work out?"

"We just haven't known each other for that long," she said.

"But I don't want to lose you."

"I won't go out there on a hope," she said. There was a pause. "I mean, if you're really serious, then . . ."

"Then what?"

"I think you can figure it out, Mr. Sherlock."

THE CRUISE LINER carrying the Krugers docked in Tel Aviv in early October. They hailed an English-speaking taxi driver and showed him the scrap of paper with the Jerusalem address the young man courting their daughter had given them.

As they climbed the dusty steps to the tiny immigrant apartment — this was no Greenwich Village high-rise — Codman and Jeannette Kruger had no way of knowing that Yona's letter alerting his parents to their visit had yet to arrive.

Fifteen-year-old Shalom opened the door. The shy boy was struck dumb. He had never seen two more elegantly dressed people: the tall man in a blazer with a row of gold buttons at each sleeve, the woman in a white blouse with wide blue stripes, like the kind he'd seen sailors wear in the movies. He raised his hand over his forehead, as if to shade his eyes from a light. Then he wheeled around and ran to his mother in the kitchen.

"Hey, boy," the taxi driver said, in Hebrew. "Come back here. These are friends of Yona Sabar."

When Miryam emerged from the kitchen, drying her hands with a dish towel, she bowed and nervously invited them in.

Shalom and Ayala quickly folded the beds in the dining room and pushed them against the wall, so there was room for Miryam to set out plates of nuts and yellow raisins and fill a few glasses with orange soda. Miryam then ordered the children to the bathroom to wash and put on cleaner clothes. She had not forgotten the Kurdish code of hospitality: Anyone who stops at your house is to be welcomed, fed, and allowed to rest, even if a total stranger.

For most of their half-hour visit, the Krugers and the Sabars just stared at each other across the table and grinned. Ayala, in a pretty white sleeveless dress, put on her brightest smile. Shalom, mortified by a fresh bout of acne, hung his head. The taxi driver, translating, tried to explain that Yona had written about their arrival and was a "very good friend" of their daughter. But as far as Jeannette Kruger could tell, Miryam remained in a state of high perplexity. Nothing seemed to register.

"Tourists?" she asked at one point, through the taxi driver.

"We tried to tell her through this driver that Stephanie was probably going to marry Yona," my grandmother Jeannette, now ninety-six, recounted recently. "I don't think she understood us."

So they stuck to the only word in the Hebrew lexicon that both the Sabars and the Krugers understood.

"Shalom," the Krugers kept saying, shaking hands with everybody at least twice. "Shalom. Yes, very well, Shalom."

"Shalom," Miryam kept saying, nervously nodding and politely making only the briefest flashes of eye contact.

On the sun-baked walkway outside the apartment, Mr. Kruger asked Ayala and Shalom to stand together for a photo. But when he asked Miryam to join the children for another shot, she looked down and waved him away.

"They're like that," said the taxi driver, taking a drag on his cigarette. "It's their religion."

The Krugers said a final round of shaloms and then vanished into their shiny black taxi. Then, like earthling witnesses to a UFO landing, astonished Kurds spilled out of their apartments and up to the entryway to 1 Rashbag Street.

"All the neighbors came up to us afterward, trying to figure out who they were," Ayala remembered. "*We* didn't know who they were."

Not until a few days later did Yona's letter arrive, warning them to prepare a grand meal for a visit of the parents of the girl he was planning to marry.

I can only wonder about my father's reaction when he received this description of the visit, in an October letter from his fifteen-year-old brother: "They asked if your letter about them got here; the answer was negative," Shalom reported. "They brought a bottle of Cognac. And to me and to Ayala, the only ones at home except Mom, the man gave a pen with an advertisement for his factory. And they left us a business card. And because we had nothing to give them, they fled after ten or fifteen minutes."

YONA'S FIRST LETTER about Stephanie was a sales pitch; even his youngest siblings could see that. He wrote breathlessly that she would follow him to Israel: "'Wherever you go, I will go,' Stephanie says, just like [the biblical figures] Ruth to Naomi." He was already teaching her Hebrew words, he wrote, and she was a quick study. And guess what? She could even pronounce the word *chapchapiske*, Aramaic for "butterfly." Yona said he had chosen a Hebrew name for her, so she'd fit right in in Israel: *Kehleelah*, "crown," which is what Stephanie means in Greek.

Even little Ayala tittered when she read that last part. *Kehleelah?* That was a stretch. Kehleelah was a literary word that a high-falutin' writer might use in a poem. It wasn't a name. (It was like an American saying he had renamed his new immigrant bride Coronet.)

"When he said her name was now Kehleelah, I thought it was the best joke," she recalled recently. "Oh, okay, he wants to make us happy."

Shalom was equally dubious. "I didn't know anyone by this name," he recalled. "Only a linguist would come up with it."

When the family wrote back, Rahamim sent congratulations. But Yona's brothers were more guarded. "Yona, lately many articles about

Yona and Stephanie in Ephrata,
Pennsylvania, September 1966.

yordim were published and even one about Rafael Bashan, an academic,"
thirteen-year-old Uri wrote. *Yordim* means "those who step down" and is
a pejorative for Jews who emigrate from Israel. "He married an American
girl and he gets the influence of the wife and stays in America and doesn't
come back to his country. We hope that it won't happen to you and that
you will come to Israel after you finish studying."

Yona and Stephanie, who had met in September, were engaged by
Thanksgiving and preparing for a January wedding. There was little time
and even less money to fly the Israeli family to America for the ceremony. It was a bad time for travel: the middle of winter, with snow on
the ground and the crush of a new semester. Yona worried about finding
time for them. He worried how they'd manage on their own. And if he
and Stephanie did raise the money, there would be enough only for a few
to visit — how could he choose?

"Sara, I was surprised a little that Abba was insulted that I didn't invite
him or someone from my family to my wedding," Yona wrote to his sister
in late November 1966.

You have no idea how much I wrestled with this problem. Stephanie's parents are rich, and they could quietly pay to bring you all here. But . . . we were ashamed to ask them directly.

In the end, there was no practical way to bring the Sabars to Connecticut.

Rahamim stewed for a while but then forgave his son. "I ask you to please forget all the business with me about America," Rahamim wrote in December. "We are afraid of the snow. There will come a day when we will see each other and will be happy together. I bought a beautiful bracelet for Stephanie. . . . You asked for a cookbook but we didn't have it in the printing plant. I would send you one if I did. Your mother cooks without a book. Your wife can cook without a book, too. It's better."

Nothing about this wedding would be easy. Yale's Jewish chaplain had scribbled the wrong date in his calendar and was an hour and a half late. With Middle East tensions on the rise after an Israeli attack on Jordan, four of Yona's Arab friends from Yale sent word that they'd congratulate him later in private; they could not in good conscience attend a Jewish wedding. And a punishing snowstorm buried New England under a foot of snow, snarling traffic and convincing not a few guests to stay home.

But as they nibbled on lox and crackers and waited for the rabbi, Yona Sabar and Stephanie Kruger were lost in a world of their own making. "When I was a kid I always wondered, where, right now, is the person I'll marry?" Stephanie, in her simple white gown, said as she squeezed her fiancé's hand. "I would never have guessed that he was playing by a river in Zakho."

44 ❖ Missions

Israel was in a state of euphoria after its victory in the Six-Day War. Radios everywhere played "Jerusalem of Gold," and people sang along in the streets as if it were a new national anthem. Yona saw their honeymoon in Jerusalem that summer of 1967 as a dry run for the life in Israel they had talked about. But his hopefulness soon gave way to gloom. He watched his wife's reactions — subtle but real — to the cramped spaces, the unforgiving heat, the sharp-elbowed crowds. Was that a wince when the Kurdish *ba-buskha*s swung a live chicken over her head as a *kappara*, a sacrifice, to scare off evil spirits? "I love it here," Stephanie assured him. But on a late-night ride home from a wedding, the driver of the open truck stopped short and, as Stephanie braced herself, the metal seat supports sliced a flap in her left calf. She spent nearly a month in a Jerusalem hospital, recovering from multiple rounds of plastic surgery and slowly learning to walk again.

Back in New Haven they both waded back into their studies. My mother took the train to Yeshiva University in New York City a couple of times a week to work on a master's degree in social work. Yona holed up in Yale's Semitic Reference Room and tunneled into his research on Aramaic and the Jews of Kurdistan. Yale's vast collection of ancient books and manuscripts opened breathtaking vistas into what he had always assumed was uncharted territory.

Others had gone before him, he saw now. But he wondered about their methods, and their sincerity. Over the centuries, the few Jewish travelers courageous or crazy enough to trek among the mountains of Kurdistan often expressed outright contempt for the state of Jewish learning. None was more caustic than the thirteenth-century Spanish Jewish poet Judah Alharizi. In *The Book of Tahkemoni*, his famous rhymed prose account of his travels, he describes arriving at a Mosul synagogue on a Friday night to find a congregation of buffoons and a dimwitted cantor tripping over his prayer shawl.

According to an English translation, "His zeal mounting, [the cantor] made errors beyond counting. Instead of *It is our duty to bless and hallow Thy name* he said *It is our duty to blast and hollow Thy name*; instead of *Exalt the Lord our God*, he said, *Assault the Lord our God*; instead of *Praise the Lord, O my soul*, he said *Prize the Lard, O my soul*... And on he went until I grieved that I had ever seen that place; *a-a-rgh*, the disgrace! I pressed my palms against my burning face."

Yet the worshippers — "towers of pride, each with a belly wondrous wide, a Gargantuan backside, and a beard as flowing as high tide" — believed they were in the presence of genius.

"Some of them sat there, others lay and slept like the dead. . . . Others again fled and did not return, leaving the house of prayer. . . . There remained only four asses, who screamed and brayed with the cantor, and thought that they were singers."

Six centuries later Joseph Israel Benjamin, a twenty-seven-year-old Romanian who gave up the timber trade to search for the Lost Tribes, visited Kurdistan and looked down his nose in much the same way. In Barzan, he wrote, "the ignorance of our Jewish brethren here is so great that they are not even capable of reciting a prayer; nowhere, I must confess with pain, did I find them in such a debased state, and sunk in such moral turpitude."

Another visitor in the 1800s, David D'Beth Hillel, a Lithuanian rabbi with a bad case of wanderlust, made it all the way to Zakho, only to yawn. "I have nothing particular to say about this town," he wrote. "It is very ancient, the houses being built of hewn stone, but of a miserable appearance, and the streets and markets are narrow. . . . There are about 600 families of Israelites. . . . They are ignorant both of the Hebrew language and customs."

The leitmotif of the mountain primitive with the barest grasp of Jewish custom and history pervaded the works even of early-twentieth-century academics such as Erich Brauer. "[A fellow scholar's] experience with his Kurdish Jewish informants was the same as mine: None of them knew anything about the ancient history of their people," Brauer wrote in his landmark ethnographic study, *The Jews of Kurdistan*. Brauer's work was respected, but he never visited Kurdistan. The earlier visitors didn't speak the local language and, Yona saw, never spent enough time with the Jews there to pull off more than a caricature of their customs.

The Westerners who had tried to get a handle on Neo-Aramaic were another curious bunch. As far as Yona could tell, they fell into two categories: the Christian missionaries and the long-bearded German linguists.

The missionaries got there first. Eager to translate scripture and to preach in new languages, a crop of Christian evangelists — Americans, Britons, Dominicans, French Lazarists — set up camp in Kurdish Iran and Iraq and set about researching the local dialects. The first serious Western student of the language was David Tappan Stoddard. Born in Northampton, Massachusetts, Stoddard went to Yale before seeking ordination as a minister. In 1843 he joined an American mission in Orümīyeh, Persia, preaching among the Nestorian churches and running a school for boys. He saw no way to make inroads without fluency in Syriac, the Aramaic dialect spoken by Mesopotamia's ancient Christian communities. "As Mr. Stoddard expresses it, he finds himself *tongue-tied*," a biographer wrote in 1890 in *American Heroes on Mission Fields.*

> He has a message, but no medium through which to communicate it. . . . After one year of patient study he began to preach in Syriac. It was to some forty or fifty women and children in the house of one of the missionaries. "Of course," says he, in speaking of it, "it was a feeble effort, but it *was* an effort, and encouraged me to try again. By God's blessing I shall be able to preach next summer. I cannot yet pray in the language, but it is quite time I was learning."

In 1855, two years before his death from typhus, Stoddard's formal study of Aramaic, "A Grammar of the Modern Syriac Language, as spoken in Oroomiah, Persia, and in Koordistan," was published in the *Journal of the American Oriental Society.*

"The small *Grammar* . . . was the first attempt to acquaint the world with the structure and grammatical peculiarities of this hitherto unknown tongue," one nineteenth-century reviewer wrote. Still, it was a modest effort: "The urgent demands of missionary operations in those early days forbade the devoting [of] much time to purely linguistic pursuits. A too short life for the brilliant young graduate of Yale doubtless deprived the world of riper studies which might reasonably have been expected of one who began so promisingly."

Others soon came along. The German Theodor Nöldeke, the greatest Orientalist of his day, published a "Grammar of New Syriac" in 1869. And other German linguists with similarly impressive facial hair, Albert Socin at the University of Leipzig and Karl Eduard Sachau at the University of Berlin, followed with their own studies of this exotic language. But it was again a missionary, this time a Briton, who made the next big stride. Soon after graduating, a star student at Cambridge, the Reverend Arthur John Maclean, landed a spot as head of the Archbishop of Canterbury's prestigious Mission to Eastern Syria. "The field for investigation before him was a wide one," one Reverend Benjamin Labaree wrote in 1899 in the *American Journal of Semitic Languages and Literatures.* "It is almost a Babel of dialects one meets in passing between Urumiah and the Tigris, presenting many difficult problems. But the dean [Maclean] brought to the task a scholarly relish for such pursuits, careful habits of observation, and a definite aim to harmonize the linguistic differences of the various tribes." After five years in Kurdistan, the Reverend Maclean had absorbed enough of the language to publish, in 1901, the first known Neo-Aramaic dictionary. Glancing at the cover one day at the Yale library in his graduate-school years, Yona did a double take. The subtitle promised not just Christian dialects but "illustrations from the Dialects of the Jews of Zakhu."

The missionaries and the linguists had done a commendable job with an extremely arcane language whose very existence some scholars at first denied. (Aramaic, those scholars believed, could not have survived the seventh-century Muslim conquest that made Arabic the lingua franca of the Middle East.) But their work only scratched the surface. The missionaries had other duties, and their linguistic inquiries were often cursory. They often drew few distinctions among dialects, seeking instead a kind of Aramaic esperanto that missionaries across Kurdistan could preach. The Germans based their studies on samples of just one or two speakers, which cast doubt on the validity of their findings. Their studies focused almost exclusively on Christian dialects, leaving the language of the Jews in the dark. Some viewed their inquiries as purely intellectual exercises, barely disguising their contempt for the cultures and people behind the words. Nöldeke, though one of the most revered Semitic linguists and Islamic scholars of the last several centuries, infamously said that his studies of the Eastern races only reinforced his belief in the superiority of Western civilization. "My studies as an Orientalist," he wrote in 1887, "have been the very means of increasing my philhellenism, and I think that the same experience will befall anyone who makes a serious but open-minded attempt to acquaint himself with the nature of the Eastern peoples."

The history of the Kurdish Jews was similarly neglected or, worse, maligned. Yona winced to read Jews as far back as the thirteenth century heaping scorn on their brethren in Kurdistan. The biases of European Jews were not, he saw now, of recent vintage. Looking up from his books in a Yale library one afternoon, Yona saw his calling more clearly than ever.

45 ⬧ A Memorial Candle

A year after his wedding, Yona finally made the down payment on that apartment on the hill in Katamonim. But instead of sketching plans to settle there with his new wife, he moved his parents in, so that they could finally rise above the squalor of their government-subsidized apartment on Rashbag Street. Rahamim and Miryam, in turn, gave their Rashbag apartment to Avram, who had just married.

Yona was lifting up his family from halfway across the globe. Yet the letters from his siblings took on an increasingly desperate tone. Everyone sensed him slipping deeper into the American murk. Avram, twenty, who had rarely written before, was now laying it on thick:

> To the famous Yona Sabar, It's an honor that you are so smart for the family. . . . But you have to remember always that mother who raised you and nurtured you and who gave you the knowledge and wisdom. You abandoned her. You're considered a traitor, in every sense of the word. And not in the sense of patriotism or nationalism. But just one word: justice. . . . Tell me the difference between there and here. There is one difference: Here, is the Jewish state. And there is a foreign country, especially for you, Yona.

Miryam, meanwhile, dreamed at night that her son and daughter-in-law had moved into the new apartment in Katamonim and were happy. "In the dream, she was speaking Aramaic with Stephanie," Uri reported in a letter to his brother. "She told you and Stephanie, 'Now that I know what you like to eat, I can make you anything.' But somehow the only thing she was able to offer you was green lettuce." Uri, then sixteen, had always been the wiseacre, too arch and cynical to betray his heart. But in June 1969, he wrote again: He was quitting his prestigious high school under the strain of an increasingly turbulent home life. After six hours

in school, he had to work at the small Katamonim grocery his father
had just bought. He'd sit there, he wrote, while customers "belittled" his
father, who agreed too quickly when deadbeats asked for more credit or
the poor pleaded for a break on prices. And then, after work on Fridays,
he was expected to iron the family's clothes and shine shoes. He couldn't
focus on his school work; the apartment was too noisy, too crowded. So
he'd leave the house "nervous and angry" and come back after everyone
was asleep. His grades suffered, he stopped turning in homework, and
finally he dropped out. He was desperate and didn't know what to do.

These letters, Yona eventually saw, amounted to more than just sentimental pinings. He had been away so long here in leafy New England
that he had forgotten the trials of his old life. The family still struggled to
pay their bills. His father was growing increasingly bitter as yet another
business venture faltered. His mother continued to suffer his vicious accusations in silence.

Should he just go back to his family? Wasn't that where his real home
was? He had made a show in his department of his love for his roots. He
had even cast his Ph.D. dissertation as some kind of majestic tribute. "A
memorial candle," he had typed in Hebrew above the preface, "for my
grandfather Ephraim and the rabbis of Kurdistan, who kept the embers
of the torah from being extinguished among those 'Lost in the land of
Assyria.'"

So why was every fiber in his body resisting a return? Was it possible
to feel a stronger bond to one part of one's ancestry, an abstract part
that encompassed language and culture, than to another? What were his
obligations, exactly? What kind of person was he to neglect his family?
Weren't they the living incarnation of his roots? He had thought that he
could take his past with him, box it up, and replant it in fresh soil. Now
he wondered whether that was just self-serving bunk.

Yona had earned honors in nearly every class at Yale, and his letters
of recommendation were glowing. "Sabar's knowledge of Neo-Aramaic,
of which he is one of the rare speakers, is considerable on a scholarly level,"
Prof. Rosenthal wrote. The department chairman, Professor Marvin
H. Pope, wrote, "He will be an asset and an ornament to the best of

academic communities, and I am envious of any Department of Near Eastern Studies that has the means and the good sense to call for him."

Past and future warred inside him. He could go home, back to his mother, his roots, his people. Or, it seemed then, he could go anywhere.

46 ❧ Are They Kings?

In the late spring of 1970 the flight carrying Rahamim and Miryam and Ayala and Uri landed in a United States in the spasms of social change. Not even Yale, with its Gothic bulwarks, could repel the antiwar and civil rights movements galvanizing restless young people across the country. Students for a Democratic Society had occupied university offices. A Yale chaplain was indicted in federal court for urging students to resist the draft. The faculty voted to withdraw academic credit from army and navy ROTC programs. The university created a black studies program, introduced a pass-fail grading system, dropped the physical education requirement, and admitted its first class of women. The alumni magazine published a student meditation on marijuana titled "Notes from a Campus Pot Smoker." And in the yearbooks, the clean-cut boys in suits and ties gave way to shaggy bohemians and concert photos of Jimi Hendrix.

The unrest reached a boiling point on May 1, 1970, when Yale's liberal president, Kingman Brewster, opened the campus green to fifteen thousand young demonstrators protesting the impending trial in New Haven of Black Panther chairman Bobby Seale on murder and kidnapping charges. Some three thousand bayonet-toting National Guardsmen were summoned to keep the peace, and police fired tear-gas canisters at protestors hurling rocks and bottles. Brewster laid bare his own sympathies — and enraged the Nixon White House — by declaring a few days before the protest that he was "skeptical of the ability of black revolutionaries to achieve a fair trial anywhere in the United States."

Few departments were more cut off from the upheaval in the streets than the one that would grant Yona his Ph.D. The Department of Near Eastern Languages and Literatures, founded in 1841, was America's first.

In a set of east-facing offices on the third floor of the Hall of Graduate Studies, professors and graduate students busied themselves not with the societal overthrow but with civilization's very first stirrings. They squinted at the cryptic inscriptions on clay tablets forged thousands of years ago from the mud of the Tigris and Euphrates. They teased out the grammar of dead languages like Akkadian, Sanskrit, and Ugaritic. They picked apart the Epic of Gilgamesh, a story etched in cuneiform on twelve clay tablets that is humanity's first known work of written literature.

Yona wanted to show his family the university, introduce them to his professors, maybe give them a tour of the department's renowned collection of forty-five thousand clay tablets from ancient Mesopotamia. But he also wanted them to see the United States, in all its unrepentant novelty.

For Rahamim, nothing was as good as Jerusalem's. Not the food, not the beaches, not the drinking water. The only thing he said he could stomach was a sweet, simple concoction Stephanie had introduced him to at a local ice cream shop. "Mitshek!" Rahamim proclaimed. "Only mitshek I will drink here. Simple, kosher, delicious. Mitshek!"

While his father was nursing vanilla milkshakes, Uri, whose hair fell to his shoulders in those days, ventured into Greenwich Village and thought he was in heaven. Hippies strummed guitars in the cafés, and street-corner prophets preached free love. Maybe someone slipped a tab of LSD into his soda; in any case, when a sudden rainstorm drenched the Village, Uri found himself dashing through the streets, arms outstretched, catching raindrops in his open mouth and not noticing when his soggy sandals peeled off. When he reached the Krugers' apartment on East Ninth Street, soaking and barefoot, the door man blocked the entrance.

"Who did you say you were here to see?" the beefy man in blue piping said, with a glance that was equal parts dubious and menacing.

"Ehh, zeh Krughers," Uri said. "Zennet and Cohdmen."

"No way, kid. Beat it."

Ayala's adventures were more personal. A few days into the trip the winsome twelve-year-old got her first period. She had overheard my mother speak once, to Sara, about being "unclean." Miryam had said that the dirty pads should be wrapped in newspapers, sealed in a plastic bag, and then shoved deep in the trash where none of the men would ever see.

So Ayala blushed when Stephanie took her aside and said, "Let's go buy you some pads." She wasn't sure how Stephanie found out.

"You know about periods, right?" Stephanie said, as they stepped out in New Haven that warm afternoon. Ayala shook her head. My mother told her.

And that's how it is here, Ayala thought, as they walked back from the drug store with a box of menstrual pads that Stephanie agreed to smuggle into the house for her. *In America, all the shameful secrets you hide back home are as pure and sweet and normal as a vanilla milkshake.*

Miryam had a rough landing, but what could you expect when you brought an illiterate Kurdish homemaker to the big city? In New York, she walked over a sidewalk vent and practically jumped out of her skin when a jet of warm air inflated her ankle-length dress like a hot-air balloon. Later that day, the family turned around after crossing Broadway and saw her tiny figure frozen with fear in the middle of traffic while horns blared and cars whizzed by in both directions.

Still, she told everyone, she loved America. It was was so clean in Washington, D.C., where they spent a few days, that "you can lick the streets," she said. People everywhere were so kind, always smiling and saying thank you. It was obvious from the way she spoke about Stephanie's father that she had a crush on him. Never before had anyone held a door for her.

Yona had feared that the hippies would scandalize his mother. But she was mesmerized by the scenes of half-naked flower children making out in public parks. She ignored Yona's warnings and let Uri take her to a screening of *Woodstock*. Afterward, to everyone's surprise, she said nothing about the bare breasts. When they asked her what she thought, she said, simply, "It was wonderful to see people so free."

Her high spirits lasted through that spring day of her son's graduation, when she put on a new white dress and headscarf and took a folding chair on a Yale green.

"Yona Sabar," one of the deans on the platform called.

Then, from a seat in the front row, her son stood, in that shimmering black gown. Applause and a few hoots rose from his classmates. With his arms outstretched, Yona took the diploma and then shook hands with a long line of deans and department chairs in velvety caps and ankle-length blue robes. He bowed slightly before each of the academic dignitaries, and some seemed to bow back. Miryam craned her neck. She had never before seen men in such finery.

"Are they kings?" she asked, standing.

"No, Ima, not kings," Uri said, rolling his eyes. "Just big professors."

She realized it was probably a foolish question. And yet on that day, for perhaps the first and last time in her life, my grandmother felt like a queen. Her prince had gone to a faraway land, slain a dragon, and married a princess. All she wanted was for her boy to come home. But she knew even then, somewhere deep inside, that he never would.

47 ❧ Some Enchanted Place

Of the universities Yona applied to in Israel, just one, a second-tier school in the Negev desert, wrote back. For a Kurd to abandon Israel, go to a prestigious institution like Yale, and then come groveling for a half-time position at a no-name university, well, he could already hear the I-told-you-sos. As he deliberated, an old Iraqi expression kept coming to mind: "Titi went to the well and came back with an empty pail."

The responses from American universities were nearly as dispiriting. So he temporized. For nearly two years, he worked contract jobs as a visiting lecturer at Yale and an assistant professor at Yeshiva University, in New York, while living with my mother in a house in Teaneck, New Jersey.

Then, in January 1972, about a year after I was born, his phone rang. It was Amin Banani, the acting chairman of the Department of Near Eastern Languages at the University of California Los Angeles. He said he was sorry they hadn't called sooner, but there was an opening now for a professor of Hebrew. Banani said he was in New York at just that moment. If Yona was still interested, they should get together.

UCLA didn't have the pedigree of Harvard or Yale, Yona knew. But it was hungry, rich, and ambitious and in the center of America's second-largest city. The university had opened its doors in 1919, and its aspirations had mushroomed almost as fast as its acreage and student body. By the mid-1950s UCLA had set its sights on competing for graduate students with America's elite universities.

By the time Banani called Yona, the Department of Near Eastern Languages, though just seventeen years old, had assembled a cracker-jack group of professors, many of them poached from major East Coast institutions. The program's offerings — in subjects as exotic as Assyrian, Aramaic, Babylonian, Turkish, Armenian, Ethiopic, Farsi, Akkadian, in addition to staples such as Hebrew and Arabic — were now as diverse as those on any Ivy League campus.

The meeting in New York led to an invitation to give a trial lecture to the faculty at Banani's house in Southern California. Yona was working then an article on Aramaic nursery rhymes; all were culled from a single source: his own mother. She had cooed them in their mud-brick home in Zakho when he was a baby, soothing lullabies about eggs and chickens, rice and halva, suns and moons. On a recent trip to Jerusalem, he followed her around the apartment with a pen and notebook as she cooed them again, to her first grandson, the newborn Ariel.

Now he was reciting them to a group of fusty scholars at Banani's pink stucco bungalow in Santa Monica. Of course, he interpreted, parsed, and dissected; he ran these baby words through the intellectual meshes he had acquired at Yale. He had feared the subject might seem too insubstanial, but when he looked up from his lecture notes, he saw he had made a few of these serious-looking men smile.

Banani, seventy-eight, his perfectly round head nearly bald, told me that he saw in my father a kindred soul. Banani was born in Tehran. In 1943, during the upheavals in occupied Iran during the Second World War, he fled aboard a U.S. troop ship to India and then the United States. He was still a schoolboy when he arrived in America. When UCLA hired him away from Harvard, Banani became the first non-European on the department faculty.

"The fact that Yona came from Zakho and did represent a living enclave — this was something," Banani said when I went to see him in 2005 in that same house in Santa Monica. "Most of my colleagues took the field as dealing with dead civilizations, dead subjects. Now here is a man who had an interest in Northwest Semitics because it was his mother tongue. This was a living culture right in front of us. I was keen to get over this Eurocentric notion that we were dealing with dead civilizations. And Yona's focus on folklore"— children's rhymes, folk tales from the likes of Mamo Yona — "made it even more human."

Were there any reservations about him? I asked.

"If there were any reservations," Banani said, laughing, "it was what I liked about Yona, which was his lack of urban sophistication. Yona struck me from the beginning as a guileless and likeable human being. He didn't have any of the airs of the urban sophisticate. There were some questions, you know, 'How's he going to fit in?'"

WHAT IMPRESSED YONA about Banani were his clothes: sneakers and no tie. What freedom, compared with the de rigueur tweed for East Coast professors! And West Los Angeles, with its glorious weather and red-tiled roofs, was a paradise. It couldn't have been more different from Teaneck, buried under snow, where the fog had been so thick on the drive to the airport that he could see only a few inches beyond the windshield.

Westwood Village, the neighborhood around campus, was an oasis of palm-lined streets and warm breezes. The gold-domed roof of the Bank of America building looked like a mosque. The houses, with their red bricks, tile rooftops, and open courtyards festooned with vines, looked as if they'd been flown in from a Mediterranean resort.

Maybe this is some consolation, he thought as he got out of the taxi that Feburary day in front of the Claremont Hotel, where a sign advertised rooms for $8 a night. *Maybe I am not in the Middle East, but maybe I have something here that is like the Middle East. It really looks like some magic enchanted place.*

ON HIS RETURN to Teaneck, six thousand miles from the small Kurdish town of his birth, Yona saw his choice. Behind him were home, family, history. Ahead, America, where, free of roots, you could fly.

In his final years at Yale, as he burrowed deeper into the history and language of his people, he had tormented himself with the paradox on which he felt his life now turned: How could a man abandon his past and hold on to it at the same time?

The Promised Land had been a disappointment. It had broken his father and his grandfather. It had humiliated and infantilized his mother. A generation of Kurdish Jews had been spit on by a society that should have known better. In a highly personal way, America had come to feel more like home. In its openness and innocence and freedom, it had more in common with Zakho than Israel ever did.

Los Angeles, he knew from his many hours in Jerusalem's movie houses, was the capital of dreams. Here, under the never-ending sun and the swaying palms and the red-tiled rooftops, he could close his eyes and be home.

FATHER AND SON

Ariel and Yona, photo booth, UCLA, late 1970s.

48 ❖ Speechless

I was thirteen years old and shrieking and in tears. "I! Want! To go! To a restaurant! Why! Can't! We just go!"

I glared at my father in his sleeveless undershirt, his face a grotesque of sweat-streaked agitation. "It's a waste of money, Ariel," he said. "Please. We have delicious chicken and rice in the refrigerator that Mommy made last night."

"I! Hate! Leftovers!" I shouted. "*I* want Chinese food! *I* want to go to Lotus West!"

My mom was around the corner, in the garage of our ranch-style house in West Los Angeles, anxiously fretting the car keys and trying to pacify me. "Yona, I'll just take him," she said.

"Do you think money grows like leaves, Ariel?" Yona said, mangling another cliché. "Once a week to a restaurant is not enough?"

"No, it's not!" I said. "You should see how much Andrew's family goes out."

"Yona, you're not in Zakho anymore," came my mother's voice from the garage. "You make a nice salary at UCLA. We can go out to eat once in a while. It won't kill us."

"This is ridiculous," I shout, my voice growing hoarse. "Why can't we just go! What's the fucking big deal?"

"Twenty-five cents off," my mom said, docking my allowance by the usual meaningless fine.

"I don't fucking care," I shouted, banging the door.

"Another twenty-five cents off," she said. "Yona, I'm just going to take him and Lani, okay?" She opened the car door, and my younger brother and I got in.

"Do what you want," my father said, shaking his head, the sweat now running down his cheeks. "Do what you want."

WE LIVED IN LOS ANGELES, and I couldn't accept my father's unwillingness to fit in. I had a friend, Ivan at Akiba Academy, my Hebrew

Ariel, left, and his brother, Ilan, at Venice Beach, California, 1979.

day school, whose businessman dad drove one of the first DeLoreans off the assembly line. He had one before Marty McFly popped open its wing-like doors in *Back to the Future*. Darren's dad was a rock-concert producer who got us front-section seats at a Billy Joel show. Eric's dad had a live-in maid, a pool, and a backyard fountain stocked with goldfish. Matthew's dad drove a Rolls *and* a Mercedes, and they had an elevator in their three-story house in Beverly Hills.

And then there was me. My dad drove a dented Chevette with hand-cranked windows. When the car radio stopped working one day, he went to Radio Shack for a battery-operated transistor radio and hung it by its hand strap from the turn signal arm, where it remained, tuned to the same station, for the next decade.

I did not have a rock 'n' roll dad. When my father took my brother, Ilan, and me for a night on the town, it was to avant-garde foreign-language films that the Associated Students of UCLA were screening — for free — in some stuffy lecture hall. He made us popcorn at home and smuggled it onto campus in plastic produce bags. And unlimited rides on an in-home elevator? If I left the light on in an empty room for more than a minute, I'd get another lecture on electrical waste. "Every second it stays on, it costs two pennies, you know that, Ariel? One day, two days, one year, two years, you know how many *moo goo gai pan*s you could buy?" In a city of $300 coiffures, my father cut his own hair. His wardrobe, a rack of ill-fitting discount suits in plaids or stripes, looked like a 1960s advertisement for golfing suits. Except he'd never swung a nine iron. Nor did he play, or watch, any other sport.

At Anna's, the Italian restaurant with the best veal parmesan, a really big cut that flopped off the side of your plate, he'd bid my brother and me to order from the children's menu to save money. I told him I didn't want chicken fingers or a postage-stamp-size pizza. "I'm not a little baby," I said.

"What? The pizza sticks look delicious!" he said. "Look, it comes with, em, it says, cold macaroni salad and carrot sticks."

"Yuck," I said.

"Okay, I have a solution," my father would say, with a look of inspiration. "You order the kids' pizza sticks, and I will eat them. I will order what *you* want from the adult menu." And when the plates came, we'd switch. Every time the waiter came over to ask if things were okay, he'd eye our plates. What the hell was the twelve-year-old doing with the monster veal, while his dad nibbled the pizza sticks?

For him to order wine off a menu was, in one of his favorite phrases, "out of the question." Why? I once had the temerity to ask. "Three dollars?" he'd say. "For a glass?" If you didn't know the subject of the conversation and had seen only his expression, you'd think someone had just suggested he donate his kneecaps to science.

That's where the travel shampoo bottle came in. At the appointed time, usually after the order was placed and the waiter was out of view, my father made his move. He plunged into the darkness beneath the table and riffled through his briefcase for the telltale ribbed texture of the plastic bottle. With his free hand, he drained his glass of ice water and lowered the glass into his lap. Then came the handiwork: He flicked open the shampoo bottle's tiny spout with his thumb, tipped it into his glass, and squeezed the bottle's sides. Out came a perfect stream of Manischewitz

Cream White Concord, plashing against the inside of the glass with a urinal-like tinkle.

The empty bottle then went back into the briefcase, and the "ice water" — now with a suspiciously golden tint — went back on the table. This is when the meal went from a humdrum night out to a game of chicken. When the waiter looked like he was homing in on our table with the water pitcher, my mother would tap my father on his hand. "Yona," she'd say, arching her eyebrows in a glance whose loose translation was "Heads up." My father gripped the glass tighter and brought it nearer his chest. His posture was one of a deeply religious man defending a holy relic from infidels.

I couldn't look.

Yon-hauser Busch, my friends and I called him behind his back, after the All-American beer company whose product he never touched. Or Indi-Yona Jones, after Harrison Ford's leather-jacket-wearing archaeology professor whose fashion savvy and skill with a bullwhip my father could never hope to match. I mocked and I pulled away. I tried to morph into the ultimate L.A. boy, some hybrid of actor, surfer, and rock 'n' roller.

But I couldn't shake him. He had given me a name that may not have been Aram but that still singled me out for ridicule.

"R-E-O Speedwagon," kids in the public-school yard taunted when I'd show up to skateboard on weekends.

"Oreo cookie."

"Isn't Ariel a girl's name?"

I held him responsible for my bristly hair, which never lay straight. I blamed him for being Middle Eastern at a time when nothing was less cool. When he took off his shirt to swim in the UCLA pool, I shrank from the sight of his bare back: It was a crosshatch of ragged scars, childhood relics, he once explained, of bloodlettings by Zakho's witchdoctors when he was sick. What would anyone want with a place like that?

As I was growing up, Iranians fleeing Ayatollah Khoumeini's 1979 Islamic Revolution were flooding our neighborhood and turning Los Angeles into one of the world's largest Iranian diasporas. The immigrants were well-to-do, driving freshly waxed Mercedeses and sporting flashy jewelry. Not long after the hostage crisis later that year, "Iranians, Go Home!" began to appear in graffiti in alleys and on school buildings. In some self-centered way, I felt the ugly words were meant for me.

While I was distancing myself from my father, the undergraduates in his classes were turning in glowing evaluations that praised his patience, warmth, and humility.

Everyone — except for me, it turns out — saw things to admire. My father became a U.S. citizen in 1976 and won tenure at UCLA in the same year. Harrassowitz, a world-renowned academic press in Germany, published his dissertation. Yale University Press paid him an advance to write a book on the folk literature of the Kurdistani Jews, which featured Mamo Yona on its cover and was reviewed in the *Los Angeles Times*. He made a perilous trip to Kurdish Iran to record Christian speakers of Neo-Aramaic. The scraps of paper from his Israeli union job, on which he had inscribed half-remembered Aramaic words as a teenager, were now the foundation for a full-fledged dictionary project that filled shoeboxes with thousands of index cards. Neo-Aramaic, the final phase of a language continually spoken for three thousand year, was in its last generation or two of speakers. "The last Mohicans," my father liked to call them. He was racing against time to document the language for the generations of scholars who would come too late to hear it firsthand.

I didn't know it as a boy, but he was almost single-handedly turning the field of Neo-Aramaic from an exotic, marginal curiosity to one commanding serious and growing attention at major academic conferences. He was gaining a reputation as the language's foremost expert and garnering invitations to speak at conferences around the world.

Every few years UCLA promoted him to a higher rank and gave him another raise, a few times even encouraging him to apply for the department chairmanship. (He refused, saying he preferred teaching to management.) But you wouldn't have known any of this to look at him. Unlike most Los Angelenos who come into a little money and fame, he was still living in the same house, still married to the same woman, still driving the same economy cars (the Chevette eventually gave way to a Toyota Tercel) and still cutting his own hair.

LOOKING BACK ON IT NOW, I see it was a cold war. I never hit my father. I never ran away from home or told him I hated him. I never said I blame you for my olive skin, my hair, my name. I never said, directly, I'm embarrassed by your bad haircuts and the funny way you speak English. I didn't know how to confront my feelings that directly. So instead, I swore horribly in front of him, ridiculed him behind his back, and took pains to avoid him, to be nothing like him.

Approaching my father about the true sources of strain in our relationship — my desire to be a part of the California mainstream, my sense that he was the only thing standing in the way — would have required a maturity I didn't possess. I think part of me suspected, even then, that a close look at the holes in our relationship may have found me more culpable than he was. And at that age, I accepted nothing as my fault.

Outwardly, it may have looked like ordinary teenage rebellion. But I knew otherwise. The scenes of revolt were not soccer practice, theater workshop, or even the awful violin lessons that my mom insisted on driving forty-five minutes to get to. They were not English class or math or social studies. The battlegrounds were places I viewed as proxies for my father's world: the Hebrew day school I attended for nine years, the Jewish summer camp, the synagogue. My targets were a long line of Hebrew teachers, Bible instructors, and rabbis who never knew what hit them.

I had grown up with a Hebrew-speaking dad and spent part of every other summer in Israel. But instead of snatching easy As in Hebrew at the Akiba Academy day school, I spent my classes drawing grotesques of the Israeli teachers or interrupting with off-color jokes that had my classmates in stitches and our teachers at wit's end.

"Out!" the teachers bellowed. "Now! To Rabbi Scheindlin's office!"

After graduating eighth grade, I enrolled in the public school a few blocks from home and felt my animus for my father grow. The strangeness that I had so effortlessly camouflaged at Akiba was as plain as a zit to the kids at Emerson Junior High. I tried to tame my unruly Jew-fro with gobs of gel. But they laughed; one student said I looked like Ed Grimley, the goofball with the shellacked frontal spike whom Martin Short played on *Saturday Night Live*. Another day, I looked behind my back in class and noticed a boy drawing a sketch of a long face with an angular nose and pointy chin. When he saw me looking, he elbowed his friend and nodded toward me with a smirk. I realized it was a caricature, and a good one. It singled out the two features that made me most self-conscious. At lunch, I wandered the rows of outdoor tables with my tray, searching for a place to eat where no one would notice me.

I see now that my father would have understood these feelings perfectly. In Israel, then in America, he was forced to adapt to bigger worlds that made him feel inferior, different, and alone. But I never told him how I felt. Instead, I just stopped calling him Abba. From there on he was just Yona, a man whose relationship to me I no longer cared to advertise.

IN THE MID-1980S, as I was entering high school, my father was struck by a paralyzing anxiety that cut his voice to a raspy whisper. When a throat doctor failed to diagnose the problem, he went to a psychiatrist, who told him the cause was probably psychological. Maybe he was right, my father thought. The stress of a coming promotion for which he felt unworthy had sunk him into a sense of purposelessness and melancholy. "Subconsciously," he told me recently, "some part of my brain told me, 'You will not make it, you shouldn't be here.'" His vocal chords tightened. At times he felt like he was choking. His voice sounded like sand sifting through an hourglass, and he worried that he'd never be able to teach again.

The psychiatrist put him on antidepressants, and the throat doctor prescribed morning voice exercises, asking him to come up with mantras and repeat them at various pitches. One of his favorites was Psalm 137, which he would recite in Hebrew: "By the rivers of Babylon, there we sat down and wept when we remembered Zion. . . . How shall we sing God's song in a strange land?"

Voicelessness. It was one of the curses of exile. But my father had known from an early age how a state of grace could end, finally and without warning. Zakho was his Eden. It was a place where a boy could leap across rooftops, swim all afternoon in the river, learn psalms from a grandfather who spoke to angels. It was a place where Muslim, Jew, and Christian looked after one another. Yona Beh Sabagha had been too young when he left to see it any other way.

Rahamim had celebrated his son's bar mitzvah nearly a year before the boy's thirteenth birthday and just a week before their departure for Israel. His decision seems puzzling, unless he knew then what seems obvious now: that Yona Sabar's childhood would end the day he left Zakho.

The metaphysics of his boyhood, the angels, ghosts, and spirits who were as real a part of Zakho as the roar of the Habur River, never survived the journeys to Israel and America. It was nowhere to be found in the megasynagogues of West Los Angeles, where Saabs battled Audis for parking spaces and worshipers trailing designer handbags and perfumes jockeyed for front-row seats in the sanctuary.

My father went to temple every Saturday dutifully. But he often found greater comfort in an American counterpart to his grandfather's mystical teachings: the self-help aisle. My father may be the only man in America whose stack of coffee-table books include both *The Akkadian Influences in Aramaic* and Naomi Judd's *Naomi's Breakthrough Guide: Twenty Choices to Transform Your Life.*

On a recent visit to my parents in Los Angeles, I found other supermarket-grade self-help books and, on a scrap of paper tucked into a corner of the bathroom mirror, my father's handwritten dictum: "Just today — Live your best!" I was always a little amazed — and embarrassed — to see the homespun bromides of the heal-thyself gurus touch him so deeply. My father recently showed me a stash of advice columns he had clipped over the years from Dear Abby, synagogue newsletters, and in-flight magazines. To me, the headlines "The Art of Intelligent Surrender," "Making Peace with Fear," "Feast (Slowly) on the Buffet of Life" were corny and a little ridiculous. For my father, they were . . . well, chicken soup for the Kurdish soul. I know because along with the clippings were notes he had written to himself over the years, a catalog of fears and apprehensions that stemmed mainly from a belief in his own inadequacy.

"We <u>cannot</u> be right, neat, efficient, etc. <u>all the time</u>." Or, paraphrasing Nathaniel Hawthorne, "Happiness is like a butterfly. The more you chase it, the more it will elude you. But if you turn your attention to other things, it comes and softly sits on your shoulder."

The inner turmoil never boiled to the surface. His colleagues at UCLA told me that in times of departmental crisis my father was a calming influence. "Those qualities that were genuine about Yona were ones that brought people together," said Amin Banani, the professor emeritus who had recruited him to UCLA. "During some periods, when the department didn't get along, the professors turned to Yona as an unbiased, fair person, who didn't share their partisan passions."

His closest associates thought his reluctance to join the fray was a product of a Kurdish upbringing that eschewed open conflict. He'd rather keep a relationship than be right, they told me. He'd sooner spend twenty minutes in a chat with the department's computer tech or janitor than two minutes discussing campus politics with the department chairman.

"He's a person of the folk, not an elitist," Nancy Ezer, a longtime Hebrew lecturer, told me when I visited her office a few years ago. "He talks to people from the salary and computer office the same way he talks to people from the academy. In a university, which is very hierarchical, this stands out. It's not naïve — it comes from a certain kind of values."

"What values?" I asked.

"Part of his culture is not to expose yourself too much," she said. "It's part of his modesty. You battle the devils in private. Otherwise, it's considered exhibitionism. Western culture is geared to success, rewarding people with money, power, and prestige. In Middle Eastern culture, it's about being loved."

When my father suffers a setback — a book publisher's snub, a cancelled public lecture — he refuses to make a stink, often to the dismay of colleagues spoiling for a fight. "The assumption that people are good is something fundamental in his way of thinking," Ezer told me. "Let's say he asks for funding and it doesn't work out. He'll say, 'What was I thinking? Why would I need it? God wants it this way.' He resorts to his folk wisdom."

While I was growing up, my father rarely spoke to me of his work. But occasionally and without comment he handed me copies of his students' evaluations, anonymous bubble-filled forms rating his teaching ability. His scholarly work may have been less than glamorous. (A thief who broke into his Tercel one day left only one thing behind: his book on the folklore of the Kurdish Jews.) So I wonder now if showing me those evaluations was his way of asking for my approval, of saying that it was possible for people my age to like him.

I dug through his files recently and found a few I remembered as typical. "Professor Sabar is one of the most gracious, warm and intellectually stimulating professors (needless to say human beings) I have ever been fortunate to learn under," a senior in one of his classes wrote. He has "a humaneness that touches your heart."

"I love Prof. Sabar as a teacher and as a human being," another wrote. "If there were more people like him, life would be eternal because we'd already be in a perfect heaven with perfect people."

On a recent visit to Los Angeles, I tagged along to one of his classes and saw firsthand why so many students adored him: He was one of them. Their struggle to grasp a new language and culture had been his own. You could see it in the way he guided them through difficult passages. You could see it in how often he applauded students, even for easy answers. You could see it in how often he asked students for help with English, as though they had as much to teach him as he, them. ("Is there something in English called a grandpa clock?" he asked at one point.)

In a classroom, if nowhere else in America, he found common ground with people a world away from his own childhood. He had recently been promoted to the highest of nine steps for full professors at UCLA, a station accorded only to those with an international reputation for significant advances in their field. He was routinely invited to present papers at the world's most renowned universities. But to walk into one of his classrooms, you might think he was just an older, slightly more knowledgeable undergrad who had taken over while the professor was out.

"My mood changes after I teach," he told me as we walked to his car after class.

"Why do you think it gives you such a lift?"

"Psychologically, this is an encounter where I know what to say and people listen," he said, fastening his seatbelt. "Unlike some other kinds of social encounters, where the rules are not as easy to follow." We pulled out of the parking garage into the crisp afternoon light. "In class, I'm transmitting something from the past and giving to the future," he went on. "The past is part of me. But the future, I am not really a part of."

"What do you mean?" I said.

"I still don't always feel at home in this country. I don't understand everything. The classroom is one area where that conflict is minimal."

For my father, I saw, the classroom is a refuge, like Zakho's synagogue was for his grandfather.

We drove in silence for a minute, down the tree-lined street that winds from campus to the house where I grew up.

"Teaching is a bridge between my past and my present, I think," he said. "It gives my presence in America an additional dimension. Materially, here, you can get anything.

"But spiritually — "

He reached up to the sun visor and clicked the garage door remote, not finishing the sentence.

TOWARD THE END of ninth grade, I started sitting at the same lunch table with the two Mikes, giggling blond troublemakers with well-off parents and a yen for criminal mischief. They tolerated me because we had skateboarded together in the neighborhood while I was still at Akiba. They let me into their world because I had access to a car.

In retrospect, it was one of the lowest periods in my childhood. But the two Mikes and I had an unspoken deal: If I provided the wheels, they'd take me places. So I drove them to the house of a drug dealer named Juan in Compton and waited on a couch as if I were in a doctor's office while they handed over a stack of bills for a cantaloupe-size bag of marijuana. (They presumably resold it at school; I never asked.) I shuttled them down the streets of our own neighborhood, so they could break into parked cars and pilfer cassette tapes and removable radios.

In return, they introduced me to a Los Angeles that had been out of reach: wild keggers full of beer and beautiful girls at houses that parents had somehow vacated for the weekend. I mostly just skulked in some corner or in a chair by the pool, watching the surfer boys talk to the pretty girls and wondering what I might say if I ever got the chance.

Even if I made no waves, being seen at the parties lifted my social standing. I had become the cool kid in the advanced-placement classes, the smart dude who sort of had a life. I made new friends, and a girl in trigonometry began passing me flirtatious notes.

When I told the Mikes I was through with the chauffeur service, they shrugged.

"Whatever, dude," one of them said, walking away.

It had been a Faustian bargain, a deal with the devil that I later came to see as cowardly and shameful. But all I thought at the time was, *It worked. I'm in.* My father and his hair and his accent and his strange Jewishness? It was as if they never existed.

After my high-school prom, my girlfriend, Summer, and I went to the Mondrian Hotel on the Sunset Strip. Summer, a striking half-Swede who'd been in a few advanced classes with me, ran with a crowd of club-goers in which I thought I never stood a chance. When we made it to the Mondrian at about 4:30 A.M., a few of her friends were leaning over a glass coffee table, sniffing lines of white powder through rolled-up hotel note paper.

A guy I'd seen at school but never met sat up and brushed a few specks from beneath his nostrils. "Ah! Ree! El!"

"Hey," I said.

Coke Boy, with a plastered-on grin and exquisitely moussed hair, looked me up and down and then cocked his chin toward Summer. "*Nice,* bro," he said to me.

"Shut up, asshole," she sputtered, before turning to me. "Don't listen to him."

"Yeah, don't listen to me," Coke Boy said, winking. "I'm just the guy with the supply. So you guys want some or not?"

And there it was. Full citizenship in 1980s Los Angeles lay before me in a Hollywood hotel suite. All I had to do was sit down and inhale. But I couldn't do it. I saw a girl sprawled unconscious on the bathroom tile, and a classmate in a ripped tux giggling maniacally as he leaned out a ninth-story window, and I knew I didn't belong here, either.

I rejected my father's pleas to go to a University of California campus (where we'd qualify for what he called a "discount") and chose a New England college clear across the country.

DURING MY SOPHOMORE YEAR at college, I met Meg, the daughter of a small-town Connecticut librarian and her Dutch-born husband, a farmer. Her family had little money. To help pay for college, Meg worked at the cafeteria, standing behind a row of banquet trays in her white chef's cap and ladling blobs of turkey tetrazini and crunchy baked scrod onto students' plates. She was down-to-earth, eccentric, and sultry. I was in love.

When I told my parents about her over the phone, they listened patiently.

"It's okay to go on some dates with that Meg, she sounds very smart and nice," my mother said over breakfast one morning, when I went back to L.A. on break. "But Abba and I were talking about this, and we would like you not to get too serious about someone who is not Jewish."

My father wouldn't look up from his Raisin Bran.

I looked at him and sensed some of the old feelings come rushing back. Here I was, a college student, all the way across the country, and I was still expected to do certain things, renounce certain things, because of who *he* was.

"It's too late," I said. "I'm sorry."

49 ❖ Hollywood on the Habur

A decade passed. I graduated from college, played drums in a professional band in California, landed a magazine internship, and then moved East again for my first newspaper job, at the *Providence Journal*, Rhode Island's largest newspaper. Meg and I married at her parents' farm and rented a house in Connecticut.

I seldom spoke to my father. I was privately impressed when he traveled back to Zakho in 1992 for the first time since his childhood: He had actually gotten his butt out of the house and adventured into a snake pit of a country, like a real Indi-Yona Jones. But I never found the right opportunity to ask him about the trip or watch the videos he had taken there. And the years passed.

Then, in early 2000, my mother called with some news. A producer for the hit TV series *The X-Files* had just phoned my father. The show, then at the height of its popularity, was working on a scene in which Jesus utters the words "Lazarus, come forth!" in Aramaic. Could my father help?

I was in my fifth year as a reporter at the *Journal*. I had covered murders, plane crashes, political scandals, and corruption. I loved my job. If more than a few days passed without the adrenaline shock of a big news story, I went into a kind of withdrawal.

But I had recently left my apartment in Providence, to move with Meg to a house in Groton, a drab submarine-building town in southeastern Connecticut. We were there for one reason. It was the midpoint between my job in Providence and hers in New Haven. We commuted an hour in opposite directions. We had no friends or family there. We were so exhausted by the time we returned home that there was only time enough for dinner and a little reading before our eyes grew heavy. We were newlyweds, but we barely had a moment for each other. And the blank sixty-mile drive up I-95 to work only reinforced my sense of isolation.

I was in a no-man's-land. Some nights I came home, held Meg, and cried.

If I had been anywhere else, I might have let my mom's news about my father pass as just one more bizarre turn in his life, an anecdote to tell friends over a beer. But in the rootless environment of an anonymous commuter suburb, far from anything that felt like home, I picked up the phone one Saturday and called my father. What was life like in Zakho? I asked him, looking out my small home office at the empty street. Who still speaks Aramaic? Did you know anything about Hollywood or Los Angeles as a young boy? I started to glimpse in his responses the outlines of a newspaper story and fished a notepad from my desk. Did they even have electricity in Zakho? So if there were no movies there, what did you do for entertainment? Have you ever even seen *The X-Files*?

I had started our chat with the same measured tone I used in interviews with sources for my newspaper articles, but soon I was starting to slip. I couldn't find a good place to stop. Each of my father's answers inspired more questions. I went through a whole notepad in half an hour and began scribbling incoherently on old credit-card receipts.

The idea of any link between Hollywood, the epitome of L.A. cool, and

Yona Sabar, the anti–Los Angeleno, appealed to my instincts as a journalist. But something more was going on: The story of my father adrift in a slick Hollywood production studio was a strange parable of our relationship. It was the Manischewitz in the shampoo bottle. It was the tacky J. C. Penney suits at the UCLA faculty club, the transistor radio dangling from the turn signal in a world of Boston Acoustics and Blaupunkt. Yet here, now, as I listened to my father, my embarrassment gave partway to bemusement.

Yes, he told me, he did know of Hollywood as a boy. As a teenager in Israel, he had escaped the rigors of life in a new country in the darkness of Jerusalem's movie theaters. He still remembered the way those dazzling actresses sang in *Oklahoma!* and *Seven Brides for Seven Brothers*. "The world in those musicals was such a beautiful world compared with the difficult life of new immigrants," he recalled. "My dream as a child was to someday be in Hollywood. Just to see it, even. It looked like some Shangri-la." High-school classmates had even given each other Hollywood names: Yona Sabar had become John Savage.

I laughed. "So what do you think of *The X-Files*? I didn't realize you watched it."

"To tell you the truth, Ariel, I never really heard of it." So after getting the call from the producer, he did a little informal research among his UCLA students. "They say it's like *Twilight Zone*, that type of TV," he said. "Half mysterious, half realistic."

For weeks after the producer's call, he said, he found himself the subject of adoring chatter in the department. "I thought no one would care," he said. "But all these secretaries got quite excited to hear I will be on *X-File*," he said, dropping the *s* in another of his reconfigurations of American culture. "Teaching assistants are coming up to me in the hall and saying, 'We heard you were on *X-File*!'"

I sat down on the floor with my scraps of paper and closed the door. "Tell me the story of the day you went to the studio," I said.

When he arrived at the gates of Fox Studios, my father told me, a guard consulted a clipboard and waved him to a special parking place. "Yes, sir, we're waiting for you," the guard said.

"For me?" my father asked.

"Yes, sir, please direct your vehicle to the row on your left."

He parked his Tercel between a Fiat and a BMW.

Inside the big sound studio, a producer asked him to read, in Aramaic, the words with which Christ raises the dead man from his grave. This was easy. The part that threw him was when the producer asked him to say "I am the Walrus" in Aramaic. The writers, it seemed, wanted to have a little fun at the expense of Beatles fans. Better acquainted with Israeli folk albums than he was with the Magical Mystery Tour, my father didn't get any of this.

"Em, may I ask," my father said, timidly, "what is the connection between this 'I am a walrus,' and Lazarus?"

The producer replied with a curt, "Don't worry."

The trouble, my father explained, was that walruses were not native to Aramaic-speaking lands, which were mainly mountainous.

"A synonym?"

My father thought for a moment. Then, as the tapes rolled, he delivered a line perhaps never before spoken in Aramaic history. "*Ana kalbid maya,*" he said. I am the dog of the sea.

The experience grew even more disorienting when the producer asked him to say "goo goo g'joob," from the same psychedelic Beatles song. Typical Hollywood, my father thought. This must be its bastardized idea of a levitation chant. Not wanting to embarrass the producer, he politely offered to improvise something a little more biblical-sounding.

"Best, I think, to stick to the script," the producer told my father.

"I assumed," my father recalled later, "that this must be some kind of mystery episode and that he doesn't want to divulge the secrets of it even to me. He wants me to do my share without knowing what I'm doing. And I followed. I asked him once or twice, but he didn't respond really."

As the recording session wound down, the producer said he was impressed with my father's delivery. He asked where he'd learned to speak so dramatically. My father didn't mind the compliment but wanted to come off as modest. He said anyone could have done the same, so long as he was familiar with the way God spoke to Moses in *The Ten Commandments*.

"What do they usually pay you?" the producer asked.

Unschooled in the ways of Hollywood dealmaking, my father told the producer to decide. A check for $500 arrived in the mail a few days later.

My father smiled. This was a raise, he told me. He had gotten considerably less the last time Hollywood had required his services.

When was that? I asked.

In the mid-1970s he had received a call from the producers of *Oh, God!*, the comedy starring George Burns as the Supreme Being and John Denver as the earnest supermarket manager to whom He appears. In one scene, a panel of doubtful clergy ask Denver for "documentation" that the Almighty would actually appear on Earth in the guise of a cigar-champing octogenarian. They hand Denver a questionnaire "in the ancient tongue of Aramaic," a language only His Holiness could understand.

"You want me to get God to take a quiz?" Denver's character asks.

They do, and my dad wrote it: What's the true origin of the universe? Did man fall from Grace in the Garden of Eden? Will there be a Judgment Day for Man? For penning the questions in large Aramaic script, my father received payment of $100 and a set of deluxe felt-tip pens.

As the 9 p.m. show time for *The X-Files* neared, the anticipation in my parents' house in West Los Angeles grew.

Over the phone, I learned that my father had checked *TV Guide* and found that a reviewer had given the episode a 9 out of 10 rating. He was getting ready to record the program on two VCRs. "I'm going to make two copies, at least," he said. "Just in case I have to lend it to two people at the same time. Just in case."

My mother joked. "You always wondered what to do in retirement," she said. "Here's your chance."

But up until the final moments before the show, my father worried that it would either be embarrassing or offend the devout. He took some comfort from the producer's assurances that no four-letter words would be used in connection with Jesus. By Sunday afternoon, I found myself getting excited, too. My TV set in Connecticut had bad reception. So I called a roadside motel nearby with two questions: "Do you have cable TV?" And, "Do you rent by the hour?"

When I showed up with $20 to claim the room, the motel clerk, an older woman, gave me the once-over. Her suspicions no doubt grew when a young woman drove up in a separate car a few minutes later. It was Meg, in her station wagon, rushing from her Sunday shift as a psychiatry resident.

The clerk looked just as wary when I returned with the key, an hour later. I wanted to explain about my father — how the children walked barefoot in Zakho, how a career as an Aramaic scholar means a life of obscurity, how excited the secretaries were about his moment in the lime-light, how he'd be so proud that I paid $20 to hear him raise Lazarus from the dead. But I walked into the dark parking lot in silence.

Because of the different time zones, there were two hours left before the show would air in Los Angeles. So when I got home, I called my father. "You're a star" was the first thing I said.

"Really?" he asked, his voice rising.

THE FOLLOWING DAY I sat down at my computer and began to write. The words tumbled onto the page, as if I had been waiting my whole life to tell this particular story. The piece ran in May 2000 on the *Providence Journal*'s op-ed page, under the headline "Scholar Dad goes Showbiz: 'I am the Walrus' in Aramaic." In all my years as a journalist, I had received no more than two or three letters in response to an article. Far more often I received none, making me wonder whether anyone had bothered to read my stories at all. Now e-mails, letters, and phone calls poured in.

"I've noticed your by-line for some time now, covering such exciting events as the agenda of the East Providence School Board," one Providence doctor wrote. "Then, suddenly, out of the blue, you write this stunningly affecting piece on your father's Aramaic scholarship and his fascination with Hollywood and immortality. Your affection and admiration for him shine forth."

Some wrote that they laughed out loud, others that they were touched. My father, too, was getting e-mail . . . and job offers. An employee in the antiquities department of Christie's auction house had seen the article and wanted to hire my father to translate Aramaic markings on a seventh-century bowl.

I was startled at who bothered to read the piece. In late 2002, after taking a job at the *Baltimore Sun*, I went to the Pentagon for a high-pressure interview with a senior defense official and a group of his aides. Afterward, as I left the conference room and stepped into one of the interminable hallways, the official's assistant, an efficient woman with a big smile and a Southern drawl, dashed out after me. "Hey, I just wanted to tell you," she said. "I loved the piece you wrote about your father."

I stood there stunned. Nearly three years had passed since its publication. "I knew you guys did background checks," I said, jokingly, wondering whether being an Iraqi's son had set off any alarms, "but really . . ."

"Well, yes, we do," she said. "But no, I'm just gabbin' at you as a person here. What an amazing dad you've got."

Most surprising of all was the response from some of my colleagues at the *Journal*. On my way through the newsroom one afternoon a couple of months after the piece, a photographer nearly tackled me. "Have you written anything else about your father?" she implored. The tone was that of someone reading a cliffhanger, angry with the author for his tardiness with the sequel.

50 ❖ Coming of the Messiah

I was Savta Miryam's eldest grandson and the first to marry. But when I went to Jerusalem in 2001, about a year after the article appeared, it had been fourteen years since I'd last seen her.

Relatives and friends had urged Meg and me to put off our trip. The Arab-Israeli violence had made for a drumbeat of headlines and bloody photos in American newspapers in the weeks before our departure. I had felt foolish for worrying. I saw myself as above the Israeli stereotype of the thin-skinned American. Besides, we had a guide: My father was in Jerusalem for the summer to deliver papers at an academic conference.

Then, on the third day of our visit, a suicide bomber detonated an explosive packed with nails inside a Sbarro pizzeria in the center of Jerusalem. Fifteen people were killed, seven of them children.

"We're not going out anymore," Meg declared.

So instead of going to restaurants or tourist spots, we spent each night with Savta Miryam.

My father had rented an apartment in Jerusalem's well-to-do Rehavia neighborhood, where many years ago his mother had gone to clean the houses of Hebrew University professors. Every evening, we made the reverse commute, walking to Savta's one-bedroom apartment in a spare building of mostly elderly tenants in Katamonim, the Kurdish neighborhood she had lived in for a half century.

The first night we climbed the dimly lit steps, we found her sitting on the couch, lost in thought. I bent over to kiss her on the head and slipped my arms around her brittle frame. She looked up at me, her eyes flickering with warm light. Then came that strange music: Aramaic. Every word seemed to begin with a throat-clearing consonant and end in a plaintive vowel, as though Italian were arm-wrestling Arabic. "Is she blessing us?" I asked my father. I had never understood her incantations, a hymn of mystical-sounding words I always imagined scrawled in hieroglyphics.

"No, not really," my father said. "She says she can't believe you're really here. When she saw you walk in, she said, 'it was like the coming of the Messiah.'"

I swallowed hard and tried to smile. A messiah returns to redeem his people. I had mostly forgotten mine. In the fourteen years since my last visit, we had exchanged just a few words. My father would hand me the phone on my visits home to Los Angeles, and I would listen as a stream of Aramaic blessings crossed ten time zones along a crackling telephone line. My father would pass me the receiver and whisper, "Just say amen every so often. It will make her feel good." I said my amens and returned to my life.

The truth was, I wasn't the only one who found it easy to ignore Savta. She said little. She refused to take part in the gossip that animated the other old ladies in her apartment complex, especially the three crones who manned a bench near the front door and cast what my father suspected was the evil eye at neighbors they felt had a prideful number of visitors.

During our visits to the building, people stopped in Savta's apartment to greet my father and meet my wife. They left without so much as a nod to the stooped figure in the corner. She had long ago perfected the art of disappearing. The one night we brought dinner, a Sabbath evening feast prepared by my aunt, Savta Miryam refused to eat with us. She sat in a small chair by the balcony, about as far away as it was possible to get from the supper table.

"Please, tell her to join us," my wife pleaded.

"Don't bother," one of my aunts said. "She won't do it."

Savta was too weak now to cook her Kurdish grape leaves, her flatbread stuffed with bubbling-hot cheese, her sour kubeh soup. But she could still observe the custom of foregoing her own meal until others had finished. Only after we had all left the table did she pick up a small plateful of leftovers.

IN 1988 RAHAMIM had fallen into a months-long coma, succumbed to pneumonia, and died a few days before Yom Kippur. Never able to get a business off the ground in Israel, he ended his working years as a cashier at the employee cafeteria at Ta'as, the large Israeli defense contractor.

Retirement brought a measure of comfort. He joined a pensioner's club, went to lectures there, and swam laps in the pool. "When he died, Miryam said, 'Pour water on his grave. You know how he liked water,'" my aunt Ayala told me over coffee one day. "But even as she said it, I could hear a note of jealousy. As if he had had too much fun." The poison of those long-ago accusations had never fully dissipated.

Life alone was not easy, either. Because she had trouble understanding prices and counting money, trips to a supermarket or bank were small trials. She saw few people besides the group of tenants who met mornings in the hall downstairs. When she joined them, she mostly just sipped tea and listened while they clucked about their children.

Miryam's had done well by any yardstick: My father and his younger brother Shalom were well-known university professors; Sara taught Hebrew to adults in Los Angeles, and Ayala to Jewish-school kids in Cherry Hill, New Jersey; Uri was vice principal of a school near his *moshav* farm co-op in northern Israel; Avram worked as a bank loan officer. But at the gatherings at the social hall, she never spoke of them. All these miles from Zakho, she still believed that boasts tempted the evil eye.

She missed the apartment Yona had bought for her and Rahamim. When Rahamim had brought her here, to this spartan home for retirees a few blocks away, she felt uprooted and alone. She missed the voices of children. She hated the thought of having other people look in on her.

"But you're getting old, Mom," Ayala had told her.

"But not old like them," Miryam said of her new neighbors.

For a short time after Rahamim's death, she continued to cook. On Friday afternoons, before the Sabbath, she would take a plate of food to a blind neighbor's apartment and set it on his table, often without saying a word. But now even that Friday errand had become too difficult. Blood circulated poorly through her legs, and her calves ached. She developed ulcers that had to be swabbed with antibiotics. She refused to take the medicine the doctors prescribed. Unable to find a comfortable position in bed, she would get up and sit on a plastic chair on her balcony, surveying the stars.

It stung when relatives showed up with food, for the kitchen had been the one place where no one could challenge her authority. Though she never said so, relatives knew she saw their take-out food as a rebuke. It was also, I suspect, a stabbing reminder of the past. At the end of her life, as at the beginning, her body had robbed her of the ability to nourish her children.

As her calves swelled and her strength drained, Miryam asked my father to pray for her death. He couldn't. This illiterate woman was his muse and senior consultant. He had risen to the highest ranks of academia through his own hard work, but it was his mother he called in the lonely years he spent assembling his Neo-Aramaic-to-English dictionary, when the meaning of a word eluded him, when some nuance of the language hovered just beyond reach.

She had loved reminiscing with her family, spinning stories from a time and place that now lived only in memory. But in recent years, after her friends died and her children scattered, most people had lost interest.

"So, what do you remember about your childhood?"

It was our second evening with my grandmother. My wife was asking the question, with my father translating. "I heard you had twelve children," Meg continued. "What do you remember about their births?"

Meg was in the last year of her residency in child psychiatry. "You're on vacation, sweetheart," I was about to tell her. But before I could say a word, Savta's body straightened and her eyes widened, as if she were a long-ago abandoned marionette feeling a welcome tug at the strings. Over the next four nights, she let us inside a life of great miseries and small triumphs: The surprise marriage to a first cousin she barely knew. The kidnaping of her firstborn. The five children who didn't survive childhood. The six who did.

She shined like an oil-fed flame.

On our fourth night, Yona told his mother that Meg loved to swim and that we had gone to a hotel earlier that day for a few laps in the pool.

"Ah," my grandmother said, in Aramaic. "Meg is a kalbid maya."

My father did a double take. "Dog of the sea" was precisely the phrase he had cobbled together when the producer asked him for an approximation of *walrus* for *The X-Files*. He had assumed — incorrectly, it now seemed — that it was a new coinage.

"Mom, I'm sorry, what does kalbid maya mean exactly?" my father asked, plucking a pen and a slip of paper from his shirt pocket.

"Like Meg," Miryam said. "Someone who loves the water."

"A swimmer? Someone who loves to swim."

"Yes, yes," Miryam said, waving her hand in front of her face as if nothing could be plainer.

My father scribbled furiously.

We couldn't go the next night. My uncle Uri had made plans for a tour of villages near his moshav. "I don't think you should go," my savta protested, flapping her hand as if she were shooing demons. "It's not a good idea." Uri's hillside perch, in a lush patch of country in northern Israel, was near Arab villages where tensions ran high.

"We'll be with Uri, don't worry, Ima," my father said. "We'll be back to see you the day after tomorrow."

But she persisted. "Why do you need to go?" she said. "I don't think it's a good idea."

We didn't understand her stridency. I'd visited Uri's family there many times as a kid. I supposed it was just a grandmother's nature to worry.

When we said our good-byes, Miryam was sitting on the couch where she often slept; after a couple of hours of TV, she was often too tired to walk to her bed in the next room. But on this night, something possessed her: She pulled herself up by her walker and followed us out the door, into the hallway, and all the way to the stairs. It was a journey that by rights she did not have the strength to make.

Blessings tumbled from her lips as the walker's aluminum legs scraped against the stone floor. "May God watch over your journey," she said. And then, to Meg and me, "May you have a son in nine months."

Here we were, already out on the street, and we could still hear this determined woman calling out to us — and to God — as she faded from a world that had long passed her by.

THE PHONE RANG early the next morning. I could hear my father speaking softly in the other room. Then came a knock on the bedroom door. My father, in his pajamas, was standing just beyond the threshold. His arms hung at his sides like dead weights. His face was slack.

"Savta died last night," he said. "A woman in her building found her on the couch this morning."

"I'm sorry, Abba," I said, getting out of bed and embracing him, as my eyes brimmed with tears.

We took a cab to her apartment. Her body, covered by a bed sheet, had not been moved from the spot on the couch where her neighbor had found her. My father slid the sheet down to look at her face and then re-placed it. I looked at the pillow-size lump her body made under the sheet. I realized for the first time just how small she had been and felt something tighten in my throat.

Relatives and friends came and went as funeral arrangements were made. The sun rose hot that day, and the apartment sweltered. Soon people were passing plates of food. A teenage cousin went into Savta's bedroom to take a nap. In the afternoon, the body was still there on the couch, drawing no more notice, it seemed to me, than a yellowing newspaper. Finally, two men from the Kurdish burial society turned up and loaded the body into the back of a van. The funeral was the next day, in the Givat Sha'ul cemetery in the hills of Jerusalem. Many years earlier her children had bought a plot beside my grandfather's.

There was no embalming, no casket, no vault. Just her doubled-over figure wrapped in a simple dress and dropped — dumped, it seemed — into the rocky, brown soil. Savta Miryam was now a permanent inhabitant of the part of the cemetery the Kurdish Jews called Zakho City.

No one kept track of birthdates in Kurdistan, but by my father's best estimate she had been about seventy-nine.

My relatives wasted no time in assigning meaning to her death. Miryam, they said, had died to stop our dangerous trip north. Death was one last gesture of self-sacrifice for her offspring. She was not particularly sick. She had no known terminal illness. So why else would she have chosen to go just then?

It was poetic, but I wasn't sure it was true. It was equally possible that she feared dying alone. All her life, people had abandoned her. Her mother died when she was a girl, leaving her to a cruel stepmother. She was too quick to give her firstborn to a wet nurse, and the girl disappeared forever. Yona said he would come back after Yale, but he never did. Sara followed her brother to the United States, and Ayala followed Sara. Rahamim died thirteen years earlier, but he had emotionally deserted her long before. Too many times in her life, what were supposed to be temporary absences had turned into permanent ones.

The messiah, she had called me. Now I wondered whether she meant it ironically. I was back for the first time in fourteen years. We had listened to her stories for four consecutive nights, laughing and begging for more. It had been years since anyone even cared enough to ask, my aunt told me. Our questions made her feel loved, admired, even. But now we were leaving. We told Miryam it was for just one day. But that's what people always said, wasn't it? Very soon, she knew, it would be for longer. Very soon we'd be back in America, where old grandmothers and their stories vanished into thin air.

In life, she had always felt helpless against abandonment. In death, she had perhaps finally asserted herself. For four short days she was the center of a family, and that was how Miryam Sabar wanted to leave the world.

51 ◈ Covenants

A little more than a year after we buried my grandmother, my wife gave birth to our first child, Seth: a son, as Savta had prayed that last night of her life. One thing Savta might not have prayed for was our decision not to circumcise him. My wife grew up going to a Congregational church. She didn't believe in much of anything by the time Seth was born, except that no one with a knife was going to get anywhere near his body within the first week of his life. She had no problem with our raising Seth Jewish, but no knives. "If a mohel shows up," she warned, "I think I'd grab Seth off the table, lock us in the bathroom, and just sob."

As Seth's birth neared, my parents weighed in firmly in favor of the bris. "He'll wonder why he doesn't look like his father," my mom said. My uncle Shalom, a professor of Jewish art history at Hebrew University, was more vociferous; he fired off a volley of long, argumentative e-mails from Israel about the bris being the covenant between God and the Jewish people.

I felt obliged to put up a fight on my family's behalf. But when I searched myself, I couldn't muster the conviction. I was hardly an observant Jew. I couldn't remember the last time I had been to temple. My wife was a Gentile, so in the strictest sense, Seth wasn't Jewish to begin with. What did we gain, exactly, from what was in some ways a barbaric ritual? Who were we trying to fool, except maybe ourselves?

I told my family I was siding with Meg. I cautioned them to read nothing into it. We were still committed to raising Seth Jewish. But I didn't see circumcision as the lynchpin of Jewish identity.

I resented the pressure. I found myself getting irritated with my father. Hadn't he laid the groundwork for this precise moment nearly forty years ago, when he left Israel? When you abandon the Jewish homeland and raise your children in metropolitan Los Angeles, you can't expect life to go on as it always has. Zakho may have been an insular backwater where Jews never wavered from tradition. L.A. was not.

Wasn't assimilation the logical end point of immigration? With Jews making up just 2 percent of the U.S. population, weren't intermarriage and uncircumcised children inevitable? My father talked a big game about rescuing your heritage from obscurity. But I saw now that he talked better than he walked. Just as I thought I was starting to see him more clearly, he slipped away from me. What was it he wanted from me, exactly? What ground did he have to stand on?

A few weeks after Seth's birth, my parents came to visit us in Annapolis, Maryland, where I was working for the *Baltimore Sun*. Meg and I saw no harm in my father's request that we all take the baby to a temple so a rabbi could bless him.

We found a conservative synagogue in the phone book and drove over the next Sabbath morning. After several men and women climbed the bima to say the prayer between Torah readings, the rabbi's assistant walked to our bench to ask if we wanted a turn — a customary honor extended to visitors.

Meg carried Seth and joined my father and me on the platform by the unfurled Torah scrolls. Suddenly every eye in the congregation was on us. My heart started to throb. This was a Conservative temple. There were rules.

The rabbi, an effervescent middle-aged woman, started the prayer for Seth. But when she came to the part about the covenant with God — translation: bris — she stopped suddenly. "Is he circumcised?" the rabbi asked.

The sanctuary was uncomfortably silent. I could feel the blood rushing to my face.

"Not yet," I mumbled.

But at precisely the same time, my father bent forward deeply, somewhere between a nod and a bow, and grunted something that sounded very much like "uh-huh."

I'm not sure what the rabbi heard. But she hastily launched back into the prayer over the newborn.

I was astonished. Had my father just lied to a rabbi, in full view of the open Torah scrolls? I was relieved that the public awkwardness had passed, but appalled at my father's seeming disingenuousness. I planned to confront him afterward.

In the meantime, we returned to our seats. After the final prayer, the rabbi, still on the bima, asked us to introduce ourselves.

"Ahh-hah, that sounds Sephardic," she said, brightening at the repetition of the last name Sabar. "Where are you from?" When my father said he was from Kurdistan, the rabbi looked riveted, as if a column of heavenly light had at that precise moment pierced the synagogue's skylight. "This is *very* interesting," she intoned, stretching out the "very." "I studied about the Kurdistani Jews in rabbinical school but have never met one. We've certainly never had one in our temple before." And they started a dialogue, right there in front of the congregation. The rabbi, on the dais, posed question after question about Yona's family. My father, standing in the back row, fielded them like a professor instructing a class of undergraduates.

The rabbi was rapt. "Now, listen, children," she said, casting a glance at the boys and girls in the sanctuary. "You're witnessing a piece of history right here." The children turned their heads, as did a few adults, who seemed to find this strange visitor, with his off-kilter hair and his pants pulled up too high, suddenly interesting.

Yona told the worshippers that he was the last boy bar mitzvahed in his Kurdish town before the mass migration to Israel. He mentioned that he still remembered his Torah portion from Exodus. An attractive mother on the bench in front of us turned around and said that was the same passage her son would read this year at his bar mitzvah.

"We should invite you!" she said, smiling brightly.

At the Kiddush reception moments later, the rabbi and a half dozen middle-aged women surrounded him. To look at their reverential faces, it was as if Moses himself had sauntered into their temple.

I never did confront my father about his response to the rabbi's question about Seth. To me, his behavior had seemed deliberately ambiguous. He had made a throat-clearing sound he hoped the rabbi would take for a yes. He had given a bow that might also have been a nod. Immigrants like my grandfather, who lived in a world of absolutes, set themselves up for disappointment. My father, it seems, saw that survival in a new land required a daily negotiation of past and present. There were times when it was better to favor pragmatism over orthodoxy, ambiguity over hard truth.

If this was what Yona Sabar of West Los Angeles, California, needed to do to convince himself of his grandson's righteousness, who was I to fault him? Whether or not Seth was circumcised was beside the point, for the rabbi, for me, and even, I hoped, for my father.

What was real were the stories of my father's boyhood in Kurdistan. What gripped the rabbi and the worshippers that day were his ties to the Jews exiled to Assyria some three thousand years earlier. This was the original Judaism. This was flesh-and-blood history. This, I felt, was the covenant.

What to do about my relationship to this past bedeviled me for the next couple of years. I knew time was running out. Seth was growing up all American, to parents who never knew extreme adversity, who never had to trek across borders with only the things they could carry, who never had to learn a new language just to survive.

My father was getting old. His back ached, and he had taken to wrapping his ailing knees in elastic braces. Both his parents had already died. And every few days another Kurdish Jew of their generation was laid to rest in that growing part of the cemetery known as Zakho City.

As the weeks passed, I felt a growing pressure to act. Part of what seized me was the journalist's sense for when an important story must be gone after — or forever lost. Another, deeper part was fear. Fear that my best chance for a kind of personal redemption might be getting away from me.

In the fall of 2004, I quit my job at the *Sun* to see what I could find.

THE RETURN

Road sign to Zakho, 1992.

52 ❖ River Keeps Flowing

I made a deal with Meg. Seth had been born a few months after her residency in child psychiatry ended, and she had stayed home with him for the last two years. "If you go back to work and help support us while I pursue this crazy project, we can move to Maine," I said.

It was a clear day in the late spring of 2004, and we were walking with Seth through a park near our apartment in Annapolis.

"Are you serious?" she said.

Meg had always wanted to live in Thoreau country. She bought into the lore of Maine as an unspoiled wilderness populated by rugged individualists. She dreamed of long walks through the woods, fresh milk from local farms, and night skies full of stars. I had resisted. I wanted to be a big-city journalist, and there wasn't a whole lot in the way of cities — big or small — in Maine. But now I could work from home, and it wouldn't matter where we lived as long as I had phone and Internet service.

"What do you say, Meg? I'm offering you what you always wanted."

"I'm not sure this is about me as much as it's about you," she said. "But Maine, huh?" She thought about it for a day, then bit. "I'll do it for the Kurds," she said.

That winter my parents paid their first visit to our new house. The snowy roads, bone-chilling temperatures, and the absence of a decent cappuccino were deeply troubling to my father. He was a warm-weather, urban creature, and rural Maine in the winter was not unlike his personal vision of purgatory. The upshot was that we had a lot of time to talk. We took seats in my office, at the kitchen table, in the living room, and he led me day by day through the turning points in his life. He had a surprisingly vivid memory of life in Zakho, recalling people, places, and conversations in crisp detail.

He protested occasionally that he didn't understand why I needed so much minutiae: the name of a mountain, the title of a magazine one of his childhood friends had read. He hesitated when I asked for the names of people who knew him at key points in his life — in Zakho, Israel, New Haven, and Los Angeles. He knew I planned to call and worried that I'd be bothering them. Mostly he played along, though. I asked questions until I could tell from a slightly haggard look that he was growing tired. "Thanks a lot, Abba," I said, taking pains to call him that even though it came less than naturally at first. "Let's take a break for now. We'll pick up another time."

He was ambivalent about my newfound interest, he told me later. "On the one hand, I'm really happy," he said. He never had high expectations that his children, raised in America, would care about his family's roots in Kurdistan. "I thought that would end with me and that's it," he said. "Because you are in America. I see there is a new generation. I cannot expect you to know about the past forever. I didn't expect you to become super Kurdish, wearing Kurdish pants wherever you go."

So what were your expectations? I asked.

"I thought when I taught you to say *bumbeh* — " an Aramaic baby word for "stomach" he taught me as a boy " — that was the best thing I could do. Because that was fun and practical, and because some words were funny and made you laugh, like *bisho bisho*, 'bath.' Yet, I thought you were going forward and didn't have interest and I couldn't tell you much."

But he seemed to have other, stronger misgivings. He had made it this far by keeping his head down. You don't stick out. You don't make a spectacle of yourself. You don't ask for too much. You don't show off. But quietly, when no one is looking, you work harder than anyone else. And quietly, you get ahead. "My grandfather said, 'Don't put yourself in the mouth of people,'" my father told me. "In other words, the less people talk about you the better." The same strategy had kept the Jews alive in Kurdistan for twenty-seven hundred years, and for my father, it seemed decidedly at odds with a starring role in a book. "I don't think most of my colleagues have any interest in me as a human being," he said. But then, resignedly, he seemed to understand something fundamental about my search. "This is your story, of course," he said.

Another day I asked him, "What did you think of my behavior as a boy?"

"The main thing I remember is you were very obstinate," he said. "You

wanted your own way. We thought, He's just a child, we can easily convince him to do something one way or another. But you were not easy
to convince. And you always insisted and demanded what you wanted.
There were no compromises. Occasionally we developed some negotiating language — we'd give you a choice of two or three things, and you'd
choose one. But sometimes we were immobilized because we wanted one
thing and you wanted another."

Do you think you succeeded with me as a parent?

There was a long pause. "I don't know," he said at last. "This is difficult
for me to say."

A few weeks after his visit to Maine, he called out of the blue to say
he had found a 1978 tape recording of me singing "some really beautiful
songs." He insisted on popping the tape in the recorder and playing a
snippet over the phone. I was about seven years old and singing Hebrew
prayers. "When I found this tape, Ariel, I laughed and teared at the same
time," my father said, after the tape player clicked off. "I'm sure if I send
this to any yeshiva, they'll appoint you head of the yeshiva on the spot."

I got the feeling he was trying to make up for the awkwardness of our
last conversation. He was trying to rewind to a time when he had felt
more certain of his success as a parent.

"My memory of you at that time is still very fresh," he went on. "Now,
it's difficult to connect you with that."

"Why?"

"We are all removed from those days," he said, and I wondered whether
he was talking more about me or him.

MY FATHER HAS NEVER been comfortable discussing his inner-
most feelings, particularly negative ones, and I felt he was only scratching
the surface of our relationship. I knew I would get a different perspective
from his sister Sara. She was never one to mince words, and she didn't
disappoint. "You treated him like dirt," she said, shaking her head as
we drove back to her house after lunch at a Chinese restaurant. "You
disrespected him. You made fun of him. You did not listen to him. You
disobeyed. You preferred your mother in very obvious ways. You didn't
attempt to cover it up."

I wasn't expecting her to be *this* direct. I stopped the car outside her house, near the Los Angeles airport, and turned up the air conditioning. I decided we would sit in this uncomfortably tight space until I heard her out.

Didn't you rebel against your father? I asked. She had told me earlier that she angrily defied his demands that she quit school to work. Her reasons were more noble, I said, but her actions not all that different.

"No." She was emphatic. "Although I stood up to my father, I never disrespected him in public. The worst thing I said once was 'We don't love you.'" She explained that it came after another of his attacks on her mother's virtue. "I regret it to this day."

Her judgment stung. But I suspected it was mostly true. On the drive back to my parents' house, I wanted more than ever to try to make things right with my father. If that wasn't possible, I wanted at least to understand him, to see past the template of "father" to the complicated human being I had too often kept at arm's length.

Zakho, the Kurdish border town of his childhood, was as good a starting point as any. I knew he'd only been back once, in 1992. And so after my visit with Sara, I asked him about that trip.

"Why did it take you four decades to go back?" I asked. "Had you tried going earlier?"

My father told me he had dreamed of a homecoming since the day he left as a twelve-year-old boy, in 1951. He had imagined returning to Zakho just a few years after his departure and landing his very own Israeli fighter jet alongside the old market, where Kurds would spill out of their stalls to embrace him as he leaped from the cockpit. The boyhood fantasy matured into adult longing, a dream deferred. In graduate school, my father realized that Iraq — particularly after the rise in 1968 of the Baathist Party, which had publicly hanged nine Jewish businessmen as Israeli spies — was not a safe place for Jews. He all but gave up hope.

He traveled to Kurdish Iran for linguistic research in 1975 and, feeling nostalgic one day, asked villagers to point toward Iraq. "All I saw was mountains," my father told me, and he returned home wistful.

Then came the Persian Gulf War. After the Iraqi surrender, in 1991, Saddam Hussein crushed a brief Kurdish rebellion and as many as

850,000 Kurdish refugees fled into the frigid mountains along the Turkish border. Tens of thousands were resettled a few miles south of the border, in Zakho. Coalition warplanes began enforcing a no-fly zone over Iraq's Kurdish north. Some twenty-one thousand coalition troops, seven thousand of them American, moved into the area as part of a humanitarian resettlement effort called Operation Provide Comfort. Ironically, it was the horrific suffering of the Kurds—thousands were dying from cold, disease, and starvation, moving the United States to act—that paved the way for my father's first visit.

In the summer of 1992 his high-school friend Abraham Zilkha, now a professor at the University of Texas, said a photographer he knew in Austin had extensive contacts among the Kurds and was planning a visit to northern Iraq. My father called the photographer, a brassy, larger-than-life Texan named Mary Ann Bruni, and she agreed to take him along.

Zakho was about the safest place for a Jew in Iraq. It was teeming with U.S. troops and humanitarian workers, protected by coalition fighter jets, and easily escapable via the nearby Turkish border. But as Bruni recalls, my father was still a nervous wreck. "He was frightened of being a Jew and going back after what he signed when he left," she said, referring to the forms the Jews signed in the 1950s renouncing their citizenship and vowing never to return.

I knew that he had hired a local man to work a video camera, and on a visit to Los Angeles in 2005, I suggested we put the recording in the VCR. Together we watched the grainy images of my father wandering the dusty streets of his hometown. He is clutching his briefcase under one arm and a blowup of Ephraim's Iraqi passport photo in the other. A group of children and other onlookers follow him like a comet's tail as he visits houses, churches, and the old synagogue. An elderly man in the market nods, clearly recognizing the picture. The man strokes an imaginary beard, remembering Ephraim's most distinctive feature.

Toward the end of the ten-day visit, a Zakho man invited my father to his son's wedding. The week-long celebration, with music and dancing and piles of fragrant food, makes up the longest part of the video. My father told me it was the only part of his trip that resembled the Zakho of his childhood.

"The father of the groom grabbed me and started to do a very energetic dance. The relatives were really worried, they thought he was going to have a heart attack. But he started shaking me like I was a teenager dancing rock and roll. He said, 'Let everyone here take videos and pictures and send them to Saddam Hussein, and I don't give a shit. I am dancing with my Jewish friend, and I don't care.' Afterward all the relatives invited me to their houses for breakfast and dinner. It was happiness."

Except for an old math teacher, none of the people he remembered was alive. The Habur River wasn't the raging serpent of his memory, but a small, weak stream. The boisterous Jewish neighborhood of his youth was now a slum, with sewage trickling through the alleys. The biggest Jewish house, which had belonged to the community leader, Moshe Gabbay, was in ruins. Squatters were living in the synagogues, and the old rooms were redolent of human waste.

Strangers came to visit him every day in the Kurdish Democratic Party's guest quarters. One man asked if my father could help his son get into an engineering school in the United States. Another said he had invented a fuel-efficient motor and wondered if the Americans would be interested. The requests moved my father. Saddam's dictatorship had crushed so many ambitions. But now, under U.S. protection and the beginnings of semiautonomy, young Kurds were letting themselves dream again.

In quieter moments, he thought about his older sister, Rifqa. In the streets he studied the faces of women his age. He looked for a family resemblance and saw only strangeness. Too much time had passed, he told himself.

Clicking off the VCR, I asked whether the visit had lived up to his expectations.

He looked down and drew one of his ragged breaths. "You have certain hopes," he began, the subject making him visibly uncomfortable. "You do this as a nostalgic trip, and nostalgia is you feel like you will see a place again. And when you see nothing is left, it's in a way a comment on life itself. You see that life doesn't stand still. Nothing waits for you to visit it again. The river keeps flowing. It may be smaller. But still it flows. And with it your life flows by. This is what life basically is."

We made tea, and I asked if he remembered his feelings in the taxi ride back to the airport in Turkey. "I felt that the Zakho I had in my mind was gone," he said. "Now I have a new Zakho that has replaced the older one, and the new one doesn't attract me like the old one did. Maybe in a way it erased the old one.

"I was not interested anymore in going back."

TWELVE YEARS AFTER that trip, I was sitting with my father at his favorite spot in the Century City outdoor mall in Los Angeles: the metal tables near Kelly's Coffee & Fudge Factory, where every afternoon found him sipping an ice-blended mocha and reading some tome on ancient languages.

"Abba?"

"Yes," he said, looking up from his book.

"If I went to Zakho, would you come with me?"

53 ❖ Time Travel

When I was a boy, Zakho was a nonsense word. It sounded dimly exotic but carried no more freight than words like Snuffleupagus or -expialodocious. When my father said he was born in Zakho, I could no sooner point to it on a map than I could Oz or Brobdingnag. It meant only that he was from some faraway place, a magical village, perhaps, like the ones in story books. Z was the last letter of the alphabet; so Zakho must be the farthest-away town on Earth, the last stop before you stepped off into space.

Now, though, I was handing my father what I thought was a gift: the chance to make Zakho real. We could repair our relationship over cups of cardamom tea at cafés by the Habur River. We could walk together through the streets of the old Jewish neighborhood, summoning the spirits of our ancestors. Though I didn't tell him right away, I even had plans to search for his kidnapped sister, Rifqa.

He would at last see me for the better son I felt I had become. I would see him as the father I never knew: the intrepid son of hard-luck parents who leaped borders and defied every expectation for a Kurdish Jew of his era. In Zakho, I would find the dashing alter ego of the cautious scholar I'd grown up with in the American suburbs. I would find a man, that is, more like me. I'd find a father I never had.

If my father shared any such hopes, he didn't let on. "We're not going to Iraq," he said, peremptorily. First, the Zakho of his day was gone. No Jews were left and few of the old buildings stood. As far as the family's story was concerned there was nothing to see. Second, I could get a fine picture of the city from interviews with Kurdish Jews in Israel and from the video of his 1992 visit. Third, the height of the Iraqi insurgency against the American occupation wasn't necessarily the ideal time for a sentimental journey by two American Jews, one of whose names bore an unfortunate similarity to that of Ariel Sharon, then the prime minister of Israel. The summer of 2005 was shaping up as one of the insurgency's bloodiest stretches; four hundred people were killed over a single two-week period. Around the same time, tensions between soldiers and Kurdish rebels in southeastern Turkey were escalating. Eight people were killed in clashes and landmine explosions in the very region we'd have to drive through on our way to Iraq's northern border. I pleaded. He resisted. Eventually he broke down. He said that if I accompanied him to a linguistic conference in England in July, maybe we could continue on to Iraq from there.

"It will be perfect, Abba," I said, seeing a poetic arc to the itinerary. We would travel from Aramaic's present, as a subject dissected in the antiseptic halls of a university, to its past in the wild foothills of Iraqi Kurdistan.

THE NORTHEASTERN NEO-ARAMAIC Workshop unfolded over two July days in a modern glass-walled lecture room at Cambridge University. The conference was a milestone in the life of a young discipline. When my father started his research, Neo-Aramaic didn't rate so much as a mention at leading conferences on Near Eastern languages. Over the decades, in no small part because of his efforts, it had gotten a toehold. The big annual conferences on Semitic languages began to devote special subsections to the field. The Cambridge event was notable as the first conference to focus exclusively on Neo-Aramaic, treating it as a stand-alone subject rather than a curious footnote to the older, dead forms of Aramaic. And it was happening, not in some intellectual backwater, but at one of the world's most hallowed academic institutions, the one-time home of Sir Isaac Newton, Charles Darwin, and Alfred Tennyson.

Over the next two days, nine scholars and four graduate students sat around wooden tables and presented research findings in various Neo-Aramaic dialects. By the end of the first day, my head was swimming with terms like *interdental fricative, vowel harmony,* and *ergative present tense.* My ears jangled with phrases like *possessive pronominal suffixes, clefting of interrogative pronouns,* and *BGDKPT consonants.*

The knockout punch came from Professor Geoffrey Khan, the Cambridge professor who organized the conference. "A fricative partially assimilated to a lateral results in a stop," he announced one afternoon. The other scholars nodded in solemn agreement.

As the conference ground on, I realized that for much of the last year I had gotten something wrong. My father's work, with its focus on folk tales, biblical legends, and yarns of master storytellers, had given me a distorted view of the field. I had assumed that the study of Neo-Aramaic could not be separated from the stories of its speakers. I realized now that that was true only for my father. For most of the others in the room, Neo-Aramaic was an object of dispassionate study. Their papers concerned a language, not its speakers; they were an arid description of symptoms, not a study of the patient or his family history or his village or his values. On the most basic level, the men and women in that conference room were scientists. They were dusting off and cataloging the remains of a dying language with the detachment and precision of a medical examiner at an autopsy.

At about noon on the second day, Khan summoned Professor Yona Sabar to the head of the table. In his geometric-patterned short-sleeved shirt and striped windbreaker, my father looked more like a lost tourist than an academic. Still, when he began to speak, the scholars leaned forward in their chairs. His presentation tried to explain why different Neo-Aramaic speakers had translated the Bible's Five Scrolls in different ways. Some had spiced their translations with anachronistic references to the state of Israel or to terrorists. One translator had thrown in a gratuitous

mention of prostitutes. Another began with a straightforward translation from the Book of Ecclesiastes, "And a wise woman among all these I
did not find," and then tossed in an editorial aside of his own invention:
"woman — she is long on braids, but short on brains."

"What motivates translators to deviate from the manuscript?" he asked
at one point.

My father slapped the table to punctuate points. He raised his voice.
He made goofy analogies ("the horse's name, Shapargaz, means 'wings,'
so he must have been fast, like today we have a jet plane") and managed
to work in a couple of saucy asides ("the woman in Ruth is described as
'very attractive and beautiful' — very sexy, in modern English, I would
say.")

Before long, the scholars were laughing, glad for some levity in an otherwise dry-as-a-salt-bed conference. I sat up, too, and not just because it
was my father's turn in the spotlight. This was the only talk in which I
could hear — and almost see — the people behind the words.

That afternoon bombs went off on three crowded subway trains and
and a bus 60 miles to the south, in London, killing more than fifty people. The news, delivered by cell phone to one of the scholars, cast a pall
over the room. During the afternoon coffee break, Eran Cohen, a young
Hebrew University professor with chiseled features and a shaved head,
walked over. "Are you still going to take your father to Zakho?"

Yes, I told him, trying to sound more confident than I felt.

"You could easily go back to America. It's just the other way."

"I know."

"The reason this dialect continues is your father," Cohen said. "He did
most of the work. Just bring him back. We need him."

"You know," I said, looking him squarely in his eyes, "what happened
today shows that no place is safe. Kurdistan could turn out to be safer
than London."

He must have picked up on the breathlessness in my voice. "You don't
have to justify it to me," he said.

"Maybe I'm trying to justify it to myself," I said, looking away.

Later that day Cohen gave the conference's last talk and also its most technical. Its title was "Information Structure in Jewish Zakho." Cohen had told me the night before that he was seeking to explain the Zakho dialect, my father's mother tongue, with "algorithms." A language was a kind of mathematical enigma; Cohen was perfecting a solution.

Bars of afternoon sunlight slanted through the conference room windows as Cohen passed around a handout titled "Syntactic Focus Markings in Jewish Zakho." Beside a series of charts, the page contained a laundry list of phrases in which the speaker orders his or her words in a way that underscores one element of the sentence.

As I read down the list, a few of the phrases struck me as unnervingly familiar:

"Just before him, another son had also died."

"They were Arabs who had nursed her."

"It is this one, the one who was born at Eliahu's wedding."

They were phrases from my grandmother's account of her twelve pregnancies, the oral history my father recorded some two decades ago and had recently transcribed and published as an article in a linguistics journal. I had read the transcript many times while stitching together the family's story. But the phrases looked strange on Cohen's handout, stripped of context and set in neat margins. A moment of annoyance gave way almost instantly to pride, and then to sadness. My grandmother, illiterate and self-effacing, never thought she had much to contribute to the world; she often felt she had failed her own family. Yet here a group of prominent linguists were turning to her simple words to push the boundaries of knowledge. Yes, it was pride I felt: pride in being her grandson. And sadness, that she would never know the gifts she had left the world.

As we were leaving the room at the end of the day, my father spotted Cohen smoking a cigarette outside the door.

"If my mother were alive and I told her that someone had quoted her," my father told Cohen, "you would be invited to eat hamusta at her house for the rest of your life."

The next day my father and I were on a plane to southeastern Turkey.

54 ✦ Habur

Israeli?"

The taxi drivers on the sidewalk outside the airport in Diyarbakir formed a semicircle around my father, and one of them, a tree stump of a man with a bushy mustache, stepped up and faced him almost toe to toe.

"Israeli?" he asked again.

My father was wearing loose-fitting carob-colored pants, an off-white short-sleeved shirt with raised chalk stripes, and brown shoes. Were it not for the leather pocket protector stuffed with pens and paper scraps, he might readily pass unnoticed in this sprawling Kurdish city in impoverished southeastern Turkey.

An Israeli acquaintance of my father's had been leading occasional tours of Zakho for Israeli Kurds for several years. Before we left, the man had recommended we get in touch with a taxi driver named Hassan, who had shuttled visiting Jewish Kurds from Diyarbakir to the Iraqi border for several years now without incident.

We had called Hassan the night before from our hotel in Istanbul. But my father had forgotten to ask any of the practical questions about where we should meet or what Hassan looked like. As we emerged from the small airport into the blazing mid-morning heat, he began asking every taxi driver he saw whether he was Hassan. Hassan's reputation as a driver of Israelis appeared to be no secret to the other cabbies jockeying for business. My father's request for him in rusty Kurdish must have been a giveaway.

"Israeli?" the man asked.

I was getting nervous. I waited for what seemed like a half minute for the reply. For months my father had worried about just such an encounter: someone exposing him as Jewish, or worse, Israeli, with potentially dire consequences. My father broke eye contact with the taxi man and looked down, shaking his head and sucking air through his teeth in a Middle Eastern signal for "no." There was a brief, charged silence in the arid hundred-degree heat. Then, like a bear crashing through a stand of trees, a barrel-chested giant with caramel-brown skin pushed past the other drivers and extended a beefy hand and a smile: Hassan.

We had scarcely left the outer slums of Diyarbakir for the countryside of cotton fields and watermelon groves when Hassan, a Kurdish Muslim, was slapping my father on the thigh as though they were old friends.

"The Jews lived among us and were good people," Hassan began, in Kurdish. "All of us — Muslims, Jews, Christians — lived together in peace, in harmony. Then the Jews went away. They left for Paradise. God be with them."

Hassan's driving made me wonder whether we might wind up in Paradise with them. The man (though he said he had six children) was a speed junkie, veering across the center line to pass slower cars and playing games of chicken with oncoming oil trucks. Flying road debris had honeycombed his windshield in hairline cracks. We drove south for four hours.

An air of Wild West lawlessness hung over the Habur border crossing.

Dozens of horn-happy taxi drivers bolted from their vehicles onto a broad street of unventilated offices staffed by short-fused Turkish police officers. Hassan handed us off to another cabbie, Tariq, a wiry young man with a special license to carry passengers into Iraq. Tariq grabbed our passports, wrote some numbers in a ledger, and led us to a small, airless office where a throng of taxi drivers pressed against a thick glass window for passport stamps. It was the hottest part of the afternoon, and I had to step outside to breathe. A torrid wind was scattering empty water bottles across the pavement. Knots of men squatted in languid poses against the walls, clicking prayer beads. Boys hawked warm soda from plastic buckets. I tried to sit on the curb, but the pavement burned and I sprang to my feet.

Two hours passed without progress. Tariq tried a small bribe, then a plea for pity. His fare, he told the police, was a distinguished American professor who was feeling unwell. "Please, let us get our stamps so we can get him someplace where he can rest."

A uniformed official behind the window shot out of his seat, gesturing angrily and shouting.

"What did that guy just tell Tariq?" I asked my father, my heart thumping.

"Emm," my father said, clearing his throat. "He said, 'I don't give a shit who that old man is or where he's from. He can stay in his seat and wait for his God-damned number, or he can go to hell.' Then he told Tariq to go away."

I looked at the sweat gathering at my father's temples and the way he clutched his briefcase to his chest like armor, and wondered whether the trip had been a mistake. He was nearing retirement and living a life of simple California comforts. What was I doing dragging him halfway across the world, to the edge of a war zone? The next hour saw no break in the heat. I began to despair of many things, not least ever getting across that border.

Then, all of a sudden, Tariq broke free from the scrum, grinning, our stamped passports in hand. A minute later I was looking out the cab window at a high concrete arch bearing words I thought I'd never see: WELCOME TO KURDISTAN OF IRAQ.

55 ◦ Kiss the Eyes of Your Sons

In the months before the trip, while ironing out our itinerary, I had thought it wise to let someone in Zakho know we were coming: someone we could trust, who could meet us at the border and take us under their wing. As safe as Kurdistan was said to be, we would still be in Iraq and we were still Americans, still Jews. But who? My father had told me that most of the people he had met on his 1992 visit had died or left. The others, he had no idea how to reach. At my parents' house in Los Angeles, I rummaged through a file of my father's papers from the trip. Amid various travel documents and news clippings, I found two handwritten letters in English from a man named Suleiman, of the Kurdistan Democratic Party's Zakho Public Relations Office.

"I like to write to you because we Kurds love you and your nation," a letter from December 1993 began. "We respect and love your feelings, we love Jews, because they hate Saddam and love Kurds." After incongruously wishing my father a Merry Christmas, Suleiman wrote, "I kiss your eyes and your mother's hand. I kiss the eyes of your sons." He asked for family photos and invited my father to return to Zakho anytime and stay with his family for a week. Tucked behind this was another letter, dated three months later. "My dearest brother Prof. Yona," it began, and repeated the invitation, this time asking that Yona's entire family stay with him as long as we wished. "Tell them that Suleiman is their uncle for ever." He ended with a request that my father "write for me continuously."

I wasn't sure how I felt about this business of eye kissing. But if Suleiman was still around, I thought he might be of some help. I carried the letters downstairs to the kitchen table, where my father was eating lunch with the TV on. "Who is this guy?" I asked.

My father said he had been one of the guides in 1992, a party worker charged with squiring foreign visitors around Zakho.

"He was the one who figured out I was Jewish," my father said.

"You mean you didn't tell anyone?"

He said he was too unsure of how the Kurds would greet the news and even asked to be taken to a church his first day to dispel suspicions. He kept thinking of his grandfather Ephraim's words: Keep your head down. But Suleiman had been a shrewd enough student of Zakho history to suss out the truth.

"By the way, Yona, we know that you are Jewish," Suleiman announced over dinner one night at a crowded Zakho restaurant.

"I was very afraid," my father recalled.

"So what did he do next?" I asked.

"He hugged me," my father said.

FROM SULEIMAN'S GRANDIOSE PROSE, I had pictured a jolly giant in flowing robes, coiled headdress, and Rip Van Winkle beard—someone not unlike my great-grandfather Ephraim. But the man waiting outside the KDP public relations office in the summer of 2005 when our taxi pulled up looked more like a small-town American school-teacher. He stood perhaps five feet five inches tall, with short, square-cut salt-and-pepper hair and a proud posture, and wore a short-sleeved dress shirt that looked like it came off the rack at Sears. I would have never picked him out had he not waved when my father and I pushed open the taxi door.

When I felt the pebbles of Zakho crunching underfoot, I was so fool-ishly giddy that I was afraid I'd never pry the smile from my face. I walked over to Suleiman, threw my arms around him, and squeezed, as though he really were my uncle.

"Thank you, thank you, thank you," I said. I inhaled the heat and dust of Zakho until I felt lightheaded. Suleiman kissed me on one check, then the other, then back on the first. He didn't kiss my eyes, but it would have been okay if he had.

"You are welcome," he said, and gestured toward the city crouching in the haze at the foot of the mountains. "This place is for you. You are now in your father's town." Suleiman was in fact a teacher. He taught English at a local primary school, and his speech had the decorous cadences of someone who rarely spoke or heard the language outside a classroom.

He tossed our bags into the back of his pickup, and off we drove down Ibrahim Khalil Road, the dusty highway into Zakho, a few miles to the south. We passed construction crews turning vacant stretches of land into rows of new office and apartment buildings. BMWs and Mercedeses lined up with lesser vehicles at a gleaming new Iraq Oil gas station complete with minimart. Then, on the bridge into Zakho proper, we hit traffic. Per-haps naïvely, I had expected a main drag of flyblown market stalls, side-walk cigarette vendors, and kabob stands. But here was an ambitiously modernizing city.

"Abba, were all these little restaurants and hotels here in 1992?" I asked from the backseat.

My father shook his head.

"This is the new Zakho," Suleiman said. "It is developing. Too much."

I saw now that my father had been correct about one thing: This was not the forlorn border outpost his family had fled fifty-four years before.

Not even close. Yet neither was it the depressed and chaotic haven for refugees he had visited thirteen years earalier. The growth in Kurdish autonomy since the Persian Gulf War had remade the city into a boom town, and its population had more than tripled, to 150,000. Just inside the relatively safe border with Turkey, Zakho was now *the* commercial gateway to northern Iraq. Every day thousands of trucks hauling petrol, consumer goods, and, lately, building supplies for Iraq's postwar reconstruction rumbled down its roads. There was so much traffic that a year earlier the city installed its first traffic lights. Suleiman told us that a local military academy, a university campus, factories, and a new hospital were all in the works.

Baghdadis desperate to escape the capital's violence were vacationing in Zakho. Truckers tired after long-hauls from Turkey were staying in a crop of new hotels. New housing developments, with names such as Martyrs and New Martyrs, after Saddam Hussein's Kurdish victims, were stretching across the open fields that once separated Zakho and the Turkish border. Local spring water was now bottled and sold in stores across the region. The windows of a downtown travel agency advertised trips to Norway, Germany, England, Australia, and the United States. A few doors down was an Internet hot spot called Zakho CafeNet.

"Before, it was a sleepy town," Omar Shemdin, the son of the late tribal chieftain Shemdin Agha, the region's most powerful aga in my father's day, told us when we went to see him later in the week. "This border was closed. There was no movement across it, except by smugglers. The road to Ibrahim Khalil" — the highway into Zakho — "was dirt. We used it for picnics. It all changed after the Gulf War. Saddam got isolated, and the Kurds got enterprising."

As we drove in that first day, I despaired of finding any trace of my father's past.

"That was the graveyard of the Jews," Suleiman announced before turning down the street to our hotel.

"Where?" I asked.

He nodded back at the busy four-way intersection. After Iraqi troops crushed a Kurdish rebellion in 1976, he explained, Saddam's steamrollers had come and buried the centuries-old Jewish cemetery under a layer of asphalt.

56 ❧ Turkish Delights or Jordan Almonds

After a late dinner at the hotel restaurant, my father and I headed into the faintly lit streets for a walk. Solitary men were sitting on curbs, the ends of their cigarettes glowing orange against the darkness. Shopkeepers were mopping their stalls. The smell of fresh-baked flatbread from clay ovens mingled with the stench of rotting food someone had dumped in the street. Out of the blackness came the tinkle of indistinct voices, the drone of a faraway car horn, and the rumble of heavy trucks against pavement. As we came to a bridge just beyond the hotel, I heard a flapping sound, like a propeller on a toy airplane, and looked up. Dozens of bats wheeled just overhead, their formless bodies blurring, before diving in a crazed mass into the branches of a tree on the Habur River.

Cocooned in the darkness, my father walked along the bridge and began to lose himself in memory. "Many times in my dreams, I cross this bridge again and am always stopped by a policeman," he said.

"Why does he stop you?" I said.

"He asks me to recite some Koranic verse, and won't let me go until I do," he said.

We turned back and passed a stall where the young Yona Beh Sabagha would buy fistfuls of sweets. As before, his story concerned not a childhood recollection of the place, but a dream in which it figured. "I have dreams, too, Ariel, of the candy store that was right here," he said, pointing to a shop window displaying cell-phone covers in every color of the rainbow. "In these dreams, I have to decide to buy either Jordan almonds or Turkish delights. I only have enough money for one kind. But sometimes, as a compromise, the shopkeeper gives me a little of both."

Dreams, I recalled now, had long been a refuge from his life's incongruities. During his first year in the United States, he once told me, he dreamed he was in New York, all alone in Grand Central Station. All at once, the train doors swept open and all of Zakho's Kurds poured out onto the platforms. Dreams were a place where fragments could be made whole. The Zakho we saw that first day was light-years from the place of his birth. It was bustling, forward-looking, growing, prospering, blazing toward the future. But as my father lay his head on his pillow that night, I felt sure that his dreams would be of the boy who flew across rooftops, fearless and free.

The Jewish neighborhood lay just behind our hotel. There were no more Jews there: All had left, most for Israel, by the early 1950s. (Of Iraq's former Jewish population of 135,000, only a handful had stayed, most of them in Baghdad.) But the people of Zakho still called it the mahala Juheeya. Suleiman led us there on our first morning, descending through a warren of rutted dirt alleys. It was now the city's poorest neighborhood, and in the 105-degree heat, the smells were unforgiving. Pipes poking from the crude concrete houses spewed wastewater into the alleys, washing rotten food and other garbage into the Habur River.

Watching children run barefoot through the muck, I felt a knot in my stomach. But my father was still in his dream state. He stopped with a smile, reached into his vinyl valise, and handed sticks of Wrigley's Doublemint Gum to a growing entourage of children.

"*Chawani Amerikai?*" said a sweetly grinning boy, who slipped onto the dirt road followed by two brown chickens. How are you, American man?

"*Chawani Zakholi?*" my father replied, matching the boy's Kurdish.

The mahala Juheeya was a study in the collision of ancient and modern. On the flat rooftops, gleaming satellite dishes were propped against rusting bed frames. A stooped man thumbing prayer beads wore both traditional Kurdish robes and a foam-panel trucker cap inscribed JESUS LOVES ME. A farmer on his way to market led a single sheep across four lanes of automobile traffic, using a biblical-looking goad to instill courage in the wooly beast. A grizzled codger sold apricots from a crate in front of a European-designer shoe store. Everywhere, the twenty-first century was bumping against the nineteenth, technology against tradition, the world against the village. The twentieth century—with its innovations of plumbing and clean water — seemed to have skipped over it entirely.

In the thirteen years of Kurdish autonomy since the Persian Gulf War, the city had shaken off the remnants of Saddam's regime. The bullet-riddled posters of Hussein that had stared down from buildings during my father's last visit were long gone. The frightened refugees who massed here after that war had integrated into the city or returned to the countryside.

We were trudging up a narrow alley when my father stopped suddenly in front of a concrete house with a small courtyard. "This looks like my family's," he announced.

We introduced ourselves to the owner, Dersim Rezazi, a twenty-four-year-old laborer with a deferential manner, who served us apricot juice. He showed us the main rooms, shooing out his children, who had been sleeping. Rezazi and his brother, a painter, lived there with eight relatives. There was little privacy: four tiny doorless rooms opened onto the courtyard. Most months, the family slept on a row of thin mats along the edges of two bedrooms; in the summer, they slept on a creaky four-poster frame on the roof, just as my father's family had many years before.

But as he looked around, my father said, "Everything has changed."

"Yes," Rezazi told us in Kurdish. "When I came here a few years ago, it was all mud houses. Now most are concrete."

I led my father up a flight of stairs to the flat roof and looked out over the neighborhood, a jumble of unfinished cinderblock walls, corrugated steel roofs, satellite dishes, and laundry lines. I inhaled the balmy air and tried to imagine my father as a boy, taking in the city from this vantage.

"This was definitely your house, right, Abba?" I asked, anxious to record its every detail in my notebook.

"To be honest, Ariel, I can't really be sure," my father said softly. "It was around here somewhere. But was it exactly this one? I don't know."

The bearings of memory, I had begun to see, did not always calibrate with those of the physical world.

We thanked Rezazi and returned to the rutted alleyways. The two synagogues, with their rugged stone walls, still stood, but they were houses now. A cheerful woman in a blue headscarf let us into the so-called Big Synagogue, where she lived with her construction-worker husband and their four children. The mikveh, the ritual bath where my grandmother and the other Jewish women cleansed after their menstrual periods, had been paved over with concrete and turned into a small bedroom with a TV set in the corner. Across the courtyard was the *hekhal*, the holy chamber that had housed the sacred Torah scrolls and the Elijah's chair where Jewish boys were circumcised. Now the hekhal was a storage room. A child's wooden rocker dangled from a hook in the wall. A mud-caked soccer ball lolled on a red lawn chair in a corner.

We looked up at the vaulted ceiling. "From those small windows," my father said, "light came into the synagogue and shined on the Torah scrolls." I thought of my great-grandfather, sitting there all night, with his books and his angels. The window frames, I saw, were still there. But the openings had long since been bricked over, suspending the room in a shadowy half-light.

Around the corner we found the "Small Synagogue." A sullen young woman in a long pink dress answered our knock at the metal gate. I recognized the courtyard, with its leafy fringes and large fig tree, from photographs my father had taken in 1992. In the photos an ancient stone tablet inscribed in Hebrew, a relic from the old temple, was propped against the courtyard wall by a giant Y-shaped tree branch. My father had wanted to show me the tablet up close, with its Hebrew inscription. But as we tramped through wild flowers in the garden, all we could see was that Y-shaped branch, lying on its side and buried in bramble.

My father asked the young woman if she knew what had happened to the tablet. She turned away, mumbling that she did not. My father sighed and squinted into the sun streaming through the fig tree.

A few days later, we found five of the tablets across town at the home of a Muslim family that had lived in the synagogue for three decades before moving out a few years earlier. Lufti Mohammed, the elder son of the late owner, told me the family had pried the three-foot by two-foot tablets from the walls during a remodeling project and set them aside for safekeeping.

"We knew these stones belonged to Jews and might be of interest to people one day," he said, as we ate watermelon in a room off the courtyard. But the mere presence of the slabs in their home terrified them; Saddam, he said, lowering his voice a little, had strong feelings about all things Jewish. Even in postwar 1992, when the family sold the synagogue and moved to a wealthier district, they took precautions. Mohammed said that he and his brothers slipped the Hebrew tablets into sugar sacks before ferrying them by bulldozer to their new house under the cover of darkness. Since then, he said, the family felt sure of an eventual big-money sale to an overseas museum. When I asked to see them, another son, a wild-eyed thirty-three-year-old who told me he had been imprisoned in Texas for stabbing a man in a bar fight, led me to the roof. If the tablets had ever stood a chance of interesting a museum, that time, I saw,

Shattered Hebrew tablet from one of Zakho's synagogues,
Zakho, 2005.

had passed. The heavy stones were stacked liked corpses on a wooden pallet on the rooftop, where sun and rain had worn the raised Hebrew letters into near illegibility.

57 ❖ Heaven Sent

At first glance, Suleiman had little in common with my father. He was born the year the Jews left Zakho, making him a dozen years my father's junior. He had fought Saddam's forces in the 1974 Kurdish uprisings and had twice fled with his family and other refugees to the mountains bordering Turkey. Yet I came to see in him my father's alter ego. He was the man my father would have been had he never left Zakho: educated, multilingual, the faithful and dignified son of humble beginnings on whom local leaders relied to make foreign visitors feel welcome.

Both were born to poorly educated parents and were the first in their family to go to college. Both earned advanced degrees and became teachers: Suleiman had a master's in English from Mosul University and taught at a Zakho school. Both kept a stash of pens and folded papers in their shirt pockets. Both were soft-spoken and respected for their modesty. Both believed, perhaps a little romantically, in the brotherhood of man: the idea that our common humanity trumped divisions of faith and nationality. Maybe it was their slow, soft rhythms of speech, but both also possessed a gift for imbuing routine observations — "everything changes with time," "all we have is family" — with the gravitas of original revelation.

Suleiman refused to take money, except to cover his car expenses, and reminded us daily of the town's respect for its Jews. Though long gone, he said, they still figured in folklore. When a father is trying to teach his son an important moral lesson, Suleiman told us, "the father will say 'From the mouth of a Jew.'"

Over the course of our visit, he and my father took part in a strange one-upmanship over who could say the nicer, more melodramatic thing about the other.

"You have charisma, unlike me," my father said. "I would really appoint you mayor of Zakho right now."

"Ahh, I see, professor," Suleiman said. "Then you, too, are charisma. The man who is handsome and educated, so? And who is for humanity!"

"It is good to have a friend like you," my father said.

"No," Suleiman corrected, with the injured look of a man too proud to accept a title he has not yet earned. "No. You are my teacher. You are my professor."

We moved out of the long shadows of the Jewish neighborhood onto a sun-baked embankment above the river. Down below, a shrouded woman rinsed bales of wool in the green water, and a half dozen young boys shrieked as they bodysurfed in the rapids.

My father stopped to gaze. I strode down the embankment to photograph the swimming boys, who, upon seeing the camera, paddled to the bank, all smiles, to pose. When I climbed back up, my father was still in a reverie. Sixty years ago, that woman washing wool might have been his mother; the boys, Yona Beh Sabagha and his friends.

"I feel like a tree uprooted," my father said, finally turning away from the river and toward Suleiman. "You can plant it somewhere else, but it will never be the same."

The next day a change overtook my father. I had never seen him more childlike. I began to hear something strengthen in his voice, as though the air of Zakho were easier on his lungs, infusing him with a confidence normally beyond reach.

At breakfast in the hotel restaurant, he told me that the *sirtik*, a hard fetalike cheese, was the most delicious cheese he had ever tasted. The tea the waiters served in those hourglass-shaped glasses, you could not get tea like that anywhere else. What did the Zakholis put into it that made it so good? (When I ventured that it might be the three teaspoons of sugar, he said, "No, Ariel, don't be foolish!") And frothy sour yogurt *dow* of this quality could not be found in any Middle Eastern restaurant in the United States, he insisted. "Superdelicious," he proclaimed. The same went for a beef dish stewed in tomatoes and peppers: "This *qaliserke* is just like my mother made," he said, "when I came home on hot days and she wanted to please me."

His English underwent a kind of regression. He forgot words. He reverted to shorter, simpler sentences. His accent thickened. His pronunciation grew mealy ("together" became "togezer"), the way I remembered it from his early days in Los Angeles, before he had stripped off its worst fresh-off-the-boat janglings. I noticed that he was peppering his speech with sound effects: "gish, gish, gish, gish," he said at one point, sounding like a child spraying make-believe bullets from a toy machine gun. The fact that his English could slip so quickly in a place where it wasn't needed made me wonder how hard he fought, day after day, to be understood in the language of his adopted country.

He waved and said "Chawani" to almost anyone, from the teenager who cleaned our room to the people at nearby tables in the hotel restaurant. Gone was the shy foreigner who sweated over every decision to join a colleague at a UCLA lunchtable. In Zakho he was a natural. The rules of social engagement were uncomplicated, and he grew expansive.

His lifelong tendency to play down differences among cultures, religions, nations, and even eras grew more pronounced in Zakho. In conversation after conversation, he repeated the idea that humanity, over continents and across time, stands on common ground. Teenage American girls who wear nose rings as an act of rebellion, he told one Zakho burgher, were in reality no different from their great-great-grandmothers, who no doubt wore similar ornaments in the old country as part of some traditional culture. "There is no such thing as primitive versus modern," he told Omar Shemdin, the Stanford-educated son of Zakho's onetime chieftain, who still spent part of each year in the family's compound here.

Every time a child looked at my father, I saw something inside his chest soften. He rummaged in his valise for Ziplock sandwich bags he had filled with pretzels, honeyed cashews, or almond biscotti. He gave one boy a shrink-wrapped travel toothbrush a flight attendant had given him on the British Airways flight to Istanbul. The children smiled broadly and ran off, as if they couldn't wait to show someone the strange things the *Amerikai* had brought.

I was touched to see my father so happy.

Over the next five days, we crossed the famous Nemo Delale Bridge, met a wizened tailor who remembered my great-grandfather's dye shop, and ate skewers of roasted lamb and chicken kabob in fresh-baked flat-bread. We talked to vendors in the narrow alley where my grandfather and great-grandfather once managed their shops. It was called "The Dark Market," they told me, because the stalls were so close that sunlight had to fight its way in.

"At home," my father told Suleiman when we were riding in his truck one day, "I can hardly walk. Sometimes my back hurts, my feet hurt. Here! Here, all my diseases disappear."

The next afternoon, Suleiman drove us into the hills of wild grains and dry grasses that circle the city like giant sand dunes. We stopped at a lookout spot where people were gathering for a wedding celebration. Suleiman walked over and somehow wrangled us invitations. We took seats outside an elliptical concrete dance floor where a long line of women in shimmering dresses danced with clasped hands in a growing circle. They swayed to traditional Kurdish music booming from a DJ booth. Each dancer looked as if she were holding the reins of a trotting pony, and the circle grew and grew.

On our way back to the truck, we waded into the knee-high grass on the hillside. Zakho unfurled beneath us in the pale evening light: beyond the glinting green ribbon of the Habur the checkerboard of flat-roofed houses melted into dun-colored plains until there was nothing but mountains.

I could see a redness in my father's eyes, and my throat tightened.

"Even in my wildest dreams," he said, speaking more to the city below him than to me, "I couldn't imagine sitting here with my son at this magnificent wedding and looking at Zakho. God from Heaven sent me this."

58 ❖ Chasing Phantoms

The ghost of my father's lost sister had made her first appearance on the flight to Diyarbakir, where we would catch the taxi to Zakho. The plane, crowded with Kurds heading to southeastern Turkey, had yet to pull out of the gate at the Istanbul airport when a baby somewhere behind us let out a sob.

My father was leaning back in his seat, his eyes closed.

"My sister is crying," he murmured.

"Which one?" I replied, softly, in case he was sleep-talking.

"*The* one," he said, his eyes still closed.

What we didn't know then was just how much Rifqa would haunt us in the months to come.

Rifqa, the kidnapped sister, my grandmother's firstborn. Unable to nurse, Miryam, then just fifteen, had given the spindly-legged newborn in the 1930s to an Arab wet nurse, who disappeared with the girl. Miryam never forgave herself.

"How she cried," my grandmother's sister in-law and longtime confidant, Naima, recalled when I visited her in Katamonim in 2005. "She almost killed herself. She was for a long time in a deep sorrow."

A few days before our departure for Iraq, I told my father that I wanted to try to find Rifqa, or at the very least learn the true facts of her disappearance. In the oral history my father recorded some two decades earlier, Miryam had left some tantalizing clues. The wet nurse's name was Gamra, she had said, and her husband was called Hsen. She even named the place Gamra lived: Tusani. My father had never heard of it, and the name was not on any of my maps of Kurdistan. But in a highly detailed 1921 British military map I found at the Library of Congress, there was a village perhaps twenty miles southwest of Zakho with an uncannily similar name: Tusan. It stood on the Syrian border, hard by the Tigris River.

The location was a good match: My grandmother had spoken of Gamra's taking Rifqa there by raft.

Rifqa was family, I told my father before our trip. Why not just ask a few questions? If there was the slightest chance she was still alive, didn't we owe it to my grandmother's memory to find out? I had landed enough scoops as a journalist to know that mysteries could sometimes be unraveled with a few simple questions posed to the right people.

My father sucked in one of those quavering breaths but could not bring himself to argue.

Suleiman took an avid interest in the story. Yes, he had heard of Tusani. He had never been there but knew it was a tiny farming village, not far from Zakho. (The name on the British map may have been missing a letter, but, yes, he said, it was the right place.) He told us that some Tusani farmers had fled the village after Saddam bombed the area in the mid-1970s. One, Hajji Nashwan, a seventy-six-year-old sharecropper who had farmed wheat and barley in Tusani for decades, was a next-door neighbor. Suleiman took us to see him.

Nashwan was a hulking man with sunken green eyes, a loose-fitting tribal robe, and a checked headdress. He motioned us toward a set of sitting mats. I saw no sign of comprehension as Suleiman told the story of Rifqa. But then, casually, Nashwan said, "There was a story of a small Jewish girl growing up in a tribe." It was a long time ago, he said. The girl, he had heard, was raised by Za'azza, a subset of the Sherabi tribe, Arab nomads who had farmed Tusani for as long as anyone could remember. "The girl with them, they said she was a Jew," he said. Flies flitted across the room. A ceiling fan rattled. Nashwan pulled his thick legs under him, like an old tiger who had lost the fire for the hunt.

How old were you when you heard the story? I asked.

Six or seven.

And when were you born?

In 1929.

I did the math: He had heard the story in 1935 or 1936. My heart started to race. We had not mentioned that Rifqa was born in 1936.

I looked at my father in disbelief. But his face betrayed no astonishment. My father, to my amazement, had already changed the subject.

He and Nashwan were now chatting about all the Jews Nashwan used to trade with, and Nashwan was urging my father to invite all his old friends to visit. He began ticking off a list of names of Jews he had remembered. "Ibrahim, Moshe, Eliyahu, Murdakh . . ."

I waited, squirming. And then I turned sharply to my father. I said I wanted to ask more questions about the Jewish girl. My father shot me a peremptory look, as if to say we had troubled the old man enough. But I persisted. Please ask him what else he remembers about the girl, I said. He relented, but Nashwan shrugged, turning his palms up.

"If she were alive, people would have kept talking about her," Nashwan said. "I heard the story once as a boy and never heard it again."

He must have noticed my disappointment. "Maybe she's alive," he said, stretching his feet. "But I don't know."

He told us to go see an elderly Za'azza tribeswoman in Zakho named Dhakiyah.

We found Dhakiyah living with her daughters and grandchildren in a ramshackle house at the edge of town. Chickens waddled across the cement courtyard, and a solitary cow eyed us from behind a metal gate. Dhakiyah, a stout woman, wore a long black headdress that wrapped under her chin and flared across her violet dress. Her forehead and chin were inked with faded blue tribal markings. Suleiman had told us that her husband and son had fought for Kurdish rights. Both had been locked up in Saddam's prisons, where they had been tortured, then killed. An air of grief seemed to hang over the house, laying deep creases under Dhakiyah's eyes.

My father explained the reason for our visit, and Dhakiyah and her daughters greeted each tragic turn in Rifqa's story with a click of the tongue.

"I don't know anything about *that* story," Dhakiyah said. But she said there were stories of Arab tribes absconding with Kurdish babies, including her own mother. Dhakiyah said that her grandmother, who lived just over the border in Sirnak, Turkey, had grown so ill that she could no longer care for Dhakiyah's mother. So she asked the Sherabi nomads, who worked in the nearby fields, to raise her. The grandmother soon died, and the nomads kept any knowledge of the daughter's roots from her. "The tribespeople said to her, 'You have no origin, because no one knows where you came from,'" Dhakiyah said, her voice low and harsh. Relatives came looking for Dhakiyah's mother a few years later. But the tribal leaders lied and told them she was dead. Dhakiyah's mother married within the tribe and had children, including Dhakiyah. Then, one day, Dhakiyah's granduncles set out for the tribal lands in a final search. Since there was no risk now of her desertion, the leaders acknowledged that a tribeswoman was the men's long-lost niece. Dhakiyah's mother was a grown woman with many children when she finally learned who she was: not a "girl of no origin," as she had been told many years before, but the descendant of a Kurdish nobleman in Turkey known as the Red Agha.

You're sure you haven't heard any similar stories about a Jewish girl? I asked, through Suleiman.

Dhakiyah clicked her tongue and twisted her face into a grimace. "If she were alive, people would have talked about it," she said, echoing Nashwan.

Even so, my head swam. The Sherabi had nursed a Kurdish baby and then lied to her relatives about her death. There was precedent. It was at least possible that Rifqa was alive.

The next day brought new leads. A cheese merchant named Wahab Mustafa, or simply Wahab Paneeri, Wahab the Cheese Man, had regular dealings with the Sherabi from Mosul. Suleiman told us that tribeswomen visited Wahab every week to sell him *lareek*, a kind of creamy cottage cheese.

When we found Wahab in his shop on Zakho's main street one afternoon, he was slicing a watermelon-size hunk of white cheese into quarters and haggling with customers over prices. Nearly sixty years old, he had cerulean blue eyes, tea-dark skin, and spoke in a hoarse shout, like a high-school football coach through a bullhorn.

"The Sherabi are my friends," he said, between serving customers.

Had he ever heard of a Gamra and Hsen? we asked.

Yes, he said. They raised buffalos down in Badusha, a rural district near Mosul. Gamra used to come to sell him kaimach, thick sheets of sour cheese made from buffalo milk. But she had not been around in a while. "If she is still alive, she would be around ninety," he said. The age fit, I thought.

Did he know anything more? Was she still alive? Did they have a daughter named Rifqa, who might have been Jewish? "I will check," he said, turning to help another influx of customers, "but you will have to be patient."

59 ❖ A Disaster, God Forbid

The next morning we set out for Tusani. We climbed into Suleiman's truck and rolled into the blast-furnace heat. Zakho disappeared in the dust, and we were soon alone on a narrow two-lane highway. High mountains flecked with trees rose on our left. Out the other window, I could make out the switchbacks of the Habur River. I imagined Gamra floating down it on a raft nearly seventy years ago, baby Rifqa asleep in her lap. If we followed the river, I thought, we, too, would get to Tusani. But it soon became clear that Suleiman was lost. At a military checkpoint he asked a soldier for directions. The soldier, with a machine gun across his chest, gave a shrug and a noncommittal point, as though he could be sure only of the general direction. We passed huts, women beating wool, barefoot boys running through ramshackle Yezidi and Christian villages, flocks of sheep grazing on rocky soil, rusting piles of military scrap.

Suleiman saw a couple of pedestrians and stopped again to ask for help.

My father was getting antsy. "You see, even Suleiman, a native, isn't sure how to get there. Can you imagine how scary it would have been for my father? This was the end of the world."

Wherever we were was clearly not Zakho. There were no landmarks, no signs, just a few tumbledown mud huts scattered at random intervals down the road. My grandfather came to this no-man's-land by donkey in the middle of winter, and I was starting to get a picture of how frightening the journey must have been.

"Okay," Suleiman said, sliding back into the driver's seat. "They say the area is nearby. And safe. This is good, because I left my pistol at home."

Suleiman turned right, onto an unmarked dirt road strewn with melon-size rocks. We were tossed about in our seats as the truck lurched toward the Tigris, passing rolling fields of wild grains and sunflowers. Suleiman's air conditioner was useless against the heat. I felt faint for a moment when he stopped suddenly at a fork in the road. Dust swirled around the pickup, obscuring our view.

Then we saw a cluster of indistinct objects on the muddy plain just above the riverbank. I thought it might be a mirage: From a distance they looked like bales of hay. But as we drove closer the image resolved: a small, low-lying encampment of mud-brick and cinderblock huts.

Tusani. We were probably approaching through the very pastures my grandmother had described to my father, the ones where Gamra had said they would find her those many years ago: "Just ask at Tusani. . . . As soon as you enter the village, I am right at the beginning. Yes, indeed."

A tall farmer with a mustache and movie-star looks was at work behind one of the first huts. He started at the sight of our pickup. Tusani, it seemed, was not a place accustomed to visitors. Suleiman waved and asked for the village chief. The farmer — his name was Lubayd Tusani — slid in beside me in the backseat and directed us toward a set of huts around a dirt courtyard. The whole place looked deserted. Rusting barbed wire enclosed empty coops. The openings of the huts were obscured in shadow.

Lubayd led us into a hut at the center of the courtyard. As our eyes adjusted to the darkness, we saw a slight man with gnarled hands, a stoop, and a deeply lined face. Alim Ya'qub Tusani, born in 1927, was introduced to us as the village elder. Suleiman exchanged a few words with him in Kurdish. Alim smiled, revealing a row of missing front teeth, and commanded his wife to bring a tray of fresh-cut watermelon.

"Jews!" Alim said. His eyes glowed like a child's before a jar of jelly beans. He was beside himself. The village, he told us, once traded briskly with the Jews of Zakho, and he ticked off a roster of the best-known Jewish peddlers. They had come by raft or donkey to sell clothes, sweets, tea, and buttons, and left with bundles of wool from Tusani's vast flocks. The Jews stayed as long as two weeks, negotiating deals by day and singing Kurdish folksongs with the villagers into the night.

Alim's voice softened a little as he recalled their abrupt departure in the early 1950s. The Iraqi authorities had barred Jews from taking money or gold out of the country, though rules on clothes and textiles were less strict. So several Jews came to Tusani and spent every last dinar on wool. The villagers so pitied the departing Jews, Alim said, that after the last scrap of fresh wool was gone, they cut open their pillows and sold off the wool stuffing.

The village had gone downhill since, he said. The forty huts that hugged the banks in the early 1950s had dwindled to six. Saddam's war planes had bombed the village in 1963, indiscriminately attacking ordinary Kurds in hopes of suppressing the Kurdish Democratic Party's campaign for self-rule. Alim's brother and his family were killed, and other families fled to the cities. Nowadays, many of the young saw no future in sheep farming and were seeking their fortunes elsewhere.

"We and the Jews were loving each other," Alim said at last, in Suleiman's rudimentary translation. "We were blood brothers."

I asked whether any Jews had returned to the village since the exodus. "You are the first," he said.

As he sat barefoot and cross-legged in his brick hut, Alim had been opening and closing a jackknife and running his finger over the glinting blade. He raised it suddenly to his throat, and made a slicing motion. I felt my body clench, until my father explained that this was his way of asking us to lunch. "He wants to slice a sheep's throat and roast us some mutton," my father explained.

My father declined the offer, with many thanks, and we then told Alim why we had come. Alim nodded solemnly as we spoke of Rifqa. It was noon, and the midday heat turned the brick room into a kiln. A man I hadn't seen before strode in waving a piece of cardboard and signaled that I should fan myself. Through the door frame, I watched a brown chicken peck at the parched earth.

When I turned back, I saw an uncomprehending look on Alim's face. "I do not know this Gamra or her husband," he said at last. "I am sorry."

Then Lubayd, the farmer who had met us at the entrance to the village, looked at my father suddenly and spoke. "I know the family," he said. I shot my father a look.

There were a number of Gamras and Hsens among the Arab tribes who worked in Tusani, he said; they were common names. But there was only one couple. They were members of the Za'azza tribe, and left Tusani after Saddam bombed the northern villages in 1976. The nomads went south to the safety of Mosul, a predominantly Sunni Arab city; most settled in a neighborhood near Nebi Yunis, the Shrine of Jonah, the very place my grandmother had gone after Rifqa's disappearance to repent and pray for a healthy boy she promised to name Yona. Lubayd said he moved to Mosul in the 1970s and lived next door to them for ten years. As far as he knew, he said, they were still there. For many years they came to a cheese shop across from our hotel to sell kaimach. He knew nothing about a Jewish girl—he was born in 1963, nearly three decades after Rifqa. But the couple had raised seven or eight children, some about my father's age now.

Lubayd took a cigarette from a pack of Miamis and raised a match to it. "Maybe when it's safe in Mosul, I can go to the house of Gamra and ask for you," he said. But not now, he said. Sunni Arabs were the majority, and many were loyal to the former regime of Saddam Hussein. The day before, he added, a Kurdish friend's throat was cut by insurgents. "In Mosul, there is no difference between Kurds and Jews," Lubayd said, exhaling a rope of smoke. "They say killing a Kurd is like killing a Jew."

I had read the news reports. Mosul was Iraq's second-largest city and a northern node of the Sunni-led insurgency. A few months earlier, insurgents had seized parts of the city, attacking bridges and scaring most of the five thousand police officers into desertion. Abu Musab al-Zarqawi, the Jordanian-born leader of Al Qaeda in Iraq, who was thought to operate there, had recently claimed responsibility for killing Iraqi soldiers and a Kurdish militiaman. The bodies of dozens of young men, with execution-style bullet wounds through the head, were turning up across the city. I was aware of the danger. But what if we found her? *What if?*

"Let's go to Mosul, Abba," I said, turning to my father. "We have to."

My father's look was one of utter disbelief, as though shocked that any of his offspring could propose something so preposterous. "I don't want to go, and I don't need to go," my father snapped. "If you mention it again, I'll really think you're crazy."

"I know there are risks," I said. "But we have a duty as family to do this. For your mother's sake. For Rifqa's sake. What if she's still alive?"

The heat was sapping my father's strength and he just shook his head.

"What good would it do to find out now?" he said to me. "This is the past. It's better sometimes not to know."

As we left Tusani's rolling pastures for the paved road back to Zakho, I started to see the parallels with my grandfather and his cousin's search for Rifqa nearly seven decades earlier: Two male relatives make a long and perilous journey in hopes of discovering, if not her, then at least the truth about her disappearance. They stumble on some compelling leads. But just as in the 1930s, a villager warns them it is not safe for Jews to travel further. And just like my grandfather and his cousin, they turn back. I remembered my grandmother's voice, telling my father the story of Rifqa in that recording some twenty years earlier:

That year [1936] was when the Palestine issue became known, or something like that. Murdakh said to your father, "Well then, let us go up further to search in the pasture." Your father said to himself, "I am afraid that a disaster, God forbid, may happen. . . . Somebody might kill us somewhere." People would say, Because of their tiny little thumb girl — that would be her name until she would grow up — they caused the death of a great man, actually two men. So your father said to himself, "Let me get up and take this kind fellow and go back to our own home, before anything bad happens."

Murdakh said, "My dear Kinsman, I do not want to be embarrassed before my uncle Ephraim. I want to do our duty, and find this girl wherever she may be, even if we have to turn over every stone." Your father said to him, "Murdakh, we shall go home. The world is not well. As for the girl, well, the girl has gone away. It was not our luck to have her."

In our room back at the hotel, I resolved that the family would not turn its back on Rifqa a second time. My father made clear that I was on my own. If I wanted to track these leads to their conclusion, if I wanted to risk my life for a little thumb girl whose bones were no doubt buried in the very pastures we had just left, I would have to go it alone. That night we sat down to a silent dinner of kubeh at the restaurant of the Jamal

Tourism Hotel. We were scheduled to return home the next day, and I wanted us to get back on the right track. I wanted us to feel good again about this father-son journey.

But Rifqa had driven a wedge between us.

60 ❧ Kind of a Problem

In Maine the leaves turned yellow and russet, then tumbled to the ground in brittle heaps. I couldn't stop thinking about Rifqa. I imagined her tending buffalo in a pasture outside Mosul, a lonely figure with gray-streaked hair, casting lonely eyes north toward Zakho. I wondered how much she knew of the circumstances of her abandonment. I wondered if Gamra had ever told her the truth. If she had, how had Rifqa reacted? In the weeks and months after our return from Iraq, finding the truth had come to seem essential.

In retrospect, a kind of monomania had set in. I began to feel that my very identity hinged on finding her. My identity as a son who had at last cared about his past. My identity as a journalist able to pin down any story. Turning up Rifqa would be the ultimate "get," news-business speak for a career-making scoop. But this "get" was personal. On some level, I felt that if I could find my lost aunt — breathing proof that our past still lived in Kurdistan — it would wipe clean my failings. As a son. And as a Jew.

On days when my father tried to talk me out of a return trip, I sometimes wondered why I had bothered to find common cause with him. His lack of interest in his sister's fate seemed callous and hypocritical. I could excuse my grandfather's complacency that the past was unrecoverable, that it was wiser to move forward; Rahamim was a product of his time. But my father had staked his career on a belief in the past's value. His Aramaic scholarship was rooted in the principle that a dying society was duty bound to make a record of its history and culture, even if the rest of the world shrugged. If this was true for a lost language, shouldn't it also hold for a lost sister?

When my father visited Zakho in 1992, his search for Rifqa had consisted of cursory glances at the faces of women in the street. He hadn't asked questions. He hadn't gone to Tusani; he hadn't even realized it was a real village. "Each time I saw a woman about my age," he recounted in UCLA's Jewish news magazine after the 1992 trip, "I looked at her face, wondering if she might be my lost sister. But, alas, I did not find her. She had become an inseparable part of the land of Kurdistan and a symbol of the Jewish presence there."

As I saw it then, he gave up without even trying. He was a half hour from where she was last seen, but, just like that, he wrote her off as a symbol. To my savta Miryam, Rifqa couldn't have been more real: a reminder for the rest of her life of what she saw as her inadequacy as a mother. To the children who came after, however, Rifqa was something more ethereal, a character in a curious family fable.

I had spent two years searching for enough details to turn my father's life into a story; he was the star, as he'd been his whole life. Now I needed a little time for his older sister. And his reaction? Don't do it. Was he jealous? I began to wonder if he saw my search as a threat to his status as the family's elder.

I realized even then that pursuing Rifqa would put a strain on our relationship. But if I found her, I thought, he would forgive me. If I found her, he would understand that I was doing it for his sake, not my own.

When I told friends I planned to return to Iraq alone, some thought I had gone off the reservation. A magazine journalist who had reported extensively in Iraq told a friend that Mosul was out of the question for a solo American. "Unless your friend will travel under the protection of a media outlet or other organization that has an established presence and security operation in Iraq, he shouldn't go," he wrote in an e-mail. "Kurdistan is safer, but any other place in Iraq, including Mosul, should not be visited by anyone who isn't part of an organization, or has the protection of one, that is already on the ground and knows how to operate there."

Growing frustrated, I e-mailed a Kurdish-American U.S. Army interpreter I had met in Iraq. I hoped he might accompany me on a search for Rifqa in Mosul, where he was based. He ignored my e-mails for a few weeks, then finally wrote back. "I know how much you want to find out about your aunt, but believe me now is not the time," he e-mailed in February 2006. He told me that even he wasn't permitted to leave the base without an escort of two U.S. soldiers.

I called Suleiman's son Heval, a twenty-seven-year-old interpreter in the Kurdish Democratic Party office in Zakho, and asked whether he might go to Mosul with me. He rejected the idea out of hand, saying it would be suicidal. "Okay," I said, sounding a little exasperated. "What about paying someone to go to Mosul to ask questions for me?"

"Let's put it this way," Heval said. "A local from Zakho or even an Arab that goes to that area and asks about some family that had relations with local Jewish people — no one would dare to do at this time. It's kind of a problem."

It was 2 A.M. I had stayed up because I knew the best time to reach Heval was in the morning, Iraq time. I must have sounded like I was coming unhinged. "As an American, a Jew, and a Kurd, I guess I'd make a nice target," I said. "Three strikes, right?"

"Yes, many negative points," he said, laughing morbidly. "The main idea, Ariel, we already have one loss in your family. It was a long time ago. Let's not lose another one."

Two months later I was back in Hassan's taxi, hurtling toward the Iraqi border.

61 ❖ Breakdown

It was May 2006, and things weren't going well. When I let the middle-aged translator into my hotel room in Zakho the first night to tell him why I had come, I saw the muscles in his face tense. Moments earlier, in the taxi from the border, Faheem had seemed the picture of confidence: He bragged about his B.A. in English from Mosul University, spoke of relations among the important agas, asked what Kurdish foods I liked. But his bonhomie dried up the moment I told him the reason I'd come.

An American Jew asking questions about an Arab kidnapper in Kurdistan nearly seventy years ago was not, it seemed, what he had bargained for. "I don't know any of these people," he said, after an awkward silence. "If Suleiman went with you to ask questions last time, he should go again."

Suleiman had already told me over the phone that he was too busy to help this time. He was teaching school during the day and supervising a construction project in the afternoons. And his son Heval, a good English speaker, had told me he was away for a new job. The few other translators in town were all tied down with various military operations. After many dead ends, a Kurdish diplomat I knew in Washington had referred me to Faheem. He was all I had. And now, after only a few minutes, he was trying to bail out.

"I'll be back soon," he said, and left.

One hour passed, then two. From the slot window of my room, I watched darkness fall over the rooftops. Below, in a dirt lot beside the hotel, a teenage boy was playing with a long rifle with a sniper's scope. He aimed it at the sky, then lowered it to study the trigger, then raised and pointed it at various imaginary targets. It felt like the oxygen in the room was thinning.

When Faheem finally returned, after 9 P.M., he was holding the arm of a gaunt man with sunken cheeks and a bulbous nose. "Kendo Qasim," Faheem said. "He is like a historian. He remembers the Jewish community. He knows your father. Same age."

Kendo had indeed known my father. They had sat next to each other in grade school, and he was the uncle of the groom in the week-long wedding celebration my father had gone to in 1992, the highlight of his trip.

Great, I thought. *A friend*. But after a few niceties, he was recounting an unsettling postscript to the wedding, of which my father had been unaware. Someone had secretly videotaped my father — the Jew — dancing with Kendo's family. The tape had been slipped to Saddam Hussein's security forces in Mosul, the nearest large city under his control after the imposition of the no-fly zone following the Persian Gulf War. Saddam was renowned in the Arab world for his hatred of Israel. He spoke of "scorching" the country with chemical gas and paid $25,000 rewards to the families of Palestinian suicide bombers. As president, he republished a pamphlet written by his uncle and surrogate father titled "Three Whom God Should Not Have Created: Persians, Jews, and Flies." Particularly after his 1991 defeat by the United States, Israel's best-known ally, anyone found to have hosted Jews in Iraq would have been dealt with severely.

Kendo said that a friend of his brother's, a member of Saddam's security services, had turned up at the house a couple weeks after the wedding and warned the family of dire consequences if they ever went to Mosul. "Any Kurd who made contact with any Jews was forbidden to go to the south," Kendo said as we spoke in the cramped hotel room. "He would be arrested by the regime and sentenced to hang."

After Kendo and Faheem left, I slid under the sheets and turned off the light, trying to forget where I was. I couldn't sleep. Everything was conspiring to keep me awake: the wall clock's relentless tick, the otherworldly drone of the muezzin's 4 A.M. call to prayer. My body felt as though it were breaking down. There was an unremitting pressure against my skull, a buzzing sensation around my forehead. I felt like some sort of strung-out junkie in withdrawal. I wanted to shut my mind off for just a few hours of sleep, but I couldn't find the switch.

I holed up in the hotel for much of the next day, too nervous to go outside or sleep. I was getting nowhere and getting angry at myself. As a journalist, I had gone into many difficult, even dangerous, situations to report stories. I had always delivered. But for the first time in as long as I could remember, I was stricken by a paralyzing fear.

Then, at around 9 P.M., the phone rang.

"Yes, Ari?" a kindly voice said.

"Yes?" I said, breathing hard.

"Suleiman."

I had never been gladder to hear a man's voice.

"Welcome to your father's home, my good friend," he said.

When I answered a knock at the door a half hour later, Suleiman hovered there like a vision. With a thousand-watt smile, an impeccably pressed gray suit, and a blue-and-red striped tie, he looked like nothing so much as a game-show host.

"We have dinner at my house," he said, spreading his arms with a slight bow.

As we left the hotel and climbed into his truck, he told me he had gotten time off from work and was free to spend the next day with me, tracking leads on Rifqa.

"Thank you, Suleiman," I said, on the verge of tears. "Thank you more than you know."

62 ❖ "The girl, the Jew, is alive."

Our first stop was the shop of Wahab Paneeri, the voluble cheese maker who had regular dealings with the Sherabi tribeswomen, who sold him buffalo-milk cheese. A year ago, when my father and I visited, he said he suspected Gamra had died. He said he would make further inquiries. He advised us to be patient.

When we stopped in this time, the Cheese Man flashed me a big grin, then kicked an old man out of his small shop to make room for Suleiman and me to sit.

"Do you remember me?" Wahab asked, his blue eyes twinkling. He seemed to think we just stumbled in by chance, and that my memory needed refreshing. Of course, I said, grabbing his shoulder. He went to the sink to rinse curds from his hands, then squatted on the floor in front of my chair, resting a hand on my knee.

"Here is what somebody has told me," he said. "When the Jews left Zakho, villagers in Tusani hid your aunt. That family with the aunt left to Mosul. Your aunt grew up and married."

I assumed I didn't hear him right. "Can you ask him to say that again?" I said to Suleiman, who was translating from Wahab's Kurdish.

But it was too late. A throng of customers jammed into the shop's narrow doorway, and Wahab stood up to regale them with one of his long-winded stories. I sat on pins and needles for twenty minutes, until the crowd finally dispersed.

"The Sherabi told me, 'The girl, the Jew from Tusani, is alive,'" Wahab continued. "But the family of Hsen told the Jews from Zakho, when she was a baby, that the girl wasn't alive. But the girl, Rifqa, knows she wasn't from Hsen and Gamra. Somebody told her, 'You are a Jew.'"

Wahab said that Gamra and Hsen took the Jewish girl from Tusani to the rural Badoush region outside Mosul, and the girl grew up, married, and had children.

"Did they say her name was Rifqa?" I asked.

"No," he said. "Just a Jewish girl taken from Zakho."

"This is wonderful news. Who told you all this?"

A Sherabi woman from Mosul who sells him cheese, he said. He would not tell me her name.

"What else did she say?"

"I don't have details," he said, growing suddenly cold. "When I questioned her further, she didn't want to answer. She was astonished. She asked, 'What business is that of yours?'"

It didn't make sense. For the past year, Suleiman had stopped in to check for news of Rifqa, and Wahab had mentioned none of this. Now all these details. I begged Wahab to speak with the Sherabi woman again, and asked him to send a message through her to the woman in Mosul who might be my aunt. He promised he would.

"*Galak mamnun,*" I said, in Kurdish. Thank you very much.

"I do it because your great-grandfather was Zakho's *khamdari,*" he said, using the Kurdish word for *sabagha,* or dyer. "I have always helped Jews. My name was on Saddam's list because Jews visited me. I do it for humanity."

OUR NEXT STOP was Tusani. Ten months earlier, the farmer my father and I met there, Lubayd Tusani, said he had lived next to a Gamra, who was possibly Rifqa's wet nurse, and her children in Mosul in the 1970s. "Maybe when it's safe in Mosul," Lubayd had told us, "I can go to the house of Gamra and ask for you."

His memories of Gamra had been crisper than anyone else's, and he still knew where she lived. I had high hopes. But when we arrived at Tusani, the farmers told us Lubayd wasn't around. He was in Zakho, they said, working on a construction site.

We got back in the car and reversed course. Lubayd, it turned out, had less of a connection to Tusani than we'd thought. He'd taken a job as a construction worker and was spending a lot of time in Zakho. We found him swinging a hammer on top of a house in one of the new residential districts. Gone were the traditional Kurdish pants and bare feet I remembered from our last visit. Here, in town, he was wearing blue jeans and what looked like fake snakeskin loafers, covered in dust.

When he clambered down from the roof and met us on the street, he seemed distant and older. He leaned against the wall and pulled out a cigarette with his long fingers.

"I asked around," Lubayd said, uninterestedly, taking a slow drag on the cigarette, "but didn't get any information."

Whom did he talk to? I asked.

"A Sherabi from the town of Shechan, a guy named Mutab."

Suleiman helpfully offered—maybe he was trying to drop me a hint—that Mutab was the Arabic word for "tired." Everyone, it seemed, was tired. Tired of the story. Tired, I feared, of me.

But I couldn't let go. If Lubayd hadn't made it to Mosul to get a message to Gamra, at the very least he could help paint a sharper portrait of her, so that I might render her more vividly in my family story. What did he remember about Gamra and Hsen? I asked. What were they like? What were their habits? Were they good parents?

"I didn't know them," he said flatly.

I asked Suleiman to remind him of our conversation the year before, when he said he had been their neighbor for a decade in Mosul.

"I knew them when I was a kid," he said, taking another drag and blowing the smoke out of the side of his mouth. "I'm not sure who was who. There were so many Sherabi. They all blend together."

It was as if I was talking to a different person.

Suleiman turned to me. "We can ask him to go to Gizronia and Shechan," two towns on the other side of the Tigris where some elderly Sherabi still lived. "But you'll have to pay him."

Lubayd straightened, his interest in Rifqa suddenly revived.

"Come to me in two days," he said, "and I'll tell you what I found."

The next day I acquired yet another helper. I hadn't seen Faheem, my

Tusani, Iraq, 2005.

first translator, for a couple of days. At 2 P.M., though, he appeared at my
hotel door, shadowed by a lumbering bear of a man.

"This is Hani Abdul Karim Shemdin Agha," Faheem said, smiling
sheepishly, like a ne'er-do-well who by some impossible feat had at last
redeemed himself.

Who? I wanted to ask.

"The son of Abd al-Karim Agha," Faheem volunteered, sparing me
great embarrassment.

I did a double take. Immediately I saw the resemblance to his father's pictures in the books. Abd al-Karim Agha, the hotheaded tribal leader fond of
carrying a long stick, had been the great protector of the Jews of my father's
day. He mediated disputes between Jewish and the Muslim merchants. He
chased away the Palestinian provocateur who tried to turn public sentiment against the Jews. And when the Jews left for Israel, he got into his Jeep
and escorted the buses to Mosul to assure their safe arrival.

I gave Hani a hearty handshake and offered him the only chair in the room. He was a tall, apple-chested man with short, curly gray hair, a white mustache, and a round face. His baseball cap bore the word AUSTRALIA and a stitched-on likeness of hopping kangaroos. He was a sixty-seven-year-old bachelor and said he was the third child from his mother — which was only so helpful, since his father had sixteen children by four wives.

The room was air-conditioned, but he was panting and perspiring, as if his body was working overtime just to keep a man of his size up and running. Every few minutes, he pulled a napkin from his pocket and touched the beads of sweat on his brow.

"My father loved the Jews much too much," he told me, in halting English.

When I told him why I had come, he looked galvanized. He told me to come to his house right away. He would get on the phone and make inquiries. He knew people. He would call on his family's web of contacts around Zakho to get answers. Just wait, he said, and I would see.

"Hello, mister!" he said to me, smiling confidently as we walked the couple of blocks to his house. "Hello, my dear!"

His father was long gone, but Hani was still his father's son. The sudden reappearance of a Jew in Zakho, I thought, had awakened some atavistic protective instinct. As soon as we arrived, he ordered relatives to get on their cell phones. His nephew paced back and forth in the courtyard, phone pressed to his ear, in a mimicry of furiously tracking down leads. After wrapping up his last call, the nephew smiled. "You should try Muhammad Fikri," he told me.

We found Fikri that night on a shadowy street west of the town's center. Stooped, gaunt, and toothless, Fikri, seventy-one, pulled a few chairs onto his moonlit front lawn and bade us sit. He said he was a retired wheat farmer, born into the Hseni tribe, the one the wet nurse Gamra's husband might have belonged to. His son was married to the daughter of a Sherabi chief.

Hani told Rifqa's story. Fikri shook his head. It didn't ring any bells. And in any case, the wet nurse's name was common. "There were many Gamras in that place," he said. A pale flame flickered in his eyes, which seemed the only things alive in his sunken face. "The Sherabi were poor. They were known to take other people's children."

But children are a financial burden, I said. Why would a poor family with many children take on another one?

"Sometimes," Fikri said, "they sold the children or traded them for food." A childless couple might want one, or a family in need of extra hands on the farm.

He said he could ask around Gizronia or Shechan, the same towns near the Tigris that Lubayd Tusani had spoken of.

"I have many friends — I can help," he said. "But if I do," Hani translated bashfully, "will you give me a gift?"

I handed Fikri a $20 bill. Fikri made a perfunctory gesture of refusal, then took it, gushing with gratitude. "I will ask all over for you," he said.

Back on the street, Hani had about him an air of triumph, as if the mystery were on the brink of resolution.

"Hello, mister!" Hani said, grabbing my hand. "Hello, my dear!"

But we never heard from Fikri again.

The next day Suleiman and I drove to a roadside drink stand a few miles outside Zakho to follow up with Lubayd.

Lubayd bought us both orange sodas, lit a cigarette, then squatted in the half light of the cinder-block hut. "I went to Shechan," he said.

"And?" Suleiman asked.

"People there knew of a Hsen, but he was not married to a Gamra. I did hear that in Gizronia there might be a Hsen married to a Gamra."

Why didn't you go there then? Suleiman asked.

"I didn't have time," Lubayd said. "But when I do, I will go."

Frustrated by his lack of initiative, I reminded him again that last July he had said that he had lived next to a Gamra and Hsen in Mosul. Did we mishear him?

"There was a Hsen there in Mosul, but I'm not sure if his wife was Gamra," he said, twirling a key chain around his finger.

I was beginning to wonder if I could believe anyone anymore. Did he tell the truth last time and get scared? Or was he telling the truth now?

He must have picked up on my irritation, because he looked at Suleiman with pleading eyes and said he had asked repeatedly about Rifqa since last year and had heard nothing.

I thanked him and handed him the $100 bill — U.S. currency is highly sought-after in northern Iraq — that I had promised a few days before.

"I'll ask and ask and ask," he said, as we got back into Suleiman's truck and waved good-bye. "If I find something, I'll call you. In five years' time, I'll have to know something."

In the truck on our way back to Zakho, Suleiman sighed. "Not all that glitters is gold."

"With Lubayd or Wahab?" I said.

Suleiman just shook his head. "Some people say much, but there's no act behind it."

Walking alone through the streets that evening, I noticed how much Zakho had changed in the ten months since my last visit.

There was a crop of new computer and electronics stores. A Pierre Cardin haberdashery sold natty suits. On the riverfront there was now another bustling café, with white chairs on a balcony over the water. Late-model BMWs cruised the streets; I noticed one, a gleaming SUV, with video screens embedded in the backs of the seats. A brand-new municipal headquarters was going up by the river, a modern structure with aqua-tinted windows that would be at home in any American city. A Norwegian oil company had begun drilling just outside Zakho, in a deal with the provincial Kurdish government that stood to make a number of local landowners very rich.

In a small grocery, I asked a group of teenagers about a billboard bearing the picture of a famous traditional singer from Zakho. They shook their heads and made disgusted expressions. "We like 50 Cent, Eminem," one seventeen-year-old boy said. "Tupac, Sean Paul."

"Jennifer Lopez," said another boy, leering at his friends.

Even the Jewish neighborhood felt different. I couldn't figure out why at first. Then I looked down: The uneven dirt alleys that had muddied our shoes the year before had been paved. The clerk at my hotel said the work was completed two or three months earlier. The rutted earth that

Kurdish Jews had trod for centuries was now smooth bands of clean cement.

Here was a city hurtling into the future. In a decade and a half of Kurdish autonomy, Zakho, at a strategic border with Turkey, had grown and molted several times over. If it had changed this much in ten months, what traces might be left of a newborn last seen on its outskirts seventy years earlier?

Maybe this was a fool's errand, I thought. *Maybe my father was right.* Zakho didn't even feel like Zakho without him. The whole place felt bereft. I was just an American Jew on an ill-considered personal mission to one of the world's most dangerous countries. I felt like a naïf. I worried that others had begun to see me as an easy mark. When I arrived a week earlier, I felt friendless and abandoned. Now I had the opposite problem. Every evening, often late, one or another self-appointed helper showed up at the hotel to ask about my day and hint that for a small gift he would be happy to assist. At first I felt paranoid. I wondered whether they were government minders, keeping an eye on the American claiming he was a journalist researching his past. But I came to suspect that their motives were far less sinister. Word was simply getting around about the crazy American Jew who was handing out C-notes to anyone willing to indulge his bizarre fantasies.

Just how far some would go would become clear my last night in Zakho.

63 ❖ Convenient Truths

On the evening before my departure, I was up late typing interview notes into my PDA when the phone rang. It was reception.

Downstairs, I found Hani, in a yellow baseball cap, leaning on the front counter.

"I have some good news for you," he said, grinning. He grabbed my hand and led me toward the back hall. A teenage bellhop led us into a first-floor room, set down two bottles of water, and shut the door. Hani motioned me to one of the double beds and took a seat on the other, with our knees almost touching.

"I bring for you the whole story," he said, straining a little as he breathed and mopping his forehead. "Do you have your notebook?" From his shirt pocket he withdrew a folded sheet of lined notebook paper, and began to read. "They changed her name to Sara," he said.

"What? Whose name?"

"The Jewish girl — maybe your aunt," he said.

"How do you know?"

"Today, the head of the Hseni tribe went to speak to the Sherabi families, near Syria border, on the other side of the Tigris."

"To Gizronia?" I asked. The town where Lubayd had heard a Gamra and Hsen once lived.

"Yes," Hani said. He looked back down at his note and ran his fingers over the perfectly formed Arabic letters. "An old Sherabi man in Gizronia told the Hseni chief that in 1939 Gamra and her sister took the child to Tusani village. This Gamra belonged to the Hsen family."

"Keep going," I said, dubiously.

"The people in Gizronia said the girl's name was Sara. Sara got married to an Arab Sherabi man, whose name he didn't know. Sara had two boys and three girls. The children now live in Mosul, with the Sherabi, in the mahalat Sherabi" — the city's Sherabi district.

"What about Rifqa, or Sara?"

"The people in Gizronia told the chief, 'We are very sorry, she died three years ago.' But before she died, she told her family that she had a friend or relative in Cizre, Turkey. She said she was going to visit her friend, but they found out later that she didn't really have a friend there."

"So why did she go?" I asked.

"In Cizre, they said, she called her family in Israel," he said. To try to calling from Iraq, he explained, would have been suicidal.

"But, I mean, we never heard from her."

"This is just what the people told the Hseni chief," Hani said.

I sat there, stunned.

"At the end of the meeting with the chief," he went on, "the Sherabi man said, 'If anyone goes to mahalat Sherabi in Mosul, they can meet with her sons, Ali and Saleh.'"

I should have been elated: Someone had just handed me what appeared to be my aunt's whole story. But all I could feel was doubt. After leading me down a succession of dead ends and blind alleys, how could Hani have suddenly hit pay dirt? There was just too much information, too conveniently laid out, written in too perfect a script, to be plausible. By delivering it the night before my departure, he must have known I'd have too little time to verify it.

Then again, it had detail. There were dates. Names of sons. If he was just telling me what he thought I wanted to hear, why would he have picked 1939, a date that didn't quite match what I had told him? Why did he say the girl's name had been changed to Sara? Why not just say it was Rifqa? Why give the exact names of sons or say that she had called her family in Israel, which could be easy to disprove? And didn't important parts of his story—her marriage and children; her life in Mosul; her apparently belated discovery that she was Jewish—dovetail with details from Wahab the Cheese Man and Lubayd? If there were another girl kidnapped from the Jews at around that time, wouldn't I have heard about it? The part of me that wanted the "get" was at war with my natural skepticism. Was Hani just angling for more money? People had said he was a lifelong bachelor. Was it possible he had a crush on me? Was he just a little off-kilter? Or was he just a simple man telling the truth?

Time was running out. I wanted proof, I told him. I began quizzing him on how he got the details and who his sources were. But it was clear that he expected gratitude, not an interrogation.

"I can have Ali and Saleh come to my house and I can take a picture for you," he said.

"Thank you," I said. "But I will also want to meet them for myself."

"How can you be here when they are here?"

"Tell them to come to Zakho on a specific date and we'll be here. Even my father would come."

Hani said he doubted we could get the timing right. Plus, he said, a face-to-face meeting could be dangerous, since we are Jewish.

"There is no other way," I said.

After a long pause, he said, a little disappointedly, "Okay."

I reached into my wallet and pressed the last of my American currency into his hand.

"I don't do it for money," he said. Then he took the cash.

CONCLUSION

Ariel and his son, Seth.

64 ❖ Paradise Lost

When I got back to Maine, I was afraid of calling my father. I worried he'd say, I told you so. I needed time to process what had happened. I could tell him about Hani's tale and pretend I had made some headway. Or I could just tell the truth: that I had little to show for my trip besides a deeper tan, a lighter wallet, and a shameful sense of disappointment.

When I finally got around to calling, I could hear relief at the other end of the line. He said he had prayed for my safety in Zakho but didn't understand me. "I often wonder how you have so much courage to adventure," he told me. "I don't have that kind of courage at all. I never did."

"But, Abba, all I did was spend two weeks in a hotel in Zakho, then fly home on a jetliner," I said. "I never even got up the guts to go to Mosul." He was the one who crossed borders at the age of twelve, I told him. He was the one who had forfeited citizenships, fought to learn new languages, and risen above poverty to make it as a professor in the United States. He had spent a life scaling Everest in a storm; I was just a spoiled suburban kid on a thrill ride.

"I'm surprised you see me that way," he said. He had never sought adventure or even change, he told me. He was "Diasporic." He had leapt only when sure of a soft landing. He had dreamed as a child of returning to Zakho, not abandoning it for good. His family's loss of status in Israel only sharpened his longing for the lost paradise of his youth.

"Sometimes, I'd hear about penniless Israelis who came to America to try to make it," he told me. "I couldn't do that. If I hadn't had a sure admission and scholarship to a university, I would never have come to America. I'm too fearful to do things that are not ninety-nine percent or one hundred percent sure. Taking risks is sometimes too costly."

My mother, who had picked up the phone, said, "I think it's all the changes in his life."

But my father pinpointed just one: his boyhood departure from Zakho. "Coming to Israel," he said, "I lost all my security blankets at once."

WHEN I STARTED my research I was tempted to see my father's work in Aramaic as a crusade: a fight to revive a dying language, the way, a century earlier, Eliezer Ben-Yehuda had reanimated spoken Hebrew in the Holy Land.

But a crusade takes a lust for conflict that my father never possessed. It also takes another thing he lacked: followers. Few of the Kurdish Jews I spoke with in Israel shared my father's attachments. Aramaic, as they saw it now, was a useless language, and Kurdistan a place of privation. Few Israeli Kurds my father's age still live in poverty; their children have assimilated and largely prospered. On my trips to Israel, the elderly invited me into their homes as if I were the son of royalty. But they revered my father not because he recorded their language and culture — most had little idea what he studied. It was because he was a "big professor in America." He was living proof that Kurds could make it. He was proof that they could move on.

The truth, though, was more complicated: My father had made it, but he had not moved on. In many ways he had sublimated homesickness into a career. I saw now that his work was not a crusade but the outward expression of an intensely personal struggle to reconcile past and present. Aside from a school medal in the hundred-meter dash and an old spoon, Aramaic was his only surviving childhood possession. Teaching Aramaic in America, I came to see, was how he sang God's song in a strange land.

Aramaic had hopped so many borders, infiltrated so many faiths, outlived so many empires. Why shouldn't it survive one more leap? I wonder now whether, for my father, this was part of its appeal. Was Aramaic, for him, not just a language but a metaphor? Was it proof that a common language — not only of words but of values — could heal a divided world? Was it proof that despite our differences, we all lived in the same village, by the same river, below the same mountains?

And if Aramaic is all those things, what does it mean that it is nearing the end of its run? As it enters its fourth millennium as a continuously spoken language, it has fallen to a whisper. Some 150,000 Kurdish Jews now live in Israel. But the children of the 1950s immigrants speak only a rudimentary Aramaic, and their children don't speak it at all. The ranks of Christian Aramaic speakers, known as Chaldeans, Assyrians, Jacobites, and Nestorians, are also in free fall. Two world wars, the Iranian revolution, religious persecution, and the two gulf wars produced an exodus of Near Eastern Christians to Europe, Scandinavia, and to American cities like Chicago, San Diego, and Detroit. Vestigial communities of Aramaic-speaking Christians cling to life in the tiny enclaves of Tur Abdin, in southeastern Turkey, and Ma'alula, near Damascus, Syria. But in an era of high-speed travel and the World Wide Web, they will struggle to pass Aramaic to their children. Perhaps fifty thousand native Aramaic speakers are alive today. As these "last Mohicans" die, so too will their language.

Though Aramaic's longevity is remarkable, its fate is common. Of the roughly seven thousand languages now spoken, half are expected to vanish over the next century. The latest edition of *Ethnologue*, the eminent census of living languages, already lists 516 tongues as "nearly extinct." No continent has been spared. Gooniyandi in Australia is down to its last 100 speakers; Dama in Cameroon, 50 speakers; Kavalan in Thailand, 24; Xipaya in Brazil, 2; Plains Miwok in the United States, 1.

Airplanes, television, and the Internet have bulldozed cultural borders. The young are leaving villages for cities, where they are swallowed up by the world. New generations are giving up their mother tongues for the market-ready languages of the global economy, chief among them English. Some 94 percent of the planet's population speaks a mere 5 percent of its languages.

Each time a language dies, another flame goes out, another sound goes silent. When the whispers of Aramaic and Dama and Plains Miwok are at last drowned out by the shouts, what do we do?

We should pause to mourn. But then we must tell our stories in a new tongue, so at least the stories may survive.

65 ❧ Ice-Blended Mocha

When my parents bought a ranch-style house in Westwood in 1972 — "spacious home on beautiful corner lot," said the ad in the *Los Angeles Times* — they moved into a neighborhood whose origins couldn't have been more different than Zakho's. Our street, Wilkins Avenue, was named after A. H. Wilkins, a senior sales executive for the Janss Investment Corporation. The Janss brothers had made a fortune subdividing a sprawling Mexican cattle ranch into hundreds of middle-class tract houses at almost the precise moment the University of California opened its massive Los Angeles campus in 1929. "Prove to yourself," said a Janss brochure I found in the L.A. Public Library, "that no other community development in the history of metropolitan Los Angeles, or even the entire West, has ever offered such a guarantee of safety and potential future possibilities to the Investor or Homeseeker." Sidewalk panels still bear the developer's name and circular logo.

Where Zakho was an ancient city whose byways and rhythms accreted slowly over thousands of years, Westwood was an instant community, built almost overnight by some of the shrewdest developers Southern California had ever seen. Where Zakho represented continuity and community, Westwood was a place of transience and disconnection.

Our house was on a corner lot. Otherwise, however, it occupied no special place amid the low-lying sprawl of single-family houses and hastily built condo complexes. We were a half mile in either direction from the asphalt ribbons of Santa Monica and Wilshire. These eight-lane boulevards, West L.A.'s major east-west arteries, carried our neighbors to ten-lane freeways and distant jobs. The morning exodus gave our neighborhood the look of a suddenly abandoned stage set.

After two decades in our house, we knew next to nothing about most of our neighbors. We saw them get into cars, build additions over the garage, push mowers across lawns. But something about the city kept us alien to one another. Proximity bred social exchanges no more heartfelt than a trade of insurance policy numbers after a fender bender. In a neighborhood with the slimmest of crime rates, nearly every lawn sprouted a sign announcing subscription to the local rent-a-cop service: BEL-AIR PATROL, they warned phantom burglars, ARMED RESPONSE.

Friends outside L.A. laughed when I told them we lived at 1——— Wilkins Avenue. "Must be a long street," they'd say. It wasn't. It was just a few blocks long. Our five-digit street number struck me as some city planner's cruel joke: a reminder of the insignificance of any single household in L.A.'s desert vastness.

I wonder if this blankness drew my father. Unlike Israel or even New Haven, West Los Angeles was an unmarked canvas on which to paint his dreams. In this new neighborhood near this new campus, amid the birds of paradise and bougainvillea, he had conjured a new Zakho. He had managed a series of careful if inexact substitutions. The peddlers in Zakho's market were reborn in the Mexican vendors on the median strips from whom he bought bags of oranges. The mud-brick synagogues where elders urged the young to study psalms found their equal in his brightly lit classroom at UCLA. The five-minute drive to campus, on the other side of Wilshire Boulevard's roar, was the five-minute walk to Zakho's public school, on the other side of the raging Habur. (In America's freeway capital, my father over two decades had put just forty thousand miles on his Toyota Tercel.) Zakho's riverfront teahouse was now the Century City espresso stand.

For my father, America's cultural bouillabaisse mirrored the religious pluralism of Kurdistan. When I accompanied him to an undergraduate class not long ago, he began by holding up a colorful children's Seder plate, made of molded plastic, that my mother had bought as a gift for my son Seth.

"This is my grandson's," he told the class.

"Awww," a girl said. "How cute."

"You see," Yona continued. "It has all the Hebrew words for egg, bitter herbs, parsley."

The students nodded.

"Now, let's flip it over. What does it say?" Pause for effect. "Made in China."

They laughed.

The idea that workers in China could make a Passover plate with Hebrew letters that you could buy in Los Angeles for a grandson in Maine: This, for my father, was America.

So, too, was the swirl of students — black, white, Christian, Muslim, Korean, Mexican — who took his Hebrew classes along with Jews. So, too, was the freedom to dip an oar in other faiths and cultures.

At his nephew's 2005 graduation from Loyola Marymount University, a Jesuit-affiliated institution, my father took Communion at a Catholic Mass.

I needled him: Did you consume the blood of Christ, too, or just the body?

"Both," he said. "Everyone drank the wine from the same glass, just like in Zakho. The only difference was they had a cloth last night to wipe the glass between sips."

His sister Sara, whose son Kedem was graduating that day, was shocked. But my father said he saw nothing untoward. If Zakho's Muslims ate Passover matzo ("holiday bread," they called it) with Jews, why couldn't a Kurdish Jew take Communion with Los Angeles Catholics?

These parallels sometimes strike me as fanciful, even laughable. But I have come to see how real they are for him, how necessary for a man displaced. At the Century City food court the other day, he set his ice-blended mocha on an outdoor table and settled into the industrial metal chair as though it were a jeweled throne. He had somehow tuned out the whine of the eight lanes of traffic below us on Santa Monica Boulevard. He had blotted out the neon glare of the faux-1950s hamburger joint and the blank wall of the 14-plex movie theater. For him the Century City food court was an Elysium of swaying palm trees and sunshine.

"This is like some little oasis away from the world," he said, without irony. "No telephones. No interruptions. Nothing. I like the view and the open air.

"I feel like it's some little Zakho."

66 ❖ Saba's Music

There is a counterpoint to the familiar immigrant story of opportunities won: It is the story, less often told, of cultures lost. Its trope is
not "a better life for our children" but broken bonds to ancestors, land,
identity, and history. For many immigrants, the past is painful and best
forgotten; it is the reason they left. But for my father, it was where the best
part of himself resided. It was a place where life could still be glimpsed
through a child's eyes.

Once my father left Zakho, he could never return. In going to Israel
and then America, he had set in motion a chain of events whose ineluc-
table end was a son with weaker ties to his past. My father does not regret
his choices: They did indeed afford him and his children a better life. But
unlike many immigrants, he saw value in swimming hard against the
tide. It was in the collision of past and present that he found he could see
himself most clearly.

My motives were different. I had not lost anything. I had not left anyplace. In tunneling back through time, I wanted only a better sense of my
debts to history. I grew up believing I could be anybody. But my son's birth
was a comeuppance. It was a stark reminder of continuity, that we are who
we come from as much as who we make of ourselves. Jews had carried a
flame into the hills of Kurdistan, and they carried it out, still burning, 2,700
years later. My father touched another candle to it and brought it across
continents. I didn't want it to die with me. If my children ever feel adrift,
unsure of who they are, I want that candle to still be burning.

In the search for my past, I had made a wrong turn with the hunt for
my lost aunt. I had wanted an Oprah moment, in which relatives separated at birth embrace through tears and order is restored to the world. I
see now that if I want to repair my ties to the past, to my forefathers and
father, it will take more than a "get." It will be a work of days and months
and years.

The work started the day I began this book, but will not be finished for many more. It started with talking with my father, and listening. We are the same people as before — I headstrong and thrill-seeking, he self-questioning and wary of change — but we are closer. I e-mail him articles about languages, and we discuss them on the phone afterward. I help him assemble slides for his lectures on Jewish Kurdistan. He asks me questions about the mysteries of American culture. (A July 2006 *New Yorker* cartoon shows St. Peter at the gates of heaven telling a dead man, "Just so you know — the official language of Heaven is Aramaic." Several relatives and academic colleagues had sent him copies, but the precise mechanics of the humor eluded him. "Ariel," he asked, "what do you think they mean by 'the official language of Heaven'?")

I tell him how lonely I've felt in Maine, away from friends and family. He tries to console me with memories of his own isolation at Yale. He sends me amusing e-mails from the scores of strangers with off-the-wall questions about Kurdistan or ancient languages, and asks for my advice on how and whether to respond. ("I am an archaeological researcher investigating the domestication of pigs during the early Holocene," one recent supplicant wrote, "and am hoping to determine whether modern populations of wild boar in the Middle East are truly wild or are perhaps feral and descended from domestic pigs imported from Europe during the early Iron Age. I am writing to ask your advice on how I might go about contacting Christian farmers in the Levant.")

More than anything, he tries to shake me out of the illusion that our lives were so different. "I can assure you," he said recently, "that I and many of my generation had very similar feelings toward our immigrant parents."

In a strange way, my quest for Rifqa mirrored my father's ambition to write the perfect dictionary. We were both seduced by illusions of finality. We had both hoped that a single achievement could capture — even restore — the past.

When my father visited us in autumn 2004, he sat for three nights at our kitchen table, bent over a frayed academic tome from 1974 titled *The Akkadian Influences in Aramaic*. He was checking his dictionary (published two years earlier) against the book. I soon saw him scribbling notes in the margins.

"What are you doing?" I asked. "Isn't it too late to be editing your dictionary?"

He said that he was turning up dictionary entries whose Akkadian roots he had failed to note. They weren't the only omissions, he told me. His dictionary had translated some eight thousand Neo-Aramaic words into English, the product of more than three decades of painstaking research. But every few weeks since the book's publication, he said, another Aramaic word, dimly remembered from childhood, surfaced into consciousness.

"I don't know how I missed them," he said, shaking his head.

"You can fix it for the paperback edition," I said, fishing for a smile.

He looked up and laughed. We both knew that the sorts of books he wrote never made paperback.

"What I do now is too late for my dictionary," he said. "But I do it for myself."

Then he closed the books and headed to bed. "The work can wait," he decided. "The world will go on."

AFTER RETURNING FROM ZAKHO, I sent a follow-up e-mail to Suleiman. He said he had checked in a few times with "Wahab of Cheese" but had no news about Rifqa or Gamra. Hani had given Suleiman another long letter, with another tantalizing but impossible-to-verify story about another kidnapped Jewish girl.

Other Iraqi Kurds, some in the United States, heard about my quest and said they knew elderly Muslim women who believed they'd been born Jewish in Kurdistan. There names now were Amuna, Hamsha, Sara. Could any of these be Rifqa? they wondered.

Anything was possible, I said. I thanked them and encouraged them to dig deeper. But the simple answers I had hoped for were really multi-headed Hydras, ever harder to pin down.

"Be sure if there is any new story I shall e-mail very soon," Suleiman wrote in 2006. I have heard nothing since.

I can't sleep some nights. I berate myself for not trying harder, for not staying in Zakho longer, for not risking it all and going to Mosul. I still dream of late-night phone calls or even a faint knock at the door. I dream that at the faraway end of the line, or there in the moonlight on my front step, stands a small woman with gray-streaked hair, pining for home.

Then I awake in the chill of another Maine morning. I look outside at the snow entombing the roads and the fields and everything beneath, and I see the past is gone. History had beckoned. I went after it, hungry. But I found neither flesh nor blood, just a few faded footprints and some shadows dancing on a wall. On days when thoughts of my folly get me down, I try to summon the words of my father. Even as he tried to stop its spinning, he told himself "the world will go on."

My father's happiest moments lately are the sounds of his three-year-old grandson saying a Sabbath prayer or reciting the Hebrew alphabet. I taught Seth both in the last year. His mind has so absorbed the shapes of those ancient letters — rare sights in Maine — that he has begun to see them in the unlikeliest of places. "That's a Zayin!" he said from his car seat one day, pointing to yellow road sign with a split arrow indicating a turnoff to the right. If you squinted, it did look like the Hebrew letter for Z.

In January 2006 we called Los Angeles and Seth left a message on my parents' answering machine. "Shabbat shalom," he said. And then, in his squeaky, halting voice, he sang the entire Hebrew alphabet. "Now I know my aleph-bet-gimels," he said at the end, before parroting a joke ending I once sang, "next time won't you send me an e-mail?"

A year later, my father has yet to erase the recording. Every day, after work, he stands alone in his bedroom, hits the Play button, and listens. Sometimes, my mother told me, he even talks back to the recording. He congratulates Seth — "What a clear, strong voice!" — or wishes him Shabbat shalom or good night, as if his little grandson were right there in the room with him.

I look to Seth now for signals about what part of our past might survive into the future. Some nights, before bedtime, I call him into my office and put on a CD of a Kurdish song my father sang to me as a baby.

"That's Saba's music!" he says, climbing into my lap with a big smile. "Can I see the pictures, too?"

I turn on my laptop and click through my photos of Zakho. He has seen the slide show many times but always has burning new questions.

"What's that, Daddy?" he asked one autumn night, pointing to a picture of a grizzled blacksmith in the market where my great-grandfather once had his dye shop.

"That's an old man in his store in Zakho," I said.

Seth looked thoughtful for a moment. "I want to go to store in Zakho," he said. "I *need* go."

I looked at his serious face for a long moment before speaking.

"One day," I said, pulling him closer. "One day we'll go together, okay?"

ACKNOWLEDGMENTS

A book is at bottom a collaboration, and I want to thank the many people who lent their memories, time, and insight. My wife, Meg, and my colleagues and friends Scott Calvert, Sam Loewenberg, and Jonathan Rockoff read early drafts and made invaluable suggestions. My agent, Andrew Blauner, took a chance on a first-time author because he believed in this project. My editor at Algonquin, Amy Gash, showed a painstaking eye for detail, offered incisive criticism, and cheered me on during difficult stretches of writing.

Several professors took time out of jammed schedules to answer my novice questions about Aramaic and other ancient languages: Sebastian Brock of Oxford University; Eran Cohen of the Hebrew University; Jacco Dieleman of UCLA; Geoffrey Khan of Cambridge University; Hezy Mutzafi of Tel Aviv University; Edward Ullendorff of the University of London; Michael Sokoloff of Bar Ilan University.

Scholars of the Jews of Kurdistan were extremely generous with their time and guidance. I reserve particular gratitude for Professor Haya Gavish of Hebrew Union College, who shared her vast knowledge of Zakho's Jews and offered me access to some of the primary materials for her book, *We Were Zionists: The Community of Zakho, Kurdistan*. Moti Zaken, the author of a wonderful dissertation on relations between Jewish Kurds and Muslim agas now available as a book, answered numerous questions. Donna Shai, now of Villanova University, shared the findings of her seminal sociological work on Kurds in Israel. Mordechai Yona, a Zakho native and private researcher in Jerusalem, offered memories, books, and photographs.

My trips to Yale were a joy thanks to Maureen Draicchio and Professors William Hallo and Benjamin Foster, all of whom shared memories of my father.

Dozens of relatives, some of whom I met for the first time, fielded endless questions, even when they concerned painful chapters of family history. There are too many to name here, and I am indebted to them all, particularly my father's five siblings.

My uncle and aunt, Shalom and Rina Sabar, deserve special mention for sheltering and feeding me in their small Jerusalem apartment during my research trips to Israel. They and their older children, Noa and Nadav, went beyond any notion of family duty in helping set up interviews and serving as translators and cultural guides, not to mention being great company. I also need to thank my cousin Lee and uncle Uri for having the foresight to tape-record their 1993 interview with my grandmother Miryam for a family history project coinciding with Lee's bat mitzvah.

Thanks very much to the friends, classmates, teachers, and onetime colleagues of my father's at the High School for the Working Youth, Hebrew University, the Ben-Zvi Institute, Yale, and UCLA. Without their vivid memories, I would have been unable to reconstruct the story of my father's life.

The Baxter Memorial Library is a public library in the rural town of Gorham, Maine. Its ingenious librarians tracked down obscure texts on language and history from across the country.

Many thanks to the people of Zakho, Iraq, my father's hometown, for the kindness and generosity they showed the semibewildered American who entered their midst in the summers of 2005 and 2006. A few townspeople put their lives on hold for days to serve as guides and translators and make sure my father and I felt at home. I will respect their wishes not to be named, the security situation in Iraq being what it is. In my heart I will never forget them.

My father had mixed feelings about my belated interest in family history. But he endured hundreds of phone calls and e-mails with patience and grace. I hope he feels the results were worth it. My mother, Stephanie, also answered many questions. She offered sage insights into my father and took some of the beautiful photographs that appear in this book. She and my brother, Ilan, should know that I love them as much as I do my father.

My wife was my shrewdest critic and greatest supporter. Meg agreed to return to work so I could quit my job for this risky project. When I was away from home on research trips, she cared for our young son while also working a demanding job. I am grateful for her sacrifices and unstinting encouragement.

This book took me from my son, Seth, and newborn daughter, Phoebe, for longer than any father could wish. If they read it someday, I hope they see that I wrote it for them.

SELECTED BIBLIOGRAPHY

Ainsworth, William F. *A Personal Narrative of the Euphrates Expedition*, vol. 1. London: Kegan Paul, Trench and Co., 1888.

———. *Travels in the Track of the Ten Thousand Greeks*. London: John W. Parker, 1844.

Alharizi, Judah. *The Book of Tahkemoni: Jewish Tales from Medieval Spain*. Translation by David Simha Segal. Oxford: Littman Library of Jewish Civilization, 2003.

Bellos, Susan. "Politics in Katamonim." *The Jerusalem Post International Edition*. May 10, 1977.

Benjamin of Tudela. *The Itinerary of Benjamin of Tudela*. Edited by Marcus Nathan Adler. London: Oxford University Press, 1907.

Benjamin II, J. J. *Eight Years in Asia and Africa: From 1846 to 1855*. Hanover: published by author, 1863.

Ben-Zvi, Itzhak. *The Exiled and the Redeemed*, 2d ed., rev. Philadelphia: The Jewish Publication Society of America, 1961.

Blady, Ken. *Jewish Communities in Exotic Places*. Northvale, N.J.: Jason Aronson, 2000.

Brauer, Erich. *The Jews of Kurdistan*. Completed and edited by Raphael Patai. Detroit: Wayne State University Press, 1993.

Brock, Sebastian P. "Three Thousand Years of Aramaic Literature." *Aram* 1, no. 1 (1989): 11–23.

Brock, Sebastian P., ed. *The Hidden Pearl: The Syrian Orthodox Church and its Ancient Aramaic Heritage*, 3 vols. Rome: Trans World Film Italia, 2001.

Cashman, Greer Fay. "The Pride of Being Kurdish." *The Jerusalem Post*. August 23, 1983.

Command of the Air Council, "Military Report on 'Iraq (Area 9), Central Kurdistan." Air Ministry (British), August 1929. Available at The National Archives of the United Kingdom.

Edmonds, C. J. *Kurds, Turks and Arabs: Politics, Travel and Research in North-Eastern Iraq 1919–1945*. London: Oxford University Press, 1957.

Feitelson, Dina. "Aspects of the Social Life of Kurdish Jews." *Jewish Journal of Sociology* 1, no. 2 (1959): 201–216.

Fischel, Walter J. "The Jews of Kurdistan a Hundred Years Ago." *Jewish Social Studies* 6 (1944).

———. "The Jews of Kurdistan: A First-Hand Report on a Near Eastern Mountain Community." *Commentary* 8, no. 6 (December 1949): 554–559.

Fück, J. W. "Islam as an Historical Problem in European Historiography since 1800." *Historians of the Middle East*. Edited by Bernard Lewis and P. M. Holt. London: Oxford University Press, 1962.

Gat, Moshe. *The Jewish Exodus from Iraq: 1948–1951*. London: Frank Cass, 1997.

Gavish, Haya. *We Were Zionists: The Jewish Community of Zakho, Kurdistan: A Story and a Document*. Jerusalem: Yad Ben-Zvi Institute, 2004. [In Hebrew.]

Greenfield, Jonas C. "Aramaic and the Jews." In *Studia Aramaica: New Sources and New Approaches*. Edited by M. J. Geller, et al., University of Manchester. New York: Oxford University Press, 1995.

Hacohen, Dvora. *Immigrants in Turmoil: Mass Immigration to Israel and Its Repercussions in the 1950s and After*. Syracuse: Syracuse University Press, 2003.

Hillel, David D'Beth. *Unknown Jews in Unknown Lands: The Travels of Rabbi David D'Beth Hillel (1824–1832)*. Edited by Walter J. Fischel. New York: Ktav, 1973.

Hillel, Shlomo. *Operation Babylon: The Story of the Rescue of the Jews of Iraq*. Translated by Ina Friedman. New York: Doubleday, 1987.

Izady, Mehrdad R. *The Kurds: A Concise Handbook*. Washington, D.C.: Taylor and Francis, 1992.

Josephus, Flavius. *The Second Jewish Commonwealth: From the Maccabaean Rebellion to the Outbreak of the Judaeo-Roman War*. Edited by Nahum M. Glatzer. New York: Schocken, 1971.

Lamb, Harold. "Mountain Tribes of Iran and Iraq." *National Geographic*, March 1946, pp. 385–408.

Labaree, Benjamin. "Maclean's Grammar of the Dialects of Vernacular Syriac." *The American Journal of Semitic Languages and Literatures* no.2 (January 1899): pp. 87–99.

Lewis, Bernard. *The Jews of Islam*. Princeton: Princeton University Press,1984.

Mann, Jacob. *Texts and Studies in Jewish History and Literature*, vol. 1. Cincinnati: Hebrew Union College Press, 1931.

Myhill, John. *Language in Jewish Society: Towards a New Understanding*. Clevedon, U.K.: Multilingual Matters, 2004.

Neusner, Jacob. "The Conversion of Adiabene to Judaism: A New Perspective." *Journal of Biblical Literature* 83, no. 1 (March 1964): 60–66.

Newby, P. H. *Saladin in His Time*. London: Faber and Faber, and New York: Dorset Press, 1983.

Regan, Geoffrey. *Lionhearts: Richard I, Saladin, and the End of the Third Crusade*. New York: Walker and Company, 1999.

Rejwan, Nissim. *The Jews of Iraq: 3,000 years of History and Culture*. London: Weidenfeld and Nicolson, 1985.

Roux, Georges. *Ancient Iraq*, 3rd ed. London and New York: Penguin Books, 1992.

Rosenthal, Franz. "Aramaic Studies during the Past Thirty Years." *Journal of Near Eastern Studies* 37, no. 2, (April 1978): 81–91.

Sabar, Yona. "Agonies of Childbearing and Child Rearing in Iraqi Kurdistan: A Narrative in Jewish Neo-Aramaic and its English Translation." *Studies in Semitic and General Linguistics in Honor of Gideon Goldenberg* (*Alter Orient und Altes Testament* 334). Edited by Tali Bar and Eran Cohen. Münster: Ugarit-Verlag, 2007. pp. 107–145.

———. "Aramaic, Once an International Language, Now on the Verge of Expiration." *When Languages Collide: Perspectives on Language Conflict, Language Competition, and Language Coexistence*. Edited by Brian D. Joseph, et al. Columbus: Ohio State University Press, 2003, pp. 222–234.

———. "Belief in Demons and Evil Spirits Among the Jews of Kurdistan." *Yeda-'Am* 8, no. 26 (1962): 27–28.

———. *The Folk Literature of the Kurdistani Jews: An Anthology*. New Haven: Yale University Press, 1982.

———. *A Jewish Neo-Aramaic Dictionary*. Wiesbaden: Harrassowitz Verlag, 2002.

———. "Nursery Rhymes and Baby Words in the Jewish Neo-Aramaic Dialect of Zakoh (Iraq)." *Journal of the American Oriental Society* 94, no. 3 (July–Sept. 1974): 329–336.

———. "Torah in the Mouth and Torah in the Heart: How Judaism Was Transmitted in a Minimally-Literate Near Eastern Jewish Community." *Queens College Journal of Jewish Studies* 7 (Spring 2005): 67–74.

———. "Yona Gabbay: A Jewish Peddler's Life Story from Iraqi Kurdistan; as Narrated by him in his Aramaic Dialect of Zakho (Four Episodes)." *Mediterranean Language Review* 16 (2005): 167–220.

Shai, Donna. *Neighborhood Relations in an Immigrant Quarter (A Social-Anthropological Study)*. Research report no. 149, publication no. 499. Jerusalem: Henrietta Szold Institute, April 1970.

Schwartz, Seth. "Hebrew and Imperialism in Jewish Palestine." *Ancient Judaism in Its Hellenistic Context*. Edited by Carol Bakhos. Boston: Brill, 2005.

Shiblak, Abbas. *Iraqi Jews: A History of Mass Exodus*. London: Saqi Books, 2005.

Shohet, Nir. *The Story of an Exile: A Short History of the Jews of Iraq*. Translated by Abraham Zilka. Tel Aviv: The Association for the Promotion of Research, Literature and Art, 1982.

Shwartz-Be'eri, Ora. *The Jews of Kurdistan: Daily Life, Customs, Arts and Crafts*. Jerusalem: The Israel Museum, 2000.

Simons, Geoff. *Iraq: From Sumer to Saddam*. New York: St. Martin's Press, 1994.

Smooha, Sammy. *Israel: Pluralism and Conflict*. Berkeley: University of California Press, and London: Routledge and Kegan Paul, 1978.

Ullendorff, Edward. "H.J. Polotsky (1905–1991): Linguistic Genius." *Journal of the Royal Asiatic Society*, Series 3, 4, 1 (1994): 3–13.

Wurmser, Meyrav. "Post-Zionism and the Sephardi Question." *Middle East Quarterly* (Spring 2005).

Zaken, Moti. *Tribal Chieftains and Their Jewish Subjects in Kurdistan: A Comparative Study in Survival*. Unpublished Ph.D. dissertation. Jerusalem: Hebrew University, 2003. (Zaken, Mordecai. *Jewish Subjects and Their Tribal Chieftains in Kurdistan*. Boston: Brill, 2007.)